BOB DOLE

The Republicans' Man for All Seasons

BOB DOLE

The Republicans' Man for All Seasons

by

JAKE H. THOMPSON

DIF

DONALD I. FINE, INC.

New York

E
840.8
·D64
T46
1994

for Katherine

CONTENTS

AUTHOR'S NOTE

This biography of Bob Dole is based on more than ninety interviews, including ones with the senator and his wife Elizabeth Hanford Dole; his first wife Phyllis Macey; Dole's family members; friends from his youth; those knowledgeable about his hometown; wartime friends; his adult friends and Senate colleagues; political allies and opponents; reporters who have covered Dole; Capitol Hill staff; and experts in Congressional matters and Senate history. The public record on Senator Dole is immense and the author has made use of that record, including *The Congressional Record*, daily and analytical newspaper and magazine articles, transcripts and videotapes from television appearances and the senator's own speeches. Handwritten notes from former White House domestic adviser John Ehrlichman quoted in Chapter Six were obtained from the Nixon Presidential Materials Project in College Park, Maryland.

All quotes from sources other than interviews with the author are identified with credit given to those sources. Whenever not otherwise indicated, the quotes were made personally to the author. Those quotes anonymously appear thus at their insistence. The author has confidence in the trustworthiness of comments given by those who are unnamed.

The author would like to thank Senator Dole for releasing private letters from former President Richard Nixon; and members of Dole's current and former staff who took time from their schedules to offer insight and assistance—particularly Jo-Anne Coe, Sheila Burke, Walt Riker, Clarkson Hine and Bryan Culp. It must not, however, be inferred this is an authorized biography; I am responsible for its contents.

The author also wishes to thank Art Brisbane, editor, and Mark Zieman, managing editor, of the Kansas City *Star* for granting a leave to write this book and James Kuhnhenn, Andrew C. Miller and James Worsham, my colleagues in the Washington bureau. Thanks also to Donald I. Fine, my publisher, and to Gail Ross, my agent; to my colleagues Stephen C. Fehr and Richard Tapscott and to my father-in-law, historian E.B. Potter, all of whom read the manuscript and made vital observations and recommendations for improvement; to Ralph Elder and staff at the Center for American History at the University of Texas at Austin; to the Kansas State Historical Society in Topeka; to Howard Means and Owen Ullmann; and to dozens of others who gave generously of their time to offer viewpoints and suggest sources of information to fill out this portrait of Bob Dole.

—Jake H. Thompson
Kensington, Maryland
June 1994

INTRODUCTION

MIDNIGHT OIL

One spring evening in 1960, McDill "Huck" Boyd, publisher of the Phillips County *Review,* a weekly newspaper in Phillipsburg, Kansas, was driving home late. Every weekend, after Boyd got his newspaper out on the streets, he roared off to a GOP event somewhere in Kansas. This evening the sixth congressional district GOP chairman was returning from a Republican function in Topeka, 235 miles east of Phillipsburg.

Around midnight Boyd's car rolled into Russell, a windblown oil and farming town two hours from home. He drove past dark homes and down the wide, empty red brick Main Street. He looked to his right at the Russell County courthouse and saw something odd. A light was on. Boyd was intrigued. What bureaucrat was literally burning the midnight oil?

Boyd stopped his car, walked into the courthouse and upstairs to the lighted office. There he discovered County Attorney Bob Dole, who had been elected to his post eight years earlier. The 36-year-old politician with dark hair and intense brown eyes sat at his desk combing through notecards of Republicans from whom he might seek political support. Dole told Boyd he had ambitions to serve in Congress. They chatted awhile and Boyd said good-bye. The two eventually became good friends. Boyd introduced Dole to other Republican movers and shakers, including his

1

friend, Alf Landon, the Kansas Republican governor who unsuccessfully challenged Franklin Delano Roosevelt in the 1936 presidential race.

That fall, with Boyd's help and his own hard work, Bob Dole won a seat in the United States House of Representatives, ushering him into the world of Washington politics. Boyd, in essence, had "discovered" Bob Dole. The publisher often told people that his first talk with Dole impressed upon him one solid conviction:

"Here was a young man who might someday be president."

Now thirty-four years later, Senate Republican Leader Bob Dole has become one of America's best-known politicians. He is a polarizing, intriguing and sometimes misunderstood lawmaker, famous for his blunt comments, deft quips and zealous partisanship. After decades shaping mountains of legislation, Dole is a senator's senator, a quintessential and durable member of "that damned club," as his old friend, conservative Lyn Nofziger calls the United States Senate.

To the public, Bob Dole is loved and loathed for perhaps the same reason: despite his senatorial dark suits and power ties, he's still a rough-hewn Kansan, a fearless straightshooter prowling in the nation's capital, where numbing nuance, bureaucratic mumbo jumbo and caution are the normative values.

Those who see him on the evening news, on a talk show or read of him in newspapers often see Dole as Mr. Mean, a dour, harsh, pessimistic conservative using his mastery of the lawmaking process and connections to frustrate government efforts toward helping people. He is the eclipse incarnate, dimming the agenda of Democrats and President Bill Clinton since Clinton's election in 1992. To critics, Dole practices the politics of obstruction.

"Generally, he adopts an extremely partisan view," said former Democrat Senator Alan Cranston, who retired after allegations he had sought improper intervention with federal regulators on behalf of a political contributor, former Lincoln Savings & Loan Association President Charles Keating Jr. Cranston is rare, a senator openly willing to criticize Dole and did so in a bitter article published in *Rolling Stone* magazine in 1993. "It seems to me he's become Mr. No, no, no. His funniness is usually cynical and dark."

Even so, Cranston carries a certain grudging respect for Dole. "When he gives his word on something, he keeps it. He's not deceptive. He's very blunt about his goals."

Nebraska Senator Bob Kerrey, who has sparred with Dole over health care and farm policy, said: "The indivisible principle with Senator Dole is that he loves his country. It is a common denominator that very often causes him to surprise Republicans, please Democrats, or cause Democrats to curse him."

David Wilhelm, chairman of the Democratic National Committee, sees Bob Dole at his core different from the way Kerrey sees him, and less charitably. "I think his legacy at this point seems to be one of the principal proponents of a negative brand of politics," Wilhelm said in late June, 1994. "There's always some hope he might play a positive or constructive role and go to the table and help pull together legislation that would be helpful to middle-class Americans. But at every point he pulls back from that and makes the choice instead to play the most partisan political games. Given who I am and the nature of my job, that's the usual criticism, I guess. But I'm not in the Senate. I'm a national party chair. I'm not the minority leader, who has a positive obligation to do more than filibuster, to be more than a party spokesman. And that is to roll up his sleeves and try to do something good for the American people. Every time we get to that precipice he pulls away and puts on an extremely partisan hat."

To his close Republican colleagues Dole is a complex man, not a cardboard cutout. "I'm sure there are times he'd like to twist my arm, but he never has," said Kansas Republican Nancy Kassebaum, often a maverick in Senate. "He's been supportive, but from a distance." Dole won great power not because he is lovable, but because of his bearing and drive, his all-consuming focus on politics. Pat Roberts, a Kansas congressman who now holds Dole's old congressional district, calls him "Rapid Robert."

"I think of him in the military sense, maybe because he's my captain," said Alan Simpson, the Senate Republican whip from Wyoming who has worked directly with Dole since 1984. "He commands your respect, you're ready to go over the cliff with him. His life is politics, all the shades and colors and vibrancy. He loves it, eats it, breathes it. He visits with more people in a day than I must in a week."

In the Clinton era, Dole has served as Republican Party's Last General, holding forth from the well of the Senate. His graying hair, angled face, dark eyes and rumbling bass voice provoke comparisons to an elder Humphrey Bogart. He cups his left hand over his right, for his right arm is disabled. In the heat of debate, to make a point, he often bounces forward on his toes like the basketball player he once was, always ready with the comment *du jour*.

Away from the public glare of the Senate floor, Dole routinely summons warring sides into his Capitol office. Meeting in the same room in which Thomas Jefferson was elected president in 1801, Dole steers endless hours

of sometimes angry debate between Republicans and Democrats to produce imperfect legislation, reflecting, nonetheless, the "art of the possible." Dole forcefully pushes for resolutions, yet at the same time defuses
tensions with humor.

Throughout his workday Dole strides back and forth between his office
and the Senate floor, often pausing to sit and direct behind-the-scenes
action from a large leather chair shielded from public view in the Republican cloakroom just off the Senate floor. From that throne Dole can
glimpse a swath of the Senate floor, a bank of telephones along a wall and
Republican colleagues who might be nearby politicking. Zeus of the Senate.

He shoulders responsibility for upholding Republican ideals, in daily
combat with those borne by Democrats, a process that, in time, paralyzes
government in gridlock. He has sought to be the leader, shielding, he
believes, Americans from the further encroachment and expense of Big
Government.

In a letter to the author former President Bush wrote: "In my view, and
I have stated this publicly several times since leaving the Presidency, Senator Dole is conducting himself in exemplary fashion as leader of the loyal
opposition. He supports the president where he can and is an eloquent
champion in opposition when the need arises."

James Baker III, Bush's secretary of state and longtime Texas friend to
Bush, said: "Bob has been a very good leader. He has no peer in terms of
his ability as a legislative strategist. And he has the ability to hold his troops
together pretty well. It ain't easy with the makeup of the Senate. I think
he's a very good legislative tactician."

In private, friends assert that Dole is more caring than he appears as a
public figure. "He is one of the softer, more sympathetic and emotional
people," contends Robert Strauss, the former Democratic National Committee chairman and an old friend of Dole. "And by emotional, I mean
that in the best sense, warm emotions, great personal sympathy for people.
Partially of his own making, people see him as a fellow who has a sort of
mean streak to him. He can be terribly cutting. He has a sense of humor
that is sometimes not well understood."

Then from where does his renowned sternness stem? In part, it arises
from impatience to "make things happen"—his personal mantra—riding
herd on a politically broad Republican caucus in the Senate and working
with shifting strategies in White Houses. "He's been a good leader for a
very, very mixed up group of people. They don't have a notion of what
they want, Republicans in the Senate," said Strauss, the Democrat. "And

when people in administrations see a legislative leader leading they think, 'He's after me.' But that's just his responsibility."

An astonishing determination propelled the boy who grew up in modest circumstances on the dun-colored prairie of Kansas, who pumped iron and ran sprints in high school, who survived injuries in World War II, and subsequent grave challenges through a forty-five-year political career of shifting political roles: state legislator, lawyer, House member, senator, Republican National Committee Chairman, vice presidential nominee, Senate majority leader and twice-run presidential candidate. He finally landed as Senate minority leader in the early 1990s, still working twelve-hour days at age seventy-one. He has become "Mr. Republican," an American political luminary, accomplishing all of his goals except one: winning the presidency. So far.

Dole has been at the heart, often as a protagonist, of the great upheavals of the last half century—World War II, the Cold War, the 1960s civil rights and student-protest turbulence, Vietnam, Watergate, the rise of the Republican right, the Iran-Contra scandal, the Persian Gulf War and the menace of the expanding federal deficit. Because politics involves warfare over ideas and ideology, many Americans strongly object to Bob Dole's political views and actions. For many others Dole has pursued precisely the right course.

To denizens of the media who have chronicled his public life in minute detail, Dole presents a range of different faces. Nearly all agree he's a big story. Journalists covering Dole tolerate or enjoy his humor, creativity, partisanship and outbursts, all of which make good copy. He has served himself up as the principal counterpoint to President Clinton since Republicans lost the White House in 1992. Dole's own press office churns out press releases, transcripts and background documents weekly to mate Dole's insatiable quest for media coverage with the media's increasing demands on his time in the 1990s. "I have a list of requests as long as your arm," Clarkson Hine, Dole's deputy press secretary, said one day in early 1994.

Dole enjoys parrying with the media mavens on the Sunday morning circuit, where he owns the record for most appearances on CBS's "Face the Nation" and NBC's "Meet the Press." With an adaptability that has kept him influential, Dole has appeared on alternative media fashionable in the 1990s—Rush Limbaugh's show, New York radio host Don Imus' show, "The Tonight Show with Jay Leno" and CNN's "Larry King Live" (seven times, almost a co-host). In 1993 Dole rated the third highest number of news stories on the evening network news, behind President Clinton and his wife Hillary Rodham Clinton, ahead of all members of the Cabinet, everyone in Congress and Vice President Al Gore.

Even after forty years in public life, Dole has low tolerance for probing personal questions from the media, particularly about congressional pay raises, perks and his multimillion-dollar fund-raising efforts used to boost his presidential ambitions, to campaign for other senators and to support the Dole Foundation, a charitable organization he established in 1984. Over the years, Dole has shown his irritation to reporters raising questions in those areas, frozen out several whose stories questioned him and has penned numerous letters to the editor to set the public record, as he sees it, straight.

In May, 1993, he wrote to Peter Stauffer, publisher of the Topeka *Capitol-Journal* in Kansas concerning a story focusing on Dole's fund-raising: "I knew the *Capitol-Journal* was sliding to the left, but your irresponsible, mean-spirited attack on me really went over the edge. Poorly researched, presented without *any* substantiation, other than recycling baseless smears, purposely ignoring almost all of the input from my office, and hyping it all with a reckless headline, the Dole Tainted by Own Campaign Finances story has set a new low for your newspapers." Dole's letter defended his efforts to reform campaign finance laws and his foundation's grants to help disabled Americans in the workplace.

The Wichita *Eagle* in the summer of 1993 ran a story about the Federal Election Commission fining Dole's 1988 presidential campaign and political action committee $112,000 for campaign violations. (It fined the Bush campaign $40,000 and Jack Kemp's campaign $120,000 later, in 1994. Audits of the other candidates were incomplete.) Dole told a reporter Kansans did not care about the matter; the *Eagle* editorialized that Kansans did. Soon the telephone rang at Editor Davis Merritt, Jr.'s desk. It was Bob Dole. They had two long conversations. Said Merritt: "At one point I was thinking, This man wants to be the leader of the free world. Why does he care about that story? It's classic Dole toughness. Agreeing to disagree is not an acceptable tone for the senator."

Dole's response? He has always felt compelled to fight back if something was, in his view, "totally wrong" or misunderstood. "When you get to the point where that doesn't bother you, then I don't think you're a good public servant," Dole said in an early 1994 interview. "If you let anybody, I don't care who it is, attack you personally or your judgment or your motives, your integrity, you ought to move on."

To mask his prickly temper, Dole delights in making people laugh with his famous barbed jokes. He used to shoot them mainly at others, yet learned he got bigger laughs if he turned them on himself. Following his loss of the Republican presidential nomination in 1988, Dole told audiences he wasn't much disappointed. "I went home and slept like a baby," Dole said, pausing with a stand-up comedian's timing. "Every couple of hours, I'd wake up and cry."

On CBS's "Face the Nation" program Sunday, April 10, 1994, he endorsed Senate Majority Leader George Mitchell to fill the vacancy on the Supreme Court created by Justice Harry Blackmun's retirement. Incredulous, Gwen Ifill of the New York *Times* asked why Dole, a Republican leader, was vouching for a Democrat. "Well, the president's not going to nominate *me*," Dole said. "Maybe they should nominate me." The show ended in chuckles as Dole burst out, "Tell them not to nominate me!" Clinton soon selected Judge Stephen Breyer.

Dole's such a large figure on the American political stage that at least three men have claimed to have saved him as he lay wounded on the field of battle in the Italian mountains in the waning days of World War II. "You meet some people who say, 'Don't you remember me?' " Dole said, smiling. "I tell them, 'No, don't think so.' Met a guy in Orlando: 'Aw, you remember me. We used to play golf together all the time,' " Dole added. "I know I remember I didn't play golf."

Dole has never played golf and these days has no hobbies, no abiding interests in sports, the arts, literature, philosophy or history, except if they can be related to politics. When he travels with Senate colleagues he lugs along political and other non-fiction current events books, not current best-selling works of fiction nor spy or mystery novels that many people often read to relax by. Bob Dole's idea of relaxation is forty minutes on the treadmill in the bedroom of his apartment at the Watergate hotel complex.

No one knows his workaholic habits better than his staff. For years Dole has moved around his office not as a chummy colleague but as a field general. Mike Baroody, a top staffer for Dole in the mid-1970s, said Dole "could be fairly demanding." When he asked for something he wanted it *now*. He has worn out dozens of staffers, many of whom have left for good jobs elsewhere after the Dole boot camp. Young speechwriters wilt when Dole scans their precious words and dismisses their speech with a "naahh." He tends to ignore those who have displeased him. He has a tough time firing staffers. Instead of pushing someone out the door, Dole's style is to shunt them aside in the daily flow of work until they find another job. His management style has fostered both worry and intense loyalty from his staff.

Walt Riker, who worked on press with Dole from 1981 to 1993, got an

early indoctrination into Dole's ways. In 1981, when Dole was chairman
of the Senate Finance Committee, he agreed to do three quick television
interviews one afternoon on completely unrelated topics. Riker set up the
TV crews in three separate rooms, with doors between each. Dole arrived,
walked into a fourth room, Riker handed him three staff-prepared briefing
papers, which Dole scanned for a minute.

"Okaayy!" Dole said, and handed the papers back. He walked into the
first room and gave the interview, then stepped into the second, then the
third, extemporaneously citing facts from the briefing papers.

"It was boom, boom, boom, and we were walking down the hallway
fast, going somewhere else," Riker said. "And that's the way it was for the
next twelve years."

Dole is something of a "perpetual motion machine," said Riker. "To
work for him you've got to keep up literally and figuratively. When he's
going somewhere he's striding out. He's got long legs and he's really
moving and you almost have to run to keep up with him, almost alter your
gait. That's part of the drill. And he doesn't turn around to see if you're
following."

Dole is also a perfectionist and some say a control freak. He has often
edited press releases moments before they were sent out. " 'I don't think
that's the right use of that word,' he'd say. And usually he was right," said
Riker. Reporters who covered Dole knew they did not have in their hands
a genuine Dole press release unless it bore either of Dole's favorite phrases:
"No doubt about it . . ." or "in my view . . ."

Dole likes memos from his dedicated staff to be brief, one page if possible. Staffers usually put a note at the bottom about how they will pursue a
winning strategy—a way to keep tabs. Much of that tab-keeping Dole
delegates to chief of staff, Sheila Burke, who has worked seventeen years
for Dole. "His style, which has not changed dramatically over the years, is
to focus on the things he concerns himself with and to stand back from the
minutiae," said Burke. "He's very well aware of who does what. He's not
somebody who likes bureaucracy. He doesn't go through me to people, he
deals with people directly, talks with his staff right up front, constantly
available, constantly wandering around in an ongoing process of gathering
information. If I tried to force everybody to come through me with
memos and everything else, I would have been gone years ago. That's just
not his style. He doesn't want somebody who controls access. He wants
somebody who loves the management process and makes sure the work
gets done."

Throughout his life Dole has been comfortable with strong women. His full-bore drive comes from his mother, Bina, who died in 1983. (His father contributed to Dole's dry sense of humor.) Bob Dole's second wife Elizabeth Hanford Dole is a charming southern mix of May Queen and Harvard policy wonk. She worked in the Johnson, Nixon, Ford and Carter administrations before becoming President Reagan's transportation secretary and President Bush's labor secretary. Since 1991 she has been president of the American Red Cross.

When his colleagues elected him Senate majority leader in 1984, Dole soon appointed longtime aide Jo-Anne Coe the first woman secretary of the Senate. Coe oversaw the Senate librarian, floor clerk staff and the flow of daily legislation. In recent years, the woman whom David Keene, a conservative political adviser to Dole, calls Dole's "Bradley fighting vehicle" has organized the senator's frenetic schedule of campaigning for Republicans and run Dole's political action committee, Campaign America.

His 1986 appointment made Sheila Burke the first woman chief of staff in the Senate, responsible for his staff of roughly forty people. Known for her rapid and assertive presentation of ideas and facts, Burke, a former nurse, is Dole's health care expert and perhaps the most influential congressional staff person on Capitol Hill.

Dole looks favorably on hard work. "And he likes people who are smart," says Robert Ellsworth, a longtime Kansas friend. "If he can sense you're as smart as he is, he likes that."

Keene calls him "almost unique in Washington" because he attracts loyalty by his own example of uncompromising loyalty. One night in the mid-1980s Elizabeth Dole, then transportation secretary, dedicated Washington's Union Station, restored to its railroad heyday with a multimillion-dollar renovation, in a gala affair drawing dozens of the Republican party's powerhouses. That same evening, elsewhere in Washington, the Heritage Foundation threw a ninetieth birthday party for Walter Judd, a former congressman from Minnesota. Keene, who looked up to Judd as a mentor, went to the birthday celebration, where he thumbed through telegrams and messages sent by senators and congressmen begging off because they had to attend the Union Station dedication.

"But there was one guy there at the birthday: Dole," said Keene, laughing. "Which had to be embarrassing to the people who sent these notes. I called him the next day to thank him."

"I would have gone to that dinner if it'd been in China," Dole told Keene. "Walter Judd, when I was a freshman in Congress, taught me. And I owe him."

"I'm sure he dropped in at the other thing as well," Keene added. "The coincidence of events tells you a lot about Dole. An attitude of 'Dedicate this place, I'll be back.' "

So who is Bob Dole, the loyal patriot or the grim politician? One part of the answer lies in what happened a half century ago, three weeks before the end of World War II fighting in Europe. German machine-gun or mortar fire exploded Dole's right shoulder when he lunged from a foxhole to rescue a wounded G.I. The injury ruined his dream of becoming a doctor, left him permanently disabled, drove him into politics.*

For years he has carried a rolled-up piece of paper or a felt-tip pen clenched in his right hand, perhaps to convey normalcy. It has become an essential symbol of Bob Dole's character. "I guess it's sort of a protective thing, sort of a signal to people, you know, that hand's occupied," Dole said in a 1993 profile of him on CBS's "60 Minutes." "It's sort of gotten to be a habit by now. I assume when I die there'll be a pen in my hand, when you look in the casket. I hope so. If anybody's listening, I want that done."

"I was thinking to myself, Anybody who writes a biography on Bob Dole ought to spend one day with one arm tied behind his back and the other one with sort of a glove on, because I don't have any feeling in this hand," Dole said in an interview with the author, squeezing together fingers on his left hand. "Not that that makes any difference, but it makes it a lot harder [for me] every day. I forget I'm disabled. It doesn't bother me anymore, but I keep thinking back to the time it takes just to put a shirt on. When you're taking thirty minutes to dress, I'm taking an hour. That's no big deal, but it adds up to a lot of wasted time."

But for anyone to face each day, such a disability would seem a big deal.

The second part of the answer to his character lies in Bob Dole's roots. For, despite his presidential quests and marshaling warfare on the Senate floor, meeting presidents, kings and corporate moguls around the globe, raising millions from special interest contributors and accepting the trappings of high political status—the ornate Capitol office, a chauffeur, his apartment in the Watergate Hotel, a condo near Miami, corporate jets at call—Kansas still lives in Bob Dole.

"I guess it's like everybody else, wherever you're from," Dole said in an interview. "In this case it was kind of special because it was not only where you grow up but where you have your problems, where people rally

---

* For his military service, Dole earned two Purple Hearts and a Bronze Star. He wears a Purple Heart pin on his jacket lapel every day.

around, raise money and you know they don't have it. I remember one guy bringing us a live duck when I was home from the hospital. Others were bringing vegetables and fruit. It just leaves a big, big impression. It probably would be any other small town, it just happened to be Russell, Kansas."

He added a bit later, "If you get to the point where you forget where you're from, then you've got a problem. Not only going back to visit, but when you make judgments about things, if you forget about the guy in overalls, like my dad wore for forty years, or somebody in the welfare office. You gotta know there's a lot of grief out there, a lot of poor people. Hopefully, you don't lose your perspective when you think you may be going up the ladder."

Senator Nancy Kassebaum, who has witnessed Dole sweep aside the Kansas congressional delegation to help the state, maintains respect for Dole because of his allegiance. "For me, the essence of Bob Dole, even though I can get annoyed with him sometimes when he gets out there and 'ehgh!'," Kassebaum says, scowling like Dole in full partisan wrath, "is that he has never lost sight of who he was. He can be an elegant dresser and he can move in the most powerful circles, but underneath it all is—I think anybody would say this who knows Bob—a keen sense of remembering where he came from, and the ambition and fight that has always been his."

It seems Dole has been in that fight his whole life, working perhaps to overcompensate for his modest heritage and his disability, yet reaching beyond their limitations to embrace them as fundamental origins of his strength and personal philosophy.

As one of his former top staffers said, in the world of Bob Dole "there are no magic bullets. You have to keep working despite possible pessimistic outcomes. You work within what you're given."

RUSSELL, KANSAS

Early settlers journeying to Kansas in the 1870s encountered an almost treeless, waterless, open prairie. An immense sky stretched overhead, the hard wind blew, banks of storm clouds traversed the land. For shelter, they dug into the earth, quarrying pale yellow limestone to build houses, barns, sheds, corrals and, eventually, the Russell County courthouse. They broke limestone into fence posts, roughly four feet tall and one foot square. They planted the posts upright and between them tied bands of barbed wire.

Hundreds of miles of limestone fence posts still mark off farm and ranch property throughout Kansas. Limestone structures might be viewed two ways: stubborn, immovable and imposing, or solid, grounded and enduring.

Bob Dole could have been the man from Fossil, Kansas. As a political metaphor, it might have been impossible to overcome. The story began nearly a century after the founding of the United States, when the Great Plains was home only to buffalo, wildcats, coyotes, quail, deer and prairie chickens. Nomadic Pawnee Indians and white trappers roamed through on hunting forays without setting up permanent villages. The land was arid, primordial.

In 1865 The Butterfield Trail, an overland passage west for pioneers, was established in what is now Russell County with station stops in Dorrance, Bunker Hill, Forsythe and Fossil, named for fossils found in the native limestone. Two years later in 1867 the Union Pacific railroad company bridged the prairie, opening a line from the Missouri River west to Denver. The railroad inaugurated conquests to settle the land.

On January 17, 1871, a group of citizens in Ripon, Wisconsin, incidentally the birthplace of the modern Republican Party, formed the Northwest Colony with the intent of visiting Kansas to scout a suitable location for a new home. The group's articles of incorporation were succinct: they aimed to grab cheap land, establish schools and churches, and become reasonable neighbors. Not just anyone could join. There were standards. Article No. 2 embraced adults of good disposition and industrious habits, and those who had a legitimate trade or calling.

"But no person of disreputable character or vicious habits shall knowingly be allowed to become a member of or settle in said colony, if in the power of the commissioners or their agents to prevent it, nor shall there be any gambling or tippling houses allowed to be established in said settlement, nor any intoxicating liquors sold therein as a beverage."

Seventy colonizers arrived by train on April 19, 1871, at Fossil Station on the divide between the Smoky Hill and Saline rivers. Their passenger coach car was uncoupled, and they took up residence in it and three boxcars the railroad had left for them. The only buildings in the county were a frame depot, a section house and a dugout. The life, reflected in the photographs of pioneer photographer Solomon Butcher, looked bleak. Butcher's photographs of the era show dugouts and single-story frame homes and unsmiling faces, sun-browned and stunned, the prairie settlers.

The newcomers met on May 2 to vote on their town's name. Miscellaneous names received nine votes, Fossil received seven and thirty-four were cast for Russell, chosen to honor Captain Avra P. Russell, a New Yorker who fought with Union soldiers, served in Kansas and died in battle, having never visited the town that would bear his name.

Thanks to Captain Russell, Dole did not have to contend with being from a community synonymous with age, decay, bygone days or hoary prehistory. Imagine for a moment Senate floor debate beginning: "The distinguished senator from Kansas proposes dramatic changes in Medicare, but they are not a vision for our future. His very hometown suggests they are dead on arrival." And one of Dole's favorite phrases using Russell would ring tinny in the ear: "That's not how we do it in Fossil, America."

Russell serves well, figuratively and literally. The forceful name embraces the resilience and restlessness of the West. It kindles images of cowboy life, rodeos and county fairs, Norman Rockwellian images of American values.

The Riponites were joined in 1876 by German–Russians emigrating to the United States in search of freedom from mandatory military service. These German-speaking newcomers established farms and worked hard; Russell County boomed with an influx of land seekers. A school and several churches opened.

Pioneer life was anything but comfortable, and Kansas was far from serene. The state was born after a six-year struggle, the Bleeding Kansas period when pro-slavery and anti-slavery citizens fought to determine whether the territory would become a free-soil state or a slave state. Anti-slavery bands, Jayhawkers, grabbed control of the pro-slavery-run state government through dozens of armed battles. The anti-slavery forces eventually drove the pro-slavery forces from the state and Kansas came into the Union a free state on January 29, 1861. But during the Civil War Kansans fought off new raids into its border towns by pro-slavery Confederate troops, highlighted by William Quantrill's 1863 raid on Lawrence that resulted in the destruction of two hundred buildings.

One fortuitous event, the impact of which wasn't fully realized until decades later, was that Mennonite emigrés in the 1880s introduced a foreign crop, Turkey red wheat, notable for its ability to survive subzero-degree winters, scorching summers and drought, and flourish into waving green stalks in June. It was first tried in Russell County around 1880. Later it became the leading crop of Kansas, blanketing the western half in an undulating sea of amber grain.

Otherwise, the pioneers battled nature and the dry earth. Grasshoppers rattled over the land like hail in 1874 and decimated every green plant or shrub. Tornadoes whistled over the flat land. Snowstorms roared out of the Rocky Mountains in the mid-1880s and killed thousands of cattle and stranded people for weeks. Rain fell infrequently, even in good years. The weather was so inhospitable in the 1880s and 1890s that farming, the underpinning of the state's economy, faltered. Banks closed and land prices plunged. Covered wagons rumbled out of Kansas bearing crudely lettered signs on their canvas walls, "In God We Trusted, In Kansas We Busted," wrote Kenneth S. Davis in his book, *Kansas, A History*.

Hardship nurtured another kind of crop that took root in Kansas. Political philosophers traveled the state sowing the seeds of populism, and farmers, ranchers and small townspeople were fertile recipients. Mary Elizabeth Lease, a Wichita lawyer known as "Lady Orator of the West," became famous and drew cheers for declaring, "It is no longer a government of the people, by the people and for the people, but a government of Wall Street, by Wall Street and for Wall Street," Davis wrote. She was credited with coining the rallying cry that farmers should "raise less corn and more HELL!" Her critics called her Mary "Yellin" Lease. She and other populist leaders such as Jerry Simpson, derided by an opponent as "Sockless Jerry" because he was too poor to buy socks, founded a People's Party.

The populists exhorted the common man to fight business monopolies, boss-dominated political parties and a widening division between the rich and the poor. Although the populist movement faded in Kansas at the turn of the century, the anti-government philosophy still courses through the state's politics—and chiefly through the mind of Kansas' senior senator.

Among those who likely caught wind of the populist ferment were early settlers to Russell County, Bob Dole's paternal grandparents, Robert and Margaret Dole. They eked out a living as tenant farmers east of Russell. Ten miles south, Joseph and Elva Talbott, Dole's maternal grandparents, farmed and butchered cattle.

By the dawn of the twentieth century Russell had grown to about 2,000 residents. In typical midwestern fashion it was laid out in a grid, bisected by the railroad tracks, the east and west streets in numbers, north and south ones named for trees or locally notable families: Maple, Ash, Elm, Seitz, Ober, Grant and Holland. The young town maintained an ethic still alive today: Russell looked favorably on those who were ruggedly independent. Townspeople did not ask for much and did not expect it.

Doran Dole was born to Robert and Margaret in 1900 and lied about his age to enlist in the Army in 1917, hoping to go "Over There" for World War I. Instead, the army posted him in Illinois and Texas for the last half of the war, according to *The Doles: Unlimited Partners,* a campaign autobiography Bob and Elizabeth Dole wrote with Richard Norton Smith for the 1988 presidential race. After returning home, Doran met young Bina Talbott, an energetic girl from a family of twelve children, who had a talent for cooking. They married in 1921; Bina (pronounced Bye-na) was 18, Doran 21. Their life together began at his restaurant, the White Front Cafe on Main Street. A photograph taken inside the restaurant shows a proud, somber Doran Dole standing beside a glass cupboard in a long, wood-floored room with about a dozen stools at a lunch counter, three tables and five American flags on display.

The Doles' first child, Gloria, was born in 1921. Their second, the future senator Robert Joseph, named for each grandfather, was born on July 22, 1923. The family crowded into a two-room white frame house with a lean-to kitchen. Bina used orange crates for shelves, the kids shared a bedroom. Doran Dole's restaurant failed, so he opened a cream-and-egg station in Russell. He would buy eggs, cream and chickens from farmers and pay them with cash or by bartering and sell his goods to the towns-people.

Russell was growing; the wide Main Street running north and south through town, which had been gravel, dust or mud in its early days, was paved in red brick a mile long. That ochre brick street still survives. Dozens of small single-story homes were built in the neighborhoods north and south of the tracks.

On Thanksgiving Day in 1923 the predictable agrarian life was suddenly changed. Oil! The Carrie Oswald No. 1 site a few miles from town made the Lucky Seven, seven local investors who paid for the exploratory well, rich. By the 1930s oil development brought a gusher of greenbacks to Russell County. Oil production, which would reach a peak of fourteen million barrels in Russell County in 1948, with a tax value of $32 million, broadened the agriculture-based economy. Soon oilmen and their families swarmed into Russell, triggering a housing boom, filling out new businesses on Main Street, spawning honky-tonks and saloons on the edge of town that the Riponites forswore when they founded the town. Shocked at first, Russell natives adjusted to the twang of Texas and Oklahoma accents.

The Doles did not get in on the oil boom. In the 1920s, two more children, Kenny and Norma Jean, were born to Doran and Bina Dole. The family moved into a larger home on Maple Street. Normal American family life, without many frills, filled their days. If the parents had extra cash at the end of the week, they bought everyone ice cream or went for a drive in the country, recalls Norma Jean Steele. Doran Dole often bought a Christmas tree on Christmas Eve to save money. On the Fourth of July he'd buy fireworks, a case of soda pop and a block of ice for the neighborhood kids to have "ice cold pop," a treat, Kenny Dole recalled in an interview for a Russell High School student in 1990. Bob and Kenny were close brothers, Kenny the one who chased cats and hung out at neighbors' homes too late, Bob the one who read and dragged his younger brother off to school, holding his hand. On Christmas Eve, when they were supposed to be asleep, Kenny and Gloria mischievously would sneak into the closet to poke at the presents, guessing what was inside. "You'd better not do that," Bob would say. "You're going to get caught."

Neither Doran nor Bina Dole finished high school, there was a living to make, but they saw to it that their children attended classes in the Russell public schools. Neither parent attended church full-time, there were chores to do, but they sent their children most Sundays to the Methodist church. And Doran and Bina Dole were at God's shoulder when it came to cleanliness:

"I used to say you could eat off my mother's floors," Bob Dole recalled in an interview, smiling at the memory. "They were always just—*whiitt*— clean. And she expected us to be clean, pressed and neat. And no mess around the bed or desk or whatever."

Bina Dole was the more "vitriolic" of the two, say longtime Russell residents. She disciplined the children. She spoke fast, walked fast and drove fast. She raised a vegetable garden in the yard tended by the children. Bina charted their lives with her personal philosophy, encapsulated in a phrase: " *'Can't' never could do nothing.*"

While she waxed the floors she made the children sit at the table with their feet hiked up until the floor dried, Kenny Dole recalled in an interview with the Russell *Daily News* in 1987. At mealtimes the children were required to sit in their chairs with their arms folded until all the food was on the table. "Our mother was kind of strict," said Gloria Nelson. Yet if a family friend or neighbor died or was ill, Bina sent over meat loaf or hot rolls. She started a tradition in Russell of decorating the outside of homes at Christmas with lights and homemade ornaments. She took Doran his lunch at the creamery and later when he worked at a grain company in Russell. Because of her upbringing, she thought little of turning out feasts for her family. "They'd have more darn food than you'd get at a harvest meal," marveled Russell Townsley, the retired publisher of the Russell *Daily News*.

"We had a close-knit family," said Norma Jean Steele, Bob Dole's younger sister. Bina Dole was proud of her children, supporting each of their endeavors. A woman of limitless energy and an occasional sharp temper, Bina brought extra money into the family during the 1930s by selling Singer sewing machines. Early in the morning Bob or Kenny lifted the heavy machines into the family car and Bina drove off to towns and farmhouses throughout the region. "I wasn't in school, so I had to go with her," Norma Jean Steele recalled, not unhappily. "I colored pictures or sat in the car. We couldn't afford a baby-sitter."

If a housewife was skeptical of the Singer contraptions, Bina would whip out a piece of clothing on the spot. If the woman protested she didn't know how to sew, Bina offered to teach her. She sold a lot of sewing machines, Kenny recalled. Payment wasn't always cash. She'd bring home a couple of chickens sometimes, or a batch of eggs as a downpayment. When Bina got her hands on a hand-me-down, she'd turn it into an outfit for one of her kids.

She worried about her own appearance. "Does my dress look okay? My hair?" one friend remembered Bina Dole saying frequently, which seemed silly. She was impeccable. Bina always sent her four children to school in clean clothes, ironed and starched shirts and trousers for the boys, and ironed blouses and pleated skirts for the girls, with pleats so crisp they couldn't be pulled out. Bob Dole inherited her fastidiousness.

In contrast to Bina's pedal-to-the-floor energy, Doran Dole, a strong, taciturn man, had one gear—steady—and it ran nonstop from dawn onward. He missed one day of work in forty years. He usually got up at five o'clock in the morning to go to work and made sure his kids were up and knew their chores. He returned home around eleven at night. He was a volunteer fireman for years. First to the creamery, then to the grain company, farmers brought their strong opinions about the sad state of grain prices and laid them on Doran Dole, who took in opposite views with equanimity. He knew every farmer in the land.

"Doran was laid back," recalled Dean Banker, whose family founded one of Russell's oldest businesses, Banker's dry goods store. "He was the epitome of a public servant in private enterprise. He was very careful about stating his opinions. Doran smiled a lot. You never saw him look like he swallowed a mouthful of words. He was always neat, even in overalls and a workshirt. He changed almost daily, which was unheard of then." Every morning before stores on Main Street opened, Doran Dole had already swept out his store and the sidewalk out front.

At home, he did not openly praise his children and he expected them to listen to his orders. He was witty, though, with a kind of subtle humor that made the kids laugh, after they thought about it. But Norma Jean Steele said, "We knew if he was upset we had to behave."

"My dad always taught you to respect your elders and there never was any question about it," Kenny Dole said in 1986. "I know one thing: you never asked my dad twice. He never asked you twice. He just kind of told you and that was it. He didn't have time to horse around telling you fifteen times to do something. He was long gone, and when he came back he expected it to be done."

Gloria Nelson picked up that theme, remembering a time when Bob was about nine years old and her mother was too ill with the flu to get out of bed—a rarity. Doran, rattled, fixed dinner, got the kids to bed, then set the alarm to be sure he'd be up in time to wake them up and pack them off to school. The alarm clanged at three o'clock in the morning. "We were slow to get up," said Gloria. "I heard him tell my mom, 'I don't know what's the matter with these kids this morning, they're just slow movin'. And they've got to get to school, I'm gettin' their breakfast and I need some milk. I'm going to send Bob down.' Bob was up and dressed and ready to go. So Dad sent him down there. Well, by this time we knew. But Bob sat down there in front of that store for I don't know how long. Finally Dad realized he had the wrong time, he went down and picked him up in the old car. Brought him home. They laughed at that at the grocery store for years."

Doran and Bina agreed on two maxims they gave their children to live by: "Money isn't everything," was one. The other, "If it is worth doing, it is worth doing right."

"Obviously, [they taught] the work ethic," Bob Dole recalled. "My dad worked all the time and my mother would load up these sewing machines, take off early in the morning, come back late at night, maybe make fifteen dollars or ten dollars. It was an early example of a working couple. Never thought of it that way in those days."

The Great Depression troubled Russell, but because of the oil boom, not as much as other communities in Kansas. Still, there wasn't much money in the Dole family, nor in many families in Russell in those days, recalls Max Horn, seventy-nine, a retired banker.

In the early 1930s a new hardship confronted Kansans of all social classes: no rain. As the Dust Bowl besieged the Midwest, Russell and many communities were blasted with dust storms. Over parched, cracked earth, the western sky would fill with black clouds. Townspeople who prayed for rain realized the clouds were rolling dirt storms. Soon the land would be engulfed with wind-whipped black dust, the region's precious topsoil. Sometimes the clouds were red, from Oklahoma. "They're frightening, they're frightening!" Max Horn said, fifty years later. "Farmers had few crops, no cattle, few chickens. But not many people moved away."

"Inside the cloud darkness was total, and remained for hours after the cloud passed," wrote Ian Frazier in his book *Great Plains*. "People in the cloud's path thought the end of the world had come and went to churches to await it. Farmers watched their fields disappear before their eyes. Fence lines were so deep in dust that cattle with mud-coated lungs could stagger away over them. People crammed wet newspapers around windows and doors and slept with wet handkerchiefs over their faces. In the winter, snow mingled with the blowing dusters—'snirt' storms."

During one dust storm Russell High School played a basketball game against Hays, twenty-five miles to the west. Players couldn't see the basket on the other end of the court in the gymnasium, time-outs were called every five minutes to sweep the floor so the players could see the lines and no one was allowed to leave the auditorium that night. They stayed, sleeping on the floor. In Russell people could not see the marquee on the Dream Theater from across the street. Farmland prices blew away as well; an acre of land dropped from ten dollars to five dollars.

Like many American families of the 1930s the Doles always gathered for Sunday dinners of fried chicken, vegetables, ice cream that they froze themselves and Bina's homemade chocolate sauce. Money was so tight by 1937 that the Doles rented out their main floor rooms to oil company employees so Doran could make the house payments, and all six Doles moved into the concrete-floored basement below. They hauled out the old coal bin, installed a bathroom and Bina fixed up the basement. The family upstairs sometimes invited the kids to come up and listen to their record player and patriotic music. For years during the 1940s, after reclaiming the upstairs, the Doles rented out that basement room.

To earn spending money Gloria and Norma Jean baby-sat while Bob and Kenny had paper routes, mowed neighbors' lawns and shoveled snow off sidewalks. Max Horn, the retired banker, says the Doles were a sound family and stayed out of trouble, unlike some other struggling families in town. They were too busy working to fool around. The girls washed dishes, did chores. Bob and Kenny delivered handbills around town on Saturdays, mowed lawns, washed cars, raked leaves and shoveled snow.

"That's what pulled us through really, my mom and dad working every day," Kenny Dole said in 1986. "So us kids came by work pretty naturally. You were expected to. You don't sit at home and watch TV and order pizza."

"We lived on the wrong side of the tracks. The north side was considered where the second-class people lived, " Bob Dole recalled. "My parents played bridge with other couples, but they didn't show up at the hoity-toity functions in Russell because they weren't that social class. It never seemed to bother them. It didn't bother us."

Doran and Bina liked to go to dances and play cards with friends—the games were played at their house, they couldn't afford baby-sitters. They did not care much for politics, though President Franklin Delano Roosevelt was struggling to pull the nation out of economic and psychological malaise with his New Deal. The Doles became Democrats not because of him but because of the way many things happened in small towns. Clifford Holland, Sr., a Russell lawyer and Democrat, was running for Congress. Doran and Bina Dole were friends. Ergo, they were Democrats.

"I'm certain my parents never gave politics five minutes thought a month," Bob Dole said. "I think they used to listen to FDR. We used to listen to Doc Brinkley, the old goat-gland doctor who had his radio station. We sat around the radio listening to Amos 'n Andy. I don't ever remember discussing politics at home through high-school days. Athletics, sports, my dad was a big baseball nut. Things like that, not politics."

Bob Dole learned about politics, though, at the epicenter of public opinion for Russell County: Dawson's Drug Store on Main Street. Owned by E.E. Dawson, the drugstore had a row of stools and a soda fountain. It was the number one stopping-off place for the town's school kids, oilfield workers, lawyers, farmers, businessmen and families. Dawson's sons, Ernie, Bub and Chet, worked there. "We made the best ice-cream sodas in the country," Bub Dawson boasted. "We had a chocolate recipe that everybody liked. The secret was made from chocolate imported from England."

Around age thirteen, Bob got a job at Dawson's as a soda jerk, serving milkshakes for fifteen cents, malts for twenty-five cents, cokes and Green Rivers, a lime drink, for five cents. The Dawson family made a practice of employing local kids who were well-liked; it drew in customers. Bob was hardworking, quick with a joke, a good athlete, said Bub Dawson, perhaps Bob Dole's closest friend in Russell. "Bob was popular as a boy, nice-lookin' kid. Well, his whole family was popular."

Dawson's was also where Dole first practiced his famous style of zinging one-liners. The store fostered camaraderie, humor came in the form of one-upmanship, and you had to learn to hold your own ground. Dean Banker remembered Chet Dawson telling one of his young employees: "Hey, kid, come over here. This man was clean-shaven when he came in and now he's got a one-inch beard waiting for you to wait on him." The Dawsons were boisterous fans of Kansas State University in Manhattan, and put up the school's purple-and-white pennants in the drugstore, not the red-and-blue ones of the larger and better-known University of Kansas in Lawrence, the cross-state archrivals.

"It was the hub of activity, the popular spot in town. And it was my first experience being out in the public. So, from that standpoint it's your first chance you have dealing with the public," Bob Dole recalled. "There were a lot of people coming in, wanting different things, wanting to visit. And you learn to sort of give and take with the customers. The Dawsons were big K-State fans and, oh, God, they'd revel when they beat KU. And every week basketball or football would be a big event at Dawson's. They'd all come down to heckle each other. I got along well with the

Dawson brothers. And I made a little spending money there, worked after school and on Saturdays. I used to clean that whole basement downstairs for a dollar, one dollar. Take about four or five hours. Takes you back a ways."

"For a dollar a day I whipped up chocolate malteds behind the soda fountain and gave curb service on weekends," Dole wrote in *Unlimited Partners*. "I picked up the comic style of the Dawson brothers, who enjoyed a local renown for their tart one-liners. I also developed an appetite for ice cream that would horrify nutritionists. In my first two weeks on the job I put on nine pounds."

It probably did not show. Long before the jogging craze, decades before Jane Fonda preached aerobics, way before Arnold Schwarzeneger pumped himself up to win world titles, Bob Dole was a jock. In high school Bob and Kenny poured concrete into cans, letting it solidify around a metal bar to make a weight-lifting set. Running was how townspeople saw Bob Dole. He'd get up at five o'clock in the morning and pound through the streets of Russell, an almost unheard of activity in those days. Not a naturally gifted athlete, he developed his body into a knot of muscle, six feet two, one hundred ninety pounds, and became a football, basketball and track star. He ran the 440 and the 880, two grueling sprints. In basketball, wearing number 99—perhaps the school used double digits to make the small student body seem larger—he was the only one from Russell picked for the Union Pacific All-Stars.

Adolph Reisig was a tackle lined up beside Bob Dole, an end, on the 1941 Russell High football team, which went 9-0 their senior year. Dole was very competitive. Reisig remembers him as "a Christian athlete" long before that phrase gained popularity. He would not take a nip of beer. "He was a good, clean-living young man," says Reisig, who worked in the alumni association at nearby Fort Hays State University. Dole, he said, could catch a ball with real skill and joked during games to break tension.

In one game one of the opposing team's running backs was black, unusual because there were few black people in western Kansas. At halftime Russell High was behind, the team was down, the coach glared at Dole. "Bob, don't you see that black halfback coming around the end?"

"Coach," Dole responded, "he comes around me so fast I didn't know he was black."

"Everybody had a laugh," said Reisig, and their spirits lifted, they won the game.

In high school Dole was the sports editor of *The Pony Express,* the student newspaper at Russell High, and he was a serious student with a sense of humor. No girlfriends, though girls liked him. Dole was shy. Reisig was in journalism class with Dole; a test was scheduled and Dole showed up with a five-gallon drum of ice cream, hoping to dissuade the teacher. "We'll have to eat fast because we're still going to have that test," Reisig recalls the teacher saying. "And then didn't give it."

Dole earned letters in football, basketball and track, and was president of Hi-Y and a member of the National Honor Society. He was a guard on the basketball team, made fewer points than most others but was good at rebounding and passing off, said Gloria Nelson. Photographs of that era show a groomed, apparently self-assured young Dole.

Of the many people stopping by Dawson's, Bob Dole saw his future in two of them, both local doctors. He knew he needed a college education to get into medical school but his family had no money. So he persuaded a banker, George Deines, to loan him three hundred dollars, which came with some free advice. "Gotta get a hat, going to be a young man," Dole recalled the banker telling him.

"So, I bought me a hat. I don't think I ever wore it. I may have worn it by the bank a couple of times so he'd see I had the hat. He wore a hat and thought anyone who amounted to anything wore a hat."

Dole, who had traveled with his family only to Kansas City in the east and Estes Park, Colorado, in the west for one summer vacation, left home at age eighteen. He and his best friend Bub Smith traveled 210 miles east to the University of Kansas, a green, open-minded state university on Mount Oread in Lawrence. It was a big change—KU, rising above the cornfields of eastern Kansas, was known as Snob Hill.

Dole was rushed by several fraternity houses because of his athletic skills, his grades and his upbeat outlook, said his Russell friend Harold Dumler. When he was checking out the Kappa Sigma house, Dole and two buddies, Bub Smith and Phil Ruppenthal, irreverently short-sheeted the older frat brothers' beds. That fall Dole enrolled in pre-medical courses and joined the Kappa Sigma fraternity. To earn spending money he waited tables at the fraternity and got up before dawn on Sundays to deliver milk. First-year students in the fraternity had to follow strict study hours. Dole was a good mixer, played on the frat house intramural team, was a social person—the kind the other pledges hung around because he was a natural leader and funny—though he did not have a girlfriend, said Harold Dumler, who was a senior during Bob's first year.

Among people who most impressed Dole was KU's legendary coach, Phog Allen, the father of modern basketball, whom he met through Allen's son "Mit" Allen, a member of an amateur basketball team in Russell.

Phog Allen accepted Dole onto his team as a freshman, though not as a starter. Bob ran track and just missed setting an indoor record in the 440-yard sprint.

THOUSANDS OF MILES from serene Lawrence, Kansas, the Nazis were now rampaging through Europe, threatening to subdue millions of people under a totalitarian, vicious regime. The news on December 7, 1941, about the horrifying destruction at Pearl Harbor by Japanese bombers signaled to many young American men they would soon be involved in a world war. The military draft was calling more midwestern young men into service during the spring of 1942. At KU good-by parties for enlisted men regularly pulled attention from classwork. For Dole, the parties were distracting. His grades were "terrible," around a C. A dean at the school called him into his office in 1942 and lowered the boom.

"You ought to enlist, you're just not making it in school," Dole recalls the dean telling him. "We had endless farewell parties, nobody really focused, certainly I didn't."

It was a story common to countless other young men at the outbreak of World War II.

ITALY AND BEYOND

IN DECEMBER 1942, a year after the United States entered World War II, Bob Dole enlisted in the U.S. Army and continued his sophomore year studies at the University of Kansas. It seemed Hitler's Third Reich would be crushed by the Allies before he was in harm's way. Called into active duty in June 1943, Dole entered basic training at Camp Barkley near Abilene, Texas. He trained in the Army Medical Corps until November, and at Camp Barkley he was briefly reunited with his brother Kenny, who had enlisted and was headed for the South Pacific. Seizing the opportunity, Bina Dole jumped aboard a train, rode from Russell to Texas and talked her way into the camp to see her two sons.

Bob Dole transferred to the Army Specialized Training Program (ASTP) at Brooklyn College in New York City. Unlike Russell's relative homogeneity, New York was exotic, a churning world of melding cultures and accents. Dole studied engineering in Brooklyn until March, 1944. He then hopped from Camp Polk in Louisiana that spring to Fort Breckenridge in Kentucky and trained as an anti-tank gunner in the 290th Infantry. He was accepted into Officer Candidate School (OCS) and traveled to Fort Benning in Georgia for his training. He entered as a corporal and graduated as a second lieutenant in the fall of 1944, months after the

D-Day invasion of Normandy that would put the war on a course toward an end in favor of the Allies.

Soon he boarded a troopship for Italy and arrived before Christmas with other second lieutenants and hung around the 24th Replacement Depot near Rome, where he rendezvoused with some Kappa Sigma brothers. They had a party, but felt a foreboding tension. Intensifying battles on the front killed and injured a growing number of American soldiers, calling for more soldiers to fill their places. "We were all sitting around waiting to be . . ." Dole mused for several seconds in an interview, "replacements somewhere."

In late February, Dole's turn came. The army assigned him to I Company, Third Battalion, 85th Regiment, Tenth Mountain Division and sent him to the front in the Italian Apennine mountains pushing northeast toward Bologna, where his job was to take over a platoon. The previous lieutenant in charge had been killed. Dole was twenty-one years old. The Allies aimed to attack German fortifications in the hills and mountains around the Po Valley, a main supply thoroughfare. If the Allies could take the valley they could cut the Germans off further south and, so the strategy went, the Germans would be forced to surrender in Italy.

The Tenth Mountain Division was already a legendary unit. In 1940, Charles "Minnie" Dole, unrelated to Bob Dole, founder of America's National Ski Patrol system, warned that a German attack on the United States could possibly begin in Maine, New Hampshire and Vermont in winter. If it happened, it was a diabolical danger; no American troops were trained to fight in snow and mountains. So in 1941 the National Ski Association began recruiting soldiers for the 87th Infantry Mountain Regiment, requiring applicants to submit three letters of recommendation. The 87th, then the 86th and 85th regiments drew in an unusual crowd— Ivy League graduates, athletes, outdoorsmen, well-educated young men. The members of what would become the Tenth Mountain Division originally trained at Camp Hope in Colorado by swooshing down the ski slopes carrying rifles and seventy-five-pound rucksacks. By late 1944 in Italy the Tenth Mountain Division had dropped its stringent requirements—Bob Dole certainly was no skier—though a strong *esprit de corps* lingered in the unit even as men died. General George P. Hayes, a World War I hero who had earned a congressional Medal of Honor, commanded the division.

The Allies' Fifth Army troops had begun an invasion of Italy in 1943 to destroy the German army, but the battle was very slow going. By early 1945 casualties had piled up on both sides. The Fifth Army's Tenth Mountain Division pushed north of Pistoia in February. It took three tries before division companies were able in March to take and hold Riva Ridge and the high, open Monte Belvedere-Monte Toracio ridge in the Apennines. The division then moved on toward a series of hills to the north, flanked by Mount della Spe and Mount Castel d'Aiano.

Al Nencioni, a sergeant in Dole's platoon, remembered the first time he saw Dole at the front in late February. Dole did not "blouse" his pants out like other soldiers; instead he tucked them into his boots. "He looked like a real rookie," said Nencioni, who became an agent for the Federal Bureau of Investigation after the war, "like a guy who was well-educated." Nencioni liked Dole anyway. "I'd rather have a company like Dole and guys who don't look tough than a battalion of John Waynes."

Another solder, Devereaux Jennings, a twenty-year-old skier from Utah who would compete in the 1948 Olympics and enter the Ski Hall of Fame, went out on several night patrols with Dole in March. Dole's platoon often came under fire from the Germans. The lieutenant was brave, said Jennings, he'd walk out to men on post at the front line even though he did not have to. He listened to the non-coms, the senior enlisted men who had more experience than newly minted lieutenants like himself. "Dole was a pretty cool, fair guy who handled himself with dignity," Jennings said. "He asked what we thought and I was happy to work with him because not all officers were like that. He wasn't an outspoken person. He just quietly did his job. I liked him. He wasn't out there to prove anything. I thought he was the best officer I'd seen."

Dole took over command of the platoon from Sergeant Frank Carafa, a battle-hardened veteran who had headed the group for several months until the next lieutenant arrived. "Dole said he wouldn't change anything right away, he'd continue everything just as we had and if he thought something needed to be changed, we'd talk about it," Carafa said. "The men loved him."

On March 18 Dole led a night patrol, triggering fire from some German positions. One of his group pulled the pin on a hand grenade and threw it. In the dark, it may have bounced off a tree and exploded. A small grenade fragment cut into Dole's leg and lightly injured several others. The men were patched up and each was awarded a Purple Heart.

On April 12, 1945, President Franklin D. Roosevelt died, not unexpected by men in the field, yet depressing. "We were all in tears," Dole recalled. "He was the president, commander-in-chief. We were all sort of a family. There wasn't any politics or any of that stuff. Hell, that was a big blow."

★ ★ ★

IT WAS FOG, not FDR's death, that delayed the beginning of Operation Craftsman, a final Allied offensive to dig Germans out of trenches and foxholes warrened into the hills above the Po Valley and take control of northern Italy. Early on April 14, only days before the end of the war in Europe, the Americans and Brazilian allies began their offensive, sending the 85th, 86th and 87th regiments, a force of hundreds of men, forward. Around nine in the morning Allied P-47 fighter planes pounded Hill 913, the objective that day, with 500-pound bombs. The fighters swung around to fire rockets and returned to strafe the hill with machine-gun fire. Artillery gunners followed, blasting away with 75-, 105- and 155-millimeter shells. After a thirty-five-minute bombardment the air was silent. As the dust cleared, Al Nencioni saw Hill 913, now nothing more than smoking gray rock. "They really plastered it," Nencioni said. "I thought, This is not going to be that bad. Mistake."

The U.S. Army field report of the division written soon after that morning suggests why: "A captured German diary revealed that they had been warned that the Tenth Mountain Division was about to attack and they would not take any prisoners. This undoubtedly accounted for the fanatical resistance that our troops encountered, which often meant digging the Germans out of their well-prepared bunkers."

From the bombing the land below Hill 913 was pocked with exploded mortar shells. Platoon leaders prepared their attack. As the division moved forward Germans who may have run off the hills during the bombardment and hidden in bunkers opened up with machine-gun fire, mortars and artillery. Dole's platoon was pinned down behind a four-foot-high hedgerow facing an open field. Hill 913 rose steeply on the far side of the field. One sergeant nearby led his men into the eerily quiet field, two hundred yards square, grass-covered and flat as a board. Machine-gun fire rattled and mines exploded in the field as the men ran for cover and died.

The machine-gun fire came from Germans holed up in a lone stone house off to the right. The American company commander ordered the I Company platoon to try to flank the house and take out the machine gunners. He requested that Sergeant Frank Carafa lead. Carafa went to tell the squad. The military's hierarchy of command said lieutenants were the head of their squads. Lieutenant Dole would lead while Carafa provided covering fire.

Dole and his men headed into a narrow grassy dip, hoping to get across an opening into a ravine. Machine-gun fire cracked and mortar shells exploded around them. Jennings, far to the right, saw the Germans crank up a mobile rocket launcher of a kind he had never seen before and fire a large artillery shell toward the Americans. "If you're intelligent, you know when you're in serious danger," said Jennings. Nencioni echoed: "I was scared, I'll admit it. You'd have to be stupid not to be."

Several of Dole's platoon were hit as Dole and the others dove into mortar craters and foxholes. His radioman moved out and was hit. Dole scrambled after him, grabbed him and pulled him back, realizing at the same time that he was dead. He crawled forward again over the rocky ground, felt a sharp pain slam into his right shoulder and collapsed. A bullet or exploding shell had ripped into his shoulder. He lay facedown in the dirt. He thought he'd lost his arms, he couldn't feel them. Only later did he realize they were stretched out above his head.

For long moments Dole yelled for help, lying on the open field. Soldiers told Sergeant Carafa that Dole was calling for him.

Finally, a full half hour later, bullets flying overhead, a terrified Carafa crawled into the battlefield, past dead men, to reach Dole, who was moaning. Dole's injury shocked him. He was laid out on his back now, right arm stretched out limp. Carafa took hold of Dole's right arm, folded it over his chest and pulled him backward out of danger behind the hedgerow. He called to Sergeant Stanley Kuschik, to get him to the medics. Carafa saw one other soldier alive about twenty yards away and scrambled out after him too and dragged him to safety.

Dole was gray, "the way they got before they died," Kuschick later remembered, in an article published in The Washingtonian magazine in 1984. "I couldn't just leave him there to die by himself." Standing orders were to leave the wounded for medics who would follow, a tough battle policy to insure a mission would move forward to its objective. But the Germans ignored human rights protocols and shot many of the medics. So Kuschick couldn't leave Dole there. He administered a dose of morphine, then dipped his finger in Dole's blood and wrote an M on his forehead, a warning to others not to give Dole another, potentially fatal dose. Soldiers were not routinely issued morphine, Kuschik had taken it off a dead medic.

Kuschick crouched beside Dole awhile, then ordered Arthur McBryar, who was slightly wounded in his leg, to stay with Dole while Kuschick joined his comrades in the attack on Hill 913.

"Stan came over and said, 'The lieutenant's been hit, bring your guys over,' " Jennings recalled. "I saw several guys gathered around Dole." Soldiers moved Dole behind the front. He lay semi-conscious on a litter all afternoon. His buddies pushed on and captured Hill 913. Dole's I Company sustained so many casualties that K company moved up and helped take the hill in the late afternoon. In all, the 85th regiment battled that day and the next to take Hills 909 and 913, suffering four hundred sixty-two casualties, with ninety-eight men killed.

"I don't remember much until being in this lineup with a whole lot of litters waiting my turn to go to an Italian hospital where they sort of check to see how you are," Dole said in an interview.

At the 170th Evacuation Hospital, army medical staff stabilized Dole's condition and on April 15 a young neurosurgeon at that hospital, Dr. Lyle French, evaluated Dole and wrote in his report that he had sustained a high-explosive shell-fragment wound to the back of his shoulder. Dr. French operated on Dole at ten in the morning April 15. He cleaned the wound, made an incision from the neck out along the shoulder, elevated the clavicle and examined the damage. With forceps he removed numerous small bone fragments around the lateral and posterior cords. The veins and artery seemed okay, but French saw several bleeding points from which a hematoma had developed, and he tried to control them with silk stitches. He sewed the wound closed and applied a plaster cast covering Dole's chest. He noted: "Postoperative condition good—evac to rear 16 April '45."

Two days later Dole was transferred to a military hospital in Casablanca, Morocco, where doctors realized the damage was more severe. French apparently had been unaware of Dole's spinal injury. Whatever hit him had fractured his clavicle, the collarbone, the scapula behind the collarbone, the humerus, the upper bone in the arm, and tore into a vertebrae, which affected his spinal cord. Now in a cast from his chin to his hips, Lieutenant Bob Dole was paralyzed.

In those first days in Morocco he struggled to keep his spirits up, dictating to Doran and Bina Dole in Russell letters that soldiers around him wrote and sent, according to The Washingtonian magazine. On April 27, 1945, Dole dictated:

"Dear Mom and Dad,

I'm feeling pretty good today. I'm just a little nervous and restless, but I'll be okay before long. I'm getting so I can move my right arm a little and I can also move my legs. I seem to be improving every day and there isn't any reason why I shouldn't be as good as new before long.

Send me something to read and something to eat.

Love,
Bob"

The war in Europe ended May 8, 1945, just three weeks after Dole was wounded. In early June he was transferred back to the United States to a hospital in Florida, then admitted to Winter General Hospital in Topeka, Kansas. Bina left home and rented an apartment in Topeka, one hundred seventy-eight miles east of Russell. Dole had now lost bowel and bladder function, was encased in the body cast and had a persistent fever. Bina Dole sat by her son's bed day and night for weeks.

One day Dole's temperature soared to 108.7 degrees and the doctors told Bina Dole her son might live only a few more hours. He recovered, but developed a kidney infection brought on at least in part because the hospital staff had moved him infrequently, allowing the sulfa drugs given him to settle in his kidneys. His right kidney was removed on July 11, 1945. His doctors believed that if he survived his injuries and complications, Dole would probably never walk again.

Confounding his physicians, Dole could move his legs by September and had reclaimed some movement of his arms. His cast came off. Soon he could stand. And he began to walk.

"Bob had learned to walk as a baby when he was between ten and eleven months old," Bina Dole said in an article published in 1984 in The Washingtonian magazine. "At Winter General I watched a nurse get him up out of bed. He walked the same way—tentatively, but with determination to learn."

He could not feed himself for a year, needed his mother to help him. Worse, he'd taken up smoking, and even though she disliked cigarettes, she would hold them for him to puff on. He had to be dressed and helped to go to the bathroom.

That fall Bina and Doran Dole brought their son home to Russell. He was an unnerving sight. He had left Russell a powerful 194-pound athlete and returned gaunt, weighing 122 pounds. Instead of running through the street, he shuffled slowly. First to the corner, then around the block, then around two blocks. He tried to project an upbeat mood, but inside it was difficult to bear. Especially looking in a mirror. He grimaced at what he saw. Nearly fifty years later, he would still look in mirrors only to shave.

Dole's parents moved out of their main floor bedroom and turned it over to him. People stopped by to say hello. "He was pretty tough about it all," his sister Gloria Nelson said. "When he came home the first time he didn't want help but he needed it. Norma Jean had to feed him. Sometimes he'd spill something and he'd just get up and walk away from the table and back into his room."

"They were very supportive, so were a lot of people in town," Dole said of his parents in an interview. "I remember going downtown for the first time, it was quite a shock going to the drugstore. I'd lost a lot of weight."

He always liked chocolate milkshakes. The Dawsons had told him, "First time you're down there, they're on the house."

"I finally got up enough courage to go downtown and do that," Dole recalled.

One day on the street a man seeing Dole, right arm in a cast and walking slowly, said, "Well, don't you think it'd been better if you'd just died?"

Dole quickly replied, "If I'da felt that way I'da been dead a long time ago."

In November, 1945, he traveled to Percy Jones Hospital in Battle Creek, Michigan, hundreds of miles from his family, for physical therapy. On the morning of December 21 he woke up to excruciating pain in his chest. The medical staff rushed in and diagnosed a pulmonary infarct, a blockage due to a blood clot. From his months of inactivity Dole's blood flow had slowed, setting up conditions for clotting. The doctors treated him with dicumarol, a blood-thinning drug. His temperature shot up and then fluctuated. Bina Dole had already come to Michigan to see her son and to be with him for Christmas; Doran Dole made the several-hundred-mile ride from Russell aboard a train crowded with servicemen, standing up most of the way. His father's sacrifice for that visit still overwhelmed Dole half a century afterward.

"When he made it his ankles were so swollen," Dole said, reaching down to his ankles in an October 1993 broadcast of CBS's "60 Minutes" taped in the backyard of his parents' Russell home. He coughed, his voice grew husky. "But . . . he made it."

On February 12, 1946, doctors stopped the dicumarol; the next day Dole felt a chill and pain in his chest. Doctors resumed the dicumarol and penicillin, but it did not seem to have an effect. His temperature climbed to 106. For a second time, his doctors thought he might die. Doran and Bina Dole were afraid that after nearly losing their eldest son in a war thousands of miles and an ocean away, they might watch him die right before their eyes.

His doctors offered one slim chance, an experimental drug used on only a handful of people around the country. The Doles had no alternative. Doran and Bina Dole signed a release allowing the staff to administer the new drug: streptomycin. The powerful drug enjoyed use for several decades thereafter before being taken off the market because some patients who received it became deaf. Four days after Dole received the streptomycin, he sat up.

By early March he was able to sit briefly in a wheelchair. Soon he stood, then walked again. His sense of humor returned. The staff wheeled him around the hospital ward to tell jokes and poke gentle fun at other patients. It seemed good for all of them—Bob Dole was famous: the soldier who didn't die when he was supposed to.

He worked hard at recovery. Each day he went to physical therapy, where he did exercises to strengthen his legs, put muscle back in his left arm and to regain as much movement as possible in his hands. He had to relearn how to eat, to dress and to write, not with his natural right hand but awkwardly with his left. His right arm remained nearly useless. To make some money Dole tried selling automobiles to patients in the hospital. Oldsmobile sold a car specially equipped with brake and acceleration controls on the steering wheel. Dole developed a pitch he aimed at paraplegics, but he sold few cars. The suffering and injury he saw around him opened his eyes to pain felt by others, Dole has said many times in interviews over the years. Men at Percy Jones had lost arms, legs and, worst of all, their mental stability through their war experiences. Though others were worse off, Dole still couldn't help feeling sorry for himself, feeling bitterness.

"Why me? I demanded—why hadn't someone been watching out for me?" he wrote in *Unlimited Partners*. "In time, I came to realize that someone *was* watching out for me, and had been from the morning of April 14. Maybe it was all part of a plan, a test of endurance and strength and, above all, of faith."

Part of his faith propelled him to scour medical facilities for a cure to heal his right arm, consumed with hope he might be restored to the whole man he had been before the war. He traveled to Wichita, Denver and to Sterling, Kansas, which had renowned clinics. No luck.

At home again in Russell, Dole pushed himself to rebuild strength. He put on his old track shoes and walked around his neighborhood, trying to increase his time every day. Wherever he went he squeezed a rubber ball in his left hand. Kenny Dole and friends set up a weight-training regimen in the garage with pulleys and small weights for brother Bob to use to rebuild muscle. His high school friend Adolph Reisig, designed physical therapy for him; he cast a twenty-five-pound lead sleeve to fit over Dole's arm. "Bob solicited help, recruited friends to help him because of his strong desire to be a whole man again," said Reisig.

One day Lamant Jahn, Dole's brother-in-law, mentioned he had heard of a doctor in Chicago with a reputation for surgical wizardry. Dole traveled to Chicago and met Dr. Hampar Kelikian, an Armenian immigrant who later became a top-rated neurosurgeon in the United States. "I'll never forget the first day I was there," Dole said in an interview. "He came rushing to greet me in the hallway in broken English. He was hard to understand and I thought, 'Maybe I'm his first patient.' "

Known as "Dr. K," Kelikian had escaped his war-torn homeland as a boy and made his way to Chicago in 1920. He worked on a farm, persuaded his boss to pay his way through college and attended medical school. After examining Dole, Kelikian said he would do some surgery, but warned the young man not to expect a miracle. Too much time had elapsed, his shoulder bones had suffered irreparable damage. Dole recalled, "I think he finally in a nice way said, 'You've got to stop chasing the rainbow. We'll do the best we can.' "

Dr. K ran his business on some simple principles: if you had no money you paid nothing for his services; if you had a lot you paid a lot. He would not accept money from Dole.

People in Russell looked for a way to reach out to Dole. Other young men in town had been killed in the war. Dole came back shattered but had not given up. Down at Dole's old soda fountain haunt Chet Dawson, a commander in the local Veterans of Foreign Wars, came up with the idea to start a collection to help pay Dole's hospital bills after Dr. Kelikian did his surgery. Dawson took an empty cigar box, put a Bob Dole Fund label on it and set it on the counter. Local banks joined in to handle contributions, which poured in, nickels, dimes, quarters, dollars, and a few hundred-dollar donations. The town pulled together a total of eighteen hundred dollars—a lot of money in those days—which they presented to Dole.

In 1947 Kelikian performed three surgeries on Dole's right arm and hand, the first of seven he would eventually do, all free of charge, to loosen Dole's right shoulder and to transplant tendons from his leg so he could have some movement. Part of the scapula was removed and muscles in Dole's neck were reconnected to his right arm. Slowly, Kelikian helped

Dole realize he would be partially disabled for the rest of his life, hard medicine to swallow.

"I don't care who it is, it takes a while to accept you have limitations you didn't have the day before yesterday or the month before or the year before," Dole said in an interview. "He was pretty good at keeping you going, thinking you had to move ahead. He'd say, 'You're doin' great.' Oh, that would make you feel like—'Boy, that was fantastic!'—Even if you did something that didn't amount to much. He was very helpful to me, he sort of adopted me as a son at the time."

Dole's dream of becoming a doctor died. In his own personal nightmare he feared he would end up an invalid selling pencils on a Russell street corner, he has said in interviews and campaign speeches. He could not let that happen. Out of that kind of despair his survival instinct bonded with his competitive drive, surged.

"I don't remember when it started," Dole said in the "60 Minutes" television broadcast. "But one day you get up and say, Okay, let's get outta here. Let's start thinking about the future instead of the past and maybe Bob Dole can do something else."

Dole returned to Percy Jones in 1947 for more therapy. One day in the mess hall in the early spring of 1948, his right arm still in a cast and elevated in front of his chest, Dole caught sight of an attractive brunette named Phyllis Holden, a New Hampshire girl who was an occupational therapist in another ward of the hospital. She in turn noted Dole. A friend warned her to stay away. "That's Bob Dole," she said. "He only has a short time to live."

Not long after, when Phyllis first spoke with him at an officers' club dance, she found out her friend was wrong. Dole was, she thought, funny, he was positive, he had a lot of push. The hall was decorated for a party, the dance floor was called "Heaven," the bar "Hell." Dole asked her to dance. He was twenty-four, she was twenty-three. She was drawn to him. "He had a good sense of humor and he was a very good-looking man," said Phyllis. "We just seemed to get along well." They dated frequently and one day, some three months later, Bob Dole came up to her and said, "Let's get married."

Phyllis was thrilled, her mother was flat opposed. Not to someone who's handicapped, she complained. Phyllis had her own ideas. She and Bob Dole were married in early June 1948.

A NEW CAREER

WITH DOLE AT the wheel of his car, the newly-married couple drove to Lake Winnepesaukee in New Hampshire for a lakeshore cabin honeymoon. Afterward they drove to Kansas to visit the Dole clan in the early summer of 1948. Bina and Phyllis hit it off. Phyllis admired Bina's energy and mothering support, and Bina seemed pleased teaching cooking to a new woman in the family. Bina never used recipes. Phyllis guessed measurements and wrote them down as she watched Bina throw together a delicious country meal.

That summer, thanks to a GI bill student loan, Bob and Phyllis Dole drove on to Arizona—Dole's doctors had suggested the warm climate might be good for his health—for Dole to enroll at the University of Arizona in Tucson. He drove the car Adolph Reisig in Russell had outfitted for him with a left-hand gearshift. Max Horn, the retired Russell banker comfortable with making pronouncements about the town he was born into seventy-nine years earlier, says getting an education, not the war injury, was the most significant event in Dole's life. Completing an education unlocked the world of opportunities in those days for young people from small towns, and Bob Dole was the only sibling in his family to attend college.

Now twenty-five, Dole took a liberal-arts program at Arizona. He couldn't write with his right hand to take notes so he wrote shorthand notes with his left. In the evening in their two-room guest house, while Phyllis was with friends, Bob would slowly make notes with his left hand. Afterward, exhausted, he went to bed. "We didn't have time to talk too much," Phyllis recalled. "But he's not that kind of a person anyway. He's not a chatterer."

Dole began to commit extraordinary amounts of ideas to memory; he couldn't write it down fast enough. He studied all the time. One evening Phyllis asked him, "*Why* do you have to make an A?"

"I've got to get it all," Dole blurted out. "I've got to learn as much as I can."

"He was very committed to doing the very best that he could," Phyllis said in an interview years later. Because of her work with other patients she understood his uncompromising motivation. "I think it goes back to the physical problem he had. Others may not have to study as hard and are not unhappy coming out in the middle. But if you're working to bring back a physical problem to normalcy, you have *got* to work as hard as you can. And I think he carried that drive over into school."

Dole's physical condition improved. He took frequent long walks in the hills around Tucson to strengthen his legs, and after a year in liberal arts he decided he wanted to go to law school. Arizona did not have a law program, so Dole thought first of the University of Kansas. He needed ongoing blood analysis, however, and Lawrence lacked a sophisticated lab. The only acceptable lab in Kansas near a law school was in Topeka. So in the fall of 1949 he enrolled in Washburn Municipal College, which later became Washburn University. The Doles moved into the Senate apartments, three-room warrens with galley kitchens and dark wood trim just across the street from the state capitol.

Dole walked the long distance to Washburn, where he pursued a bachelor's degree and a law degree. He carried a Sound Scriber to class to tape lectures. The bulky, heavy box worked like a flat record player, spinning small plastic records to pick up the lecturer's voice. Dole would plug it in near the instructor in front of the room. He was one who, instead of going to play pinball, stayed after class to talk to the professors. Ambition was his defining characteristic. Most of Dole's professors were cooperative with his limitation and gave him his exams orally. A few did not. For those tests Phyllis accompanied him and the two huddled far from the other students, Dole dictating his answers for her to write down. He would later take his Kansas bar exam to practice law in Kansas in a room full of nervous classmates, whispering answers to Phyllis, who had problems spelling legal terms.

While Dole studied law day and night, Phyllis earned money working in a center for the blind and in the Topeka State Hospital. They rarely socialized but drove out to Russell often to see Dole's family. Phyllis, they felt, was open, talkative and would pitch in to help with meals—a regular "Kansas girl," said one Russellite who especially liked her.

IN 1950 BETH BOWERS, the law librarian at Washburn, a Democrat, urged Bob Dole and three of his classmates to consider political careers. Dole listened. Politicians back home also had their eye on the twenty-seven-year-old war hero; they knew veterans made good candidates. Dole experienced a kind of fraternity rush for his political allegiance. The county Republican and Democratic party chairmen both talked to him. So did Clifford Holland, Sr., a prominent Democrat in Russell County and his parents' old family friend, and John Woelk, the county attorney and a leading Republican who had been in the state Senate. Holland and Woelk wanted him to run for state representative, a job that paid five dollars a day with an additional seven for expenses. Not exactly great money even in those days, but a stepping-stone.

"Well, Bob, if you really want to do something in politics in Kansas you'd better declare yourself a Republican," Woelk told Dole one day.

Political party registration in Russell County was two to one Republican over Democrat, Woelk continued, and the statewide registration was predominately Republican. It was a state that produced Republicans Alf Landon, the Kansas governor who ran against Franklin D. Roosevelt in 1936, and General Dwight Eisenhower, who was Texas-born but lived early years in Kansas. "In Kansas it is really hard to run for a statewide office as a Democrat," Woelk added, sensing Dole's ambition.

Even though his parents were Democrats, Bob Dole filed as a Republican, an act of pragmatism that would become a trademark of his life. That year, while still a law student, Dole defeated Democrat Elmo Mahoney, the entrenched state representative from nearby Dorrance. Dole walked into the Kansas Legislature that winter, at age twenty-seven, one of the youngest state representatives in the state's history. Seated near him in the legislature was another newcomer, William Avery, whom Dole would cross paths with later in his career. "If he hadn't of had a seat close to me I wouldn't have remembered him," said Avery, who graduated the legislature in 1954 to win a House seat in Congress. "He was just a nice guy and I liked him."

When Dole graduated from Washburn in 1952 Eric "Doc" Smith, an attorney in Russell, invited him to join his law practice. Smith did general legal work and was looking for a junior partner. Dole accepted the offer, bought a large new leather chair to put behind his big desk in Smith's second floor law office just off Main Street. "It looked like a hundred-dollar saddle on a ten-dollar horse," an early visitor to Dole's office remarked.

Bob and Phyllis Dole moved into a home in Russell, where his family kept her occupied while he worked. He did not talk much about his legal cases, but Phyllis still found Russell accepting and friendly. Some evenings she and Bob played in a bridge club. Bob worked weekdays into the night and all day Saturdays. The two regularly attended the Methodist Church service on Sunday, then gathered with others of the Dole tribe at Doran and Bina's home for Sunday dinners. Doran was quiet, Bina outgoing to Phyllis. Neither parent was touchy-warm, but they clearly were proud of their family, she thought.

In 1952 John Woelk announced he would retire as county attorney, setting off a scramble. Dole was very interested, although certain aspects of the job would belong in the liabilities column of a balance sheet. The salary was not much better than he made as a state representative—two hundred forty-eight dollars a month—four dollars *less* than the custodian at the courthouse earned. Nor was the job particularly demanding. In fact, county attorneys were expected to accept private work on the side to pad their wallets. Established attorneys generally avoided the job. It was considered a way for young lawyers to get their feet wet, a way to *become* established. Bob Dole didn't know many of the important people in Russell County, the kind who could help him win the office.

He wanted the job.

Dean Banker, a friend of Dole's, advised him to announce his candidacy in a splashy way, not follow the tradition of proclaiming from the steps of the Russell County courthouse. Dole rounded up supporters, drove nine miles east to Bunker Hill and announced his candidacy in the high school gymnasium, literally a stone's throw from the home of Ray Shaffer, the local Republican committee chairman. Shaffer was impressed. Dole had come to his turf, paid his respects, that was good.

Most people in Russell County expected the county attorney's job would go to another young lawyer, Dean Ostrum, a well-known attorney's son who had also announced for Woelk's seat. Because of his prominent family, Ostrum had political connections in the Republican party. The campaign launched, the two Republicans, friends before and after, battled for the primary election. The race turned into a poor-boy-rich-boy contest. Dean Ostrum tried to downplay his affluence by putting on dress shirts with worn collars. Dole's old friends like Bub Dawson laughed at that. "Just to kind of look poor. He didn't want to look wealthy," Dawson said. "I never will forget that frayed collar, it was really frayed." Dole didn't have to pretend. Everyone knew his modest background, knew about Doran Dole's cream station and Bina Dole's peddling Singer sewing machines, how they raised four children in their small house on Maple Street.

Bob Dole stood out for another reason. All across the country, people viewed veterans very favorably after World War II and were seeking to reintegrate the survivors into the society they had fought to preserve. Like most towns in America the war had claimed a number of young Russell men, including Dole's best friend Bud Smith, who went to KU with him. Dole's injury and disabled arm stirred sympathies. Tall, handsome with his dark hair and lean face, slightly vulnerable, his brown eyes were more serious now, his right hand was always clenched in a fist at his side.

"I ran against Dean Ostrum, who was a much better lawyer, from a family of lawyers, very fine family. He was probably a lot smarter than I was. But people thought, 'Oh, poor Bob, he needs the job,' " Dole said in an interview, wincing at the memory. He didn't try to hide his limitations, quite the opposite, according to John Woelk. "Dole always managed to display it," said Woelk. "It was an advantage he had and he exploited it."

Ostrum traveled through Russell County campaigning that summer, exerting himself as though the job meant a lot to him. At the same time Dole set out to prove he did not expect people to vote for him because of his disability; he would work for the job, listen to them, talk to them for hours, show his stamina. He campaigned from dawn until after dark in the heat, plowing back and forth across the thirty-mile-square county. Driving home at night, if Dole saw a light on inside any farmhouse he'd stop to knock on the door and introduce himself, his brother Kenny Dole recalled in 1986. Dole worked on remembering everyone's name, just as he had memorized legal cases in law school. Russell Countians gradually understood: Bob Dole was giving it his all. And wealthy families—the Driscolls, the Hollands, others—backed Bob Dole.

As the primary battle came to a vote that summer, Dole defeated Ostrum by 185 votes, barely enough for a Saturday night dance. The final tally was 1,133 votes for Dole to 948 for Ostrum. He won the hard way, by demonstrating himself more worthy at the Holy Grail of midwestern American values.

"Dole just outworked Ostrum," said Woelk.

Having won the Republican primary in the predominately Republican county, Dole's fall campaign was easier. In November of 1952, he dispatched Democrat George Holland, a son of his parents' friend Clifford Holland, Sr., and the man who had urged him to get into politics in the first place, by a vote of 4,207 to 2,065. Dole had now won a two-year term as county attorney.

In fact, a lot rode on that contest. The county attorney post was a shakeout job. "If Dole had lost his first primary it would have dimmed his political career," said Woelk. "It certainly caused Ostrum to look elsewhere." Eventually Ostrum worked his way up to a vice-presidency at Southwestern Bell Telephone Co., from which years later he retired to work in the theater in New York City.

That year of 1952 was significant for another Kansas Republican—Dwight David Eisenhower, who was elected president of the United States. Eisenhower came into office as a moderate Republican and charted the country through calmer times, the bebopping 1950s, era of the Baby Boomers, Buddy Holly, drive-ins and early television talk shows. But the decade also carried its dark undercurrent. Nuclear Armageddon menaced America, racial tensions swelled and Senator Joseph McCarthy fulminated unchecked about alleged Communists in government.

Dole, at the local level, was the hardest-working county attorney Russell, Kansas, had ever seen. He showed up at the office by eight a.m., handled county business all day and turned to his private cases only at night. He took care of the routine matters thrown at county attorneys throughout the midwest—minor crimes, liquor violations, speeding tickets. The job description also delegated some unpleasant responsibilities to the new county attorney. Dole had to sign welfare checks for recipients in the county, a practice aimed at embarrassing the unneedy who might try to take advantage of the system. In that stack of checks each month, for a while, he signed payments for Robert and Margaret Dole, his own grandparents.

"There were a lot of poor people who would come to the county," Dole said. "My grandparents were poor people."

It bothered him, too, when he had to take children away from an abusive family, Phyllis Dole recalled, even though life improved for them because of his intervention.

At home the Doles tried unsuccessfully to have a child of their own.

Doctors examined Phyllis and found nothing wrong. After more futile attempts they turned to adoption, filled out paperwork at the Kansas Children's Service League and had only a home study to pass when Phyllis found out she was pregnant. In 1954 Robin Dole, a dark-haired girl, was born and named after her father, Robert. Robin would be their only child.

DOLE RAN UNOPPOSED in the 1954 county attorney election and in 1956 defeated Clifford Holland, Jr., another of the senior Holland's sons, 3,175 to 2,317. In 1958 he beat Democrat Robert Earnest by 2,807 to 2,195. The county attorney job brought him in daily contact with the county sheriff Harry Morgenstern, whose office was next door to Dole's. "Even in a social setting, a lot of people would have a question for him and he would say he'd take care of it tomorrow. And he really did," Morgenstern said in the Russell *Daily News* in 1987. "After a social gathering, however, he would go back to work. Even if it was ten or eleven o'clock at night." Across the street Bub Dawson would close up the drugstore at eleven and see the light still burning in Dole's office.

"Aw, I left the light on and went home," Dole once said to Dawson.

But that was where Huck Boyd, the Phillipsburg publisher, found him in 1960, and decided he would help the younger man get ahead. The 6th District congressional seat was held by Wint Smith, a brash six-foot-five, three-hundred-pound Republican from Mankato, who had occupied the post since 1946. But Smith was a die-hard conservative who had trouble changing with the times. In 1958 he saw his political epitaph written when he won reelection by fewer than one hundred votes, and announced he would retire in 1960.

Boyd now approached Dole about running for the seat and introduced him to others in the Kansas Republican Party. At Boyd's suggestion Dole made a midnight pilgrimage to visit Dane Hansen in Logan, one hundred ten miles to the northwest. Hansen, a wealthy businessman and party kingmaker, had the unusual habit of working from near sundown to sunup. He was a firm Smith supporter and ally of the state's Republican Governor Alf Landon, who had run and lost the 1936 presidential race against President Franklin D. Roosevelt. Hansen was encouraging, so Dole planned his announcement at the Republican state convention in January, a sedate affair in Topeka's Jayhawk Hotel, where party pooh-bahs made backroom deals.

Unknown outside of Russell County, Dole sketched out his plan to attract attention. On January 29, the Dole convoy arrived. In marched twenty attractive young women in red skirts with matching handbags—the "Bobolinks," singing full-throated pep songs accompanied by ukulele. A football player teetered in on a tricycle, followed by a farmer wearing a huge elephant's head. Finally six distinguished men exuding a funereal mood strode in bearing an open coffin. Inside lay a Frankenstein dummy. The coffin displayed a large sign: "You have nothing to fear with Dole."

Despite—or maybe because of—his campaign theatrics, most people thought Dole would lose. He faced two experienced opponents, state senator Keith G. Sebelius of Norton, who had nearly knocked off Wint Smith in 1958, and Phillip Doyle, another state senator. Sebelius was an amiable man, well-liked for his willingness to listen for hours to people. Dole worried he also would lose to Sebelius because people would be confused between him, his wife Phyllis, and Doyle. Dole, Doyle, Phillip, Phyllis . . . how would they know who they were voting for? For starters, Dole, who welcomed Wint Smith's endorsement and campaigning on his behalf, chose a different style of campaigning from the imperious congressman—which presaged where he would later see his appeal in American politics.

"[Smith's] the kind of a campaigner who'd walk into the dime store and walk by all the clerks, go all the way to the back, shake hands with the boss and leave," Dole recalled in an interview. "Now my view is, you shake hands with all the clerks and if the boss is in you try to shake hands with him. I never pass anybody up, if I can help it. You've gotta be careful, there's a fine line between oversolicitous backslappers. I've seen some of these people pat everybody. Ugh. But I think in a nice way you can say hello to everybody. They may not want you to say hello, most people do. So when you leave that store they feel like they had your full attention for whatever, the half a second or second they shook hands.

"I guess I was very, competitive anyway and even after the disability I was more competitive," Dole added. "I was trying to prove to myself that I could still make it, still do it."

While contemporary political candidates tend to agonize over setting up attractive photo-ops, staying "on message," scrounging millions of dollars in donations, divining the heart of soulless polls, gathering opposition research—dirt—on their opponents, preaching patriotic platitudes, gleaning clues from focus groups and scheming to lure free television media coverage, campaigns back then were less contrived. You told people who you were, what you wanted to do, maybe poked at your opponents and put a few advertisements on radio and television. The art of wholesale campaigning—mass-marketing a candidate like toothpaste or soda pop—had not yet been invented.

In 1960 congressional politics was a retail affair; candidates were traveling salesmen offering their wares from town to town, in person. Dole often drove himself. What he knew in 1960 was that he needed some attention-getters, a way to separate himself from the others. Gimmicks, some might say. He chose to capitalize on his name, linking it to a common brand-name product—Dole pineapple juice. Kenny and others hurried to the grocery stores in and around Russell, buying up all the cans of pineapple juice they could lay hands on. At parades and on weekends Dole and his supporters would hit a town, set up a folding table, stack up cans of Dole pineapple juice and pass out cup after cup. Gallons of pineapple juice flooded the 6th District. Kenny Dole contacted the Dole company, asking for permission to use the juice and hinted that some free cases would be helpful. After all, they were providing free advertising. The company wrote back that it was just fine to promote their pineapple juice and thanks for buying so much of it.

"Hi, I'm Bob Dole, like the pineapple juice. I'm running for Congress and I'd like your support," Dole said a zillion times, driving some 40,000 miles during the campaign.

The Dole team cooked up other ideas and developed a method of campaigning that capitalized on Dole's willingness to seek out voters sixteen hours a day. A small Conestoga wagon toured the district bearing Dole's campaign slogan—"Roll With Dole." Everywhere, Dole supporters handed out small cards with the image of a wagon wheel in blue and red. Around the wheel's rim was: "PUT YOUR SHOULDER TO THE WHEEL AND ROLL WITH DOLE IN '60." Along each of twelve spokes was a phrase about Dole's qualifications: "Born 7-22-23; Russell Native; K.U.& Washburn; Methodist; Twice Wounded Vet.; Legislature 1951; Won 7 Elections; Boy & Girl Scouts; Sec. 4-H Fair Assn.; Ser. Off. VFW & Am. Leg; Elks-Moose-Kiwanian; Co. Atty. 4 Terms." Blue-and-red campaign posters featuring Dole's serious face were tacked up across the district, among the first color campaign paraphernalia ever used in Kansas.

The Bobolinks later became "Dolls for Dole," singing and campaigning for him in matching skirts and striped tops sewn by Phyllis and Bina. The Dolls also wore white sombreros with large letters under the brim: "BOB DOLE." Little Robin Dole, then six years old, was pressed into service. Her brown hair plaited in pigtails, Robin wore a white blouse and a red-

and-blue skirt with a small elephant on the front and a white banner stitched below declaring, "I'm for my Daddy—Are You?"

"We went around, we had Dolls for Dole, we had covered wagons, we had the Bobettes, the Bobolinks. We had a great time. You couldn't do that anymore, you couldn't have Dolls for Dole anymore. Not today," Dole said in an interview. "Lots of Dole pineapple juice. Some people put vodka in it, I learned later. That's why they were having so much fun."

Alcohol played another perhaps minor, if somewhat sour role in the campaign. Rumors floated that summer that Keith Sebelius was a drinker. In the state that had given saloon-smashing Carry Nation her start three decades earlier, drinking, especially to excess, was viewed dimly. Dole himself never drank much. A tippling problem could finish a politician. The accusation did not come up in debate between Dole and Sebelius, nor in their public appearances; it was just one of those dark comments whispered between friends. Douglas Sebelius, Keith Sebelius's son, said he had heard of the rumors after the campaign, apparently bolstered when his father was seen carrying groceries for the needy into a church. The box supposedly bore a whiskey company label.

Wint Smith, a teetotaler who backed Dole, not Sebelius, and Mildred Plummer of Downs, Kansas, another supporter who headed the Women's Christian Temperance Union, the prohibitionist group still active then, may have passed along the rumor, Dole said he had heard. But after the campaign was over he and the Sebelius family became friends. "Bob doesn't get credit for some of the benevolent things he's done," said Douglas Sebelius. "But Bob's style of campaigning was different than Dad's. He's an aggressive campaigner. It was a tough campaign."

Other bad vibes blew through the contest. The American Legion backed Sebelius because he had been state commander. The legion would not give Bob Dole its list of members, even though Doran had been a member for years and Bob had been severely wounded in Italy, and some veterans complained. The controversy hurt Sebelius.

Dole, meanwhile, barnstormed through northwest Kansas, driving himself or having Kenny drive him to Hays, Salina, Phillipsburg, Osborne, Hoxie, Oberlin, the towns with several thousand residents, and through smaller towns, such as Zurich, Paradise and Bird City. He would work all day Saturdays in windblown places like Colby with his mother after a parade, pushing pineapple juice, the campaign cards, talking to people five or ten minutes at a time for one vote.

"That's the part I like, to get out there," Dole said in an interview. "And I would not eat at a dinner. I'd go out and shake hands with everybody. My view was I could always eat. You don't want to offend a table-mate up there, but why not go out and say hello to two hundred people instead of just saying hello two hundred times to one person. It paid off—people knew I would work; I'd be the last to leave and even if people didn't agree with you they appreciated you if you worked hard. Might not vote for you, but, 'Guy works hard, say that." '

When the August 2 primary vote was tallied, Phillip Doyle won only 4,423 votes. Bob Dole outdistanced Keith Sebelius by a spare 982 votes, 16,033 to 15,051 votes, the two trading wins throughout the twenty-six counties. In his hometown of Russell, Bob Dole got 1,466 more votes than Sebelius.

After it was over Sebelius gave a gentlemen's assessment to Dole of why he lost: "Bob, you drowned me in pineapple juice."

4

FIRST YEARS IN CONGRESS

On NOVEMBER 8, 1960, Kansas gave Republican Vice President Richard M. Nixon a greater margin of votes than any other state in the union except Nebraska in his losing effort against John F. Kennedy for the presidency. That same day Bob Dole defeated Democrat William A. Davis by nearly 20,000 votes. The kid raised in a humble family on the bone-spare Great Plains was headed to the United States Congress. The Dole clan and friends in Russell were joyous, and that winter Bob, Phyllis and Robin Dole drove across country to the nation's capital.

In January, 1961, Bob Dole was sworn in to the House of Representatives. Soon the White House invited him and the other freshmen congressmen to meet the new president and his glamorous wife, first lady Jacqueline Kennedy. Phyllis badly wanted to go. Bob wouldn't commit. The eight-year Republican reign had ended and it was a Democratic White House now. Just in case, Phyllis sewed a formal dress. Not until Bob showed up at home with a rented tuxedo the day of the reception did she finally know they were going.

For the first time the Doles passed through the iron gates at 1600 Pennsylvania and up to the White House. They walked into a reception room, splendid with some of the most important people in America. It was overwhelming; Bob didn't let on, Phyllis did. The band played "Hail to

48

the Chief" and the Kennedys swept by, an arm's length away. Phyllis did not meet the Kennedys; Bob got a quick handshake from the president.

At dinner Phyllis sat between newspaper columnist Carl Rowan and a treasury secretary from a foreign country, she couldn't remember which one. Later, she dragged Bob onto the dance floor. "I wanted to be able to tell my grandchildren *I* danced at the White House," Phyllis recalled, still charged up three decades later. "I didn't know if I'd ever be back there."

In those days members of Congress met for six months of the year, not all year as they would do later, so they traveled back home when out of session. Three or four times each year the Doles drove back and forth from Washington to Russell on old U.S. Highway 40 before the interstate system was complete, a wearying journey without air conditioning that took three long days and nights. One summer it was so hot they took turns standing outside during meals in restaurants to watch over their cat and dog. Later, while they were driving through Abilene, Kansas, their dog died in the car.

Bob did not discuss politics with Phyllis, then or ever. He left for work by seven in the morning and returned home after dark. Bill Avery, who had sat near him in the Kansas House of Representatives in 1951 and was the Kansas congressional delegation's senior member, lobbied high-ranking Republicans to win Dole a seat on the House Agriculture Committee. Their congressional offices were near each other but Dole was not one to ask for help; he studied issues himself, and kept most of Wint Smith's staff. "If these people can't keep up I'm going to get rid of them," Avery recalled Dole saying. On the floor and in committee hearings Dole often was funny. "Dole seemed a kind of Bob Hope type," Avery recalled. "Nobody took him very seriously, at least I didn't and that was a problem for me later."

Dole voted and preached hard-line conservative Republicanism. In his first year, he worked up a blast of indignation over manipulation of agricultural stockpiles by Billie Sol Estes, who had links with the Kennedy White House because he was a friend of Vice President Lyndon Johnson. Bob Dole's attacks on Sol Estes put him for the first of many times in his career on the front page of the New York *Times*.

A national headline felt good to Dole, though he knew it would not mean much to folks at home in Kansas. Dole had arrived in Washington with a bull's-eye on his back, marked as a short-timer. Because of congressional reapportionment—the rejiggering of congressional districts that occurs every decade with new census figures—Kansas in 1960 had lost a congressional seat because its population had declined in proportion to growth elsewhere in the United States. So instead of six members of the House, Kansas would now have five. The Sixth District was folded into the Big First District, pitting Dole in 1962 against Republican Floyd Breeding, a Democrat popular with his constituents who had been elected to the First District in 1958. Dole could have given up then, parlaying his brief congressional experience into a comfortable law practice in Kansas City, Topeka or even back in Russell. His internal drive wouldn't let him. He welcomed politically savvy Huck Boyd as his campaign manager. They girded up to fight Floyd Breeding.

Breeding was a strong backer of President Kennedy. In his first year in Congress Dole had criticized Kennedy's agricultural policies and raised questions about the wisdom of selling American grain to communist countries such as the Soviet Union. With the Cold War at a subzero gust, Dole's stand sold very well in western Kansas. He campaigned hard against Breeding's record, and swamped Breeding on Nov. 6, 1962, 102,499 to 81,092, garnering more votes than Breeding in all but seven of the district's fifty-eight counties.

WHEN IN LATE 1963 helium and natural gas underground in southwestern Kansas were just beginning to be marketable, a group of Republican powerhouses gathered in Liberal to powwow, including Congressman Bob Dole. After the meeting the group moved to a nearby coffee shop where Dole sat all night listening to the former governor Alf Landon tell him who was related to whom in Kansas politics, what businesses people were in and what landmines to watch out for, imparting wisdom from the political network he had built for the Republican Party in Kansas. "They were the kind of things a young congressman had to know," recalled Jim French, a clothing retail shop owner in Liberal and well-connected Republican who sat with the two. Dole listened, and learned.

LYNDON BAINES JOHNSON became president after John F. Kennedy's assassination on November 22, 1963, and Dole resumed his partisan skirmishing with the new Democratic president. Dole served as chairman of a Republican committee investigating whether Bobby Baker, a protégé of Johnson, used his post as secretary to the Senate majority leader to earn a personal fortune. He tried to block Johnson from issuing memorial certificates to relatives of dead veterans, claiming they were government-paid political campaign literature. He used fiery language in those days, borne of his populist heritage, and showed his knack for turning a phrase. "No amount of press agentry or darkened rooms will hide the cracks in the sorry record of the Johnson administration," Dole railed in a speech to Republicans in Richmond, Virginia, in May 1964, as reported by the Associated Press. Johnson was "Boastful Baines" for touting economic stability, while submitting budgets leading to deficit spending. And the mood in Washington was like a "CCC" camp, full of "confusion, consternation and conniving," said Dole.

If anything, Dole's 1964 House race was more difficult than his previous two congressional campaigns. Loyal to conservatives, Dole backed conservative Barry Goldwater of Arizona for the Republican presidential nomination, an unliked man in the First District. Dole's campaign got a boost in late October when Richard Nixon flew to Pratt, Kansas, to speak on his behalf. Nixon drew a crowd of five thousand to a football field and left an indelible memory in that farming town.

Jess Kennedy, mayor of Pratt, picked Nixon up at the airport in a deep blue Lincoln Continental on loan from a local dealer. With a security man up front and Nixon, Dole and the county Republican chairman, all in dark suits, in the back seat, Kennedy drove into town nervous he might wreck. "Nixon asked about the economy in the area, about farming and about politics," Kennedy said. "Dole was just himself, congenial. Nixon was a very dignified man. He impressed me. He was what you'd expect of a leader or a diplomat. He talked on our level and he was very easy to have a conversation with."

On the airplane ride to Pratt, Nixon peppered Dole with questions about his age, interests, lay of the land in Kansas, how long Kansas Republican veteran Frank Carlson might stay in the Senate and whether Dole was interested in a Senate seat. He was.

"Former Vice President Nixon came to Pratt, stood on about five bales of hay, made a great speech to a good audience," Dole recalled on the cable television show "Equal Time" in 1994. "He got a lot of press that weekend; it was late October. I won by about six thousand votes."

That fall Dole did narrowly defeat Democrat Bill Bork by 5,126 votes; of 221,298 votes cast, Dole won 113,212 to Bork's 108,086. He won even though Lyndon Johnson defeated Barry Goldwater in the presidential race in Kansas, one of the few times in Kansas history a Democratic presidential candidate carried the state.

Back in Washington, Representative Gerald Ford, forty-nine, a Michigan Republican and head of the House Republican Conference, announced he would challenge Minority Leader Charles A. Halleck for the leadership post. Dole signed on to back Ford, a clean-cut former All-American football player at the University of Michigan who contrasted with Halleck, who had "a tippling problem." Ford represented a group of frustrated young Republicans eager for more assertive, partisan leadership. Dole talked two of his Kansas House colleagues, Robert Ellsworth and Garner Shriver, into supporting Ford, and Ford would later credit Dole for bringing in the winning margin. Dole, in his throwaway fashion, said he didn't have to do much: "I promised to pick a couple of guys up and drive them to work for a month or so."

"We won by the landslide margin of 74-67 and if we hadn't gotten those votes from Kansas it would have been a stalemate," former President Ford said in an interview. "So Bob's leadership in convincing the others from Kansas to support me instead of Halleck made a big difference in my political career. I don't think Bob regretted it and I sure appreciated it. To show my appreciation, the first political speech I made as the new Republican leader was in Kansas," Ford recalled.

Bob Dole was making headway in Washington but he worried about the narrowness of his own 1964 reelection win. On a Saturday in Kansas before Christmas in 1965, Dole met with Jim French, the southwest Kansas businessman. Dole offered French the position of district campaign chairman. French accepted and they began planning for 1966.

Early the following summer they launched his campaign. With French as his driver, Dole began each day at dawn, dressed in a sharp dark suit, made five to ten stops a day, ending around four o'clock in the afternoon to check into a hotel. While Dole changed into his fresh other suit, French would run off to the local cleaners with the first and Dole would campaign on into the evening, walking the dusty town streets and attending Rotary, Kiwanis, VFW meetings. "When Bob was introduced to somebody he'd ask how to spell their name or where they were from and he remembered almost everyone's name," French said. "He just remembered people. When you have a disability you have to develop something else, and that's what Bob Dole did. Of course, I often followed along behind him, writing down names of who we met. I would send the list to him in Washington and Dole would send out a letter: 'Nice to have met you on the streets of Liberal, Mr. Smith.' And, boy! That makes an impression."

The towns and meetings were small, groups of eight to twenty people. Dole would make his pitch and move on, just as he did running for county attorney. He rarely ate a regular meal, he'd churn along all day on peanuts, Coca Colas and an occasional chocolate milkshake. "And he had a great facility," French added, "he'd hit that car and before we'd be out of town he'd be asleep."

That season French came up with an idea to raise money—he bought four-inch-square advertisements in every weekly paper in the district and wrote the solicitation headline: "Dollars for Dole." In the ad Dole's campaign committee asked readers to send him their dollars so Dole would not have to depend on big money from corporations or unions, a sensitive point in an anti-union state.

"My God, the money just rolled in," said French. "Every day we'd get thirty to fifty letters. You could just see some farmer sitting down with his stub pencil writing a check for five dollars or three dollars." It worked so well that French put advertisements a couple of weeks later in larger papers —Garden City, Great Bend and Liberal. And the cash flowed in.

Dole was sensitive about perceptions that campaign contributions might buy his vote, according to French. He would not personally handle contributions; that was French's job. "Once, I got two checks for $200 and $250, when $100 meant a lot, from a lobbyist," said French. "Dole called up a couple days later and said: 'Still got those checks? Don't deposit them. That guy's trying to put pressure on me and I'll just send his money back.' "

Dole was not, however, above using the legitimate advantages of his office to promote his career. At that time he was receiving unfavorable press in the district, appearing to be against everything in government, particularly President Lyndon Johnson's Great Society initiatives, which included an anti-poverty program and an urban mass transit program. Dole developed a running feud with John McCormally, a columnist at the Hutchinson *News* in Kansas, who had ripped into Dole. Dole returned fire, calling the paper "Prairie Pravda." One day, Dole held up a Chicago *Tribune* profile that portrayed himself in a positive light. Dole told French, "We ought to send a copy to every registered voter in the major cities." They did exactly that, using Dole's congressional franking privilege, an allowance for taxpayer-paid mailings. In November 1966, Dole coasted to an easy win, beating Democrat Bernice Hinkle 97,487 to 44,569.

Voting records were something Kansans cared about and Dole kept his high, showing he was on the job, voting conservatively on fiscal issues and more moderately on the important issues of the day. He voted for the 1964 Civil Rights Act and the 1965 Voting Rights Act, ensuring voting rights for African-Americans, and backed creation of an independent federal consumer agency that became the Consumer Product Safety Commission.

Larry Winn, now a retired Republican Kansas House member from Overland Park, a suburb of Kansas City, used Dole as a sounding board in the 1960s for voting on agricultural issues. Dole showed up in his congressional office by seven o'clock in the morning because that was when farmers and ranchers in Kansas started their day, Winn recalled. During the congressional sessions, like many other colleagues, Winn and Dole would try to hit ten to fifteen places a day in Washington, gathering information from committee hearings, picking up legislative strategy at party functions, shaking hands with constituents visiting Washington, giving speeches to organizations or attending fund-raisers. Winn tired of the grind, Dole did not. "I'd say he's about as hard a worker as I've ever known in Congress," Winn said.

Dole did not roll into Congress the first day with the dream of occupying the White House. Nor did he, at first, think of the Senate. House reelection campaigns came rushing at him every two years, requiring him to head out to Kansas every chance he got. After a while Dole looked around. The seniority system entrenched in Congress meant that he might not be a player for years, even among Republicans. And he wanted to be a player. Why do something if you can't make a difference?

"I started thinking after a couple of terms in the House: Geeminee, this place, particularly if you're in the minority, is really a wretched place to work in, because you don't have any influence. Maybe I oughta start looking around at the Senate," Dole recalled. "Well, I didn't know if there ever was going to *be* a chance to run for the Senate."

The chance came in early 1968. Senator Frank Carlson, a veteran and popular senator, summoned Dole to his Senate office to give him a "heads up." He was retiring the following day. Carlson told Dole he would be an able replacement; he should not hesitate to start a campaign. Dole attended Carlson's retirement announcement in Topeka, and as the crowd thinned a reporter asked Dole if he was ready to announce his candidacy. "No, not today, it's Frank's day," Dole said, hinting *his* day would not be far away. "I know I didn't wait long," Dole recalled.

Dole's Republican primary challenger was his former House colleague Bill Avery, who had won the Kansas governorship in 1964 and lost it in 1966. As governor, Avery raised state income and sales taxes, and for the first time in Kansas instituted a state withholding tax on income. Prior to his proposal, Kansans were on an honor system; after Avery left office and the law was in effect, the state found 100,000 dishonorable Kansans.

They were hardly grateful. Irene Whitlock, a McPherson businesswoman active in the Republican Party, joined Dole's campaign that summer. Later she would become the executive director of the state party. On her own, she bought ten cases of pineapple juice and numerous white sheet cakes, packed them into her black Buick station wagon with boxes of Bob Dole caps and campaign buttons and drove through five congressional districts. For weeks she worked from six in the morning until eight at night. In a miasma of Kansas heat she would arrive, set up a card table, stack it with cans of Dole pineapple juice, pop one open, slice cake and push sugar *and* Bob Dole on townspeople.

"It was hot and sticky and we smelled like pineapple juice," she recalled, wincing and laughing. "Eww! It was awful!"

Whitlock and Carol Weibe, the Marion County Republican Party chairwoman, who lived twenty miles east of her, put up hundreds of Bob Dole's expensive campaign posters after hammering wooden splints for support into the backs of them. Whitlock stood on the roof of her station wagon to nail the signs high on telephone poles, where vandals, or opposing candidates, couldn't get to them.

Well into the campaign, Wint Winter, Sr., a state senator from the town of Ottawa fifty miles southwest of Kansas City, picked Dole up one afternoon at a nearby airport. Glowering as he got off the plane, Dole chewed out Winter, his Franklin County chairman. Dole had absolutely no money and did not know how to raise any; surprising news to Winter, who figured a politician who had run four races for the House and four for county attorney would have made a few moneyed friends.

"We're losing Franklin County and we're going to lose the election," Dole told him.

"Well, Bob," Winter said, "we're not going to lose Franklin County and you're not going to lose, either."

Winter brought him to town and led him into a room full of his diehard supporters, whose cheers buoyed Dole's spirits. (Dole won Franklin County in the primary, 2,066 votes to Avery's 665.)

Dole did not run a rough campaign against Avery, he did not have to. "Bob said at several joint appearances with me, 'There are no issues, just two guys trying to get to the same place,' " Avery recalled. "There was never anything personal."

As the August primary neared, the Dole campaign did borrow an idea the Democrats had used to defeat Avery in 1966. Avery had campaign signs tacked onto telephone poles throughout Kansas with his name in vertical letters. Underneath each, Dole troops added a horizontal sign, identical in appearance, with one word: "TAXES."

On August 6, Dole defeated Avery, 190,782 to 87,801 and easily dispatched his Democratic opponent in November to win a seat in the United States Senate. Phyllis Dole told friends she was happy now that they would not have to run for office every two years. At least maybe his family would see him more.

Robin understood her father was a busy man. At age thirteen, in 1965, she wanted to get her ears pierced, which was not entirely socially acceptable for nice young Kansan girls. Phyllis told her Bob would decide. Robin lined up a doctor. "I wrote him a note because he wasn't around much," Robin Dole said. "I put in all my convincing arguments. I gave him two boxes to check, yes or no. He made another box, 'maybe,' checked it and wrote a note, 'I'll talk to you tonight.' She got them pierced.

DOLE ARRIVED IN the Senate in 1969, a newcomer at age forty-five. Over at the White House, Richard M. Nixon moved in as the new president, culminating a six-year quest. He arrived at the end of a turbulent decade marked by civil rights marches, hippies and their psychedelic drugs and raging student protests on college campuses in opposition to the war in Vietnam.

As the Senate debated the Vietnam war and the budget from January into the spring, freshman Bob Dole did not speak up. The first time he asked to be recognized—the first time he spoke on the floor of the Senate —was April 14, the anniversary of his war injury. Dole delivered an analysis about the status and treatment of disabled Americans, surprising for its frankness about a subject that many Americans had not publicly faced.

"Mr. President," Dole began, addressing the Senate presiding officer, "my remarks today concern an exceptional group which I joined on another April 14, twenty-four years ago, during World War II. It is a group which no one joins by personal choice—a group whose requirements for membership are not based on age, sex, wealth, education, skin color, religious beliefs, political party, power or prestige. As a minority, it has always known exclusion—maybe not exclusion from the front of the bus, but perhaps from even climbing aboard it. Maybe not exclusion from pursuing advanced education, but perhaps from experiencing any formal education. Maybe not from day-to-day life itself, but perhaps from an adequate opportunity to develop and contribute to his or her fullest capacity. It is a minority, yet a group to which at least one out of every five Americans belongs."

Though he did not mention himself, Dole's later words seemed to come from personal experience: "Too many handicapped persons lead lives of loneliness and despair; too many feel and too many are cut off from our work-oriented society; too many cannot fill empty hours in a satisfying, constructive manner. The leisure most of us crave can and has become a curse to many of our nation's handicapped."

Dole proposed that a presidential task force be formed to examine public and private efforts, addressing eight goals: expanding employment, transportation and recreation opportunities for the disabled; establishing a central clearinghouse for information; removing barriers that blocked the disabled access to buildings; improving health care; expanding special education; offering tax deductions or other incentives to those who assist the disabled; focusing more on families who have disabled members; bettering communication between the private and government sectors to weed out duplication.

As Dole finished, Republican James Pearson, Kansas' other senator, rose to congratulate him, and others followed.

Dole's arrival in the Senate coincided with that of one other freshman, Bob Packwood of Oregon. In 1969, after the two had been sworn in, Dole brought Packwood to Topeka for a political event. Meeting at a downtown hotel, Dole introduced Packwood to Irene Whitlock, dark-haired then in her late thirties, and the three of them talked a few moments. Dole turned away to talk with someone else, and Packwood moved toward Whitlock, she recalled in an interview. "We ought to get together for a drink later," he suggested. Startled, she responded that they always met in the party's hospitality rooms at the end of these events. She did not go there that night.

(Twenty-five years later, in the spring of 1994, Dole's Campaign America, the political action committee he formed to campaign for Republican candidates, would give $10,000 to Packwood's legal defense fund to help the senator defend himself against accusations of sexual harassment by two dozen women. The day she learned of Dole's donation, Whitlock threw up her hands with an exasperated smile. "When he does things like that, it just makes you so darn mad!")

In 1969 in McPherson, Kansas, Irene Whitlock's telephone occasionally rang on Thursday afternoons.

"What's going on out there?" was the way Bob Dole said hello.

"Not much," was her expected reply.

"Busy this weekend?" he'd say. She'd reply, "Naw."

"Good, we're comin' out."

And Whitlock would drive him around all weekend long, meeting constituents, stopping only for chocolate milkshakes at roadside ice cream shops. At times Dole staffers would call and order her to pull together people for a meeting, hanging up without saying hello or good-bye. They could be gruff under pressure. Dole's schedule always changed, Whitlock's nerves jangled, worried he might not show up at an event she had scheduled. She always, she said, felt an aura of both dread and admiration associated with Dole. Whatever, she went through hoops for him.

One day in the fall of 1969 the telephone rang again. "Ever given a party for a cabinet member?" Dole asked her. "Noo," she replied.

"Thought I'd bring Wally Hickel by," said Dole of the Secretary of Interior, with whom he had made inroads. An Alaska politician, Hickel had been born in nearby Claflin, Kansas.

"Okay," Whitlock said, knowing she had just a couple of days to prepare.

In a panic, she and her friends called two hundred business and political contacts, then prepared hors d'oeuvres. On a Friday evening all two hundred showed up for a cocktail party with Dole and his guest. Everyone stayed for hours.

"I think Bob just wanted to do something," said Whitlock, ". . . because he could."

One afternoon several years later she came home and heard her son in an earnest discussion on the telephone, obviously not with one of his friends. Fifteen minutes later he hung up. "I was talking to Bob Dole," he said, explaining that one of his teachers had chided Republican policies in class and the boy had been unable to rebut, so he called Dole in Washington for some ideas. He got them.

SENATOR EVERETT DIRKSEN of Illinois, a theatrical Republican leader, "a billion here, a billion there, it adds up" . . . died suddenly in the fall of 1969, leaving a vacuum in the Senate and a loss of a legislative tactician for President Nixon. Hugh Scott, a forceful sixty-nine-year-old Pennsylvania senator, sought to replace Dirksen, as did Howard Baker of Tennessee, Dirksen's son-in-law and a moderate younger senator.

"I don't believe I knew Dole at all when he was in the House," Baker said. "And I remember talking to a number of people from the midwest about who is Dole and what is he like? And they said, Well, you got him. But he's so conservative that I don't think you can handle him. That turned out not to be the case. Dole and I struck it off instantly and well. Dole is conservative, was a conservative, but he's also flexible and realistic and I think he was keenly attuned to the times. He certainly did not turn out to be the barnstorming conservative he had been advertised to be, and perhaps was in the House." Dole signed on to support Baker's bid, but Scott eked out a win for the minority leader's post.

Dole also drew attention soon after in a zealous defense of two Nixon Supreme Court nominees. The first was South Carolina appeals court judge Clement Haynsworth, who was eventually defeated after a tough debate with Scott and sixteen other Republicans voting to reject him over criticism about his civil rights record. Nixon then sent up his second nominee, G. Harrold Carswell, a Florida appeals court judge, whom the Senate also rejected after allegations that he was a racist, which infuriated the White House. Nixon found and expected ready opponents in many Senate Democrats, but his support from moderate Republicans began slipping, too, in the fall of 1969.

DOLE SOON DISCOVERED Senate rules to be more open than the House's and as a freshman was not burdened as were senior members running committees. As a result he had free time to keep an eye on the Senate floor debate. Democrats had become accustomed to lambasting Nixon almost without challenge for his Vietnam war strategy and many other issues. Now they were met by the self-appointed "Sheriff of the Senate." From his back row desk Bob Dole jumped up to challenge Nixon detractors. So righteous was he, Dole occasionally chased Democrats out into the cloakroom to get into a face-to-face argument.

Over at the White House, the job of Lyn Nofziger, a conservative former press secretary to California Governor Ronald Reagan, was to seek out House and Senate members supportive of Nixon who were willing to rebuke the president's detractors. "I very quickly stumbled onto Bob Dole and I began writing a lot of short speeches for him," Nofziger said. "He'd call and say, 'Let's do something on thus and so.' In those days I was a very quick writer. I'd turn something out for him and he would give it. So he got this tough-guy reputation, because I write mean stuff!"

Dole's colleagues were taking note of the freshman senator from Kansas. "He's the first fellow we've had around here in a long time who can grab 'em by the hair and haul them down the aisle," Senator Barry Goldwater, the conservative Arizona Republican, observed, according to a July 12 article in the Washington *Star*. And Bob Packwood of Oregon said, "He's one of the toughest men I've ever met, the kind of guy I'd like to stand back-to-back with in a knife-fight."

In April 1970 Nixon announced U.S. troops would be attacking communist positions in Cambodia, Vietnam's neighbor, inflaming student protesters and in Washington who saw the so-called incursion as a clear escala-
tion of the war. On May 4 student protesters charged national guardsmen
on the campus of Kent State University in Ohio, triggering a volley of
gunfire that left four protesters dead. As the Senate rancorously debated
cutting off funds for U.S. military operations in southeast Asia, Dole defended Nixon's plan to wait and pull troops back by the end of June.

As that date loomed, Senator William Fulbright, the Arkansas Democrat
and chairman of the Senate Foreign Relations Committee, used the 1964
Gulf of Tonkin resolution to criticize Nixon. The resolution had often
been cited by President Lyndon Johnson as showing congressional approval
for his efforts to widen U.S. involvement in Vietnam. Fulbright hoped to
propose repeal of the resolution as a vehicle for the Senate to launch a
lengthy debate about U.S. involvement in southeast Asia. But Dole, figuring Nixon had the authority he needed to wage war, took the issue out of
Fulbright's hands by attaching repeal of the Tonkin resolution to a bill the
Senate quickly approved. Fulbright not surprisingly lashed out at Dole.
Dole responded coolly, "Is it a rule of the Senate that one must clear
everything with the senator from Arkansas?"

Fulbright later said, "You stole my cow." To which Dole rejoined,
"Naw . . . I just milked it a little."

The Nixon White House took note of Dole's emerging skills and his
partisanship. In many ways he was a stronger advocate on the floor for
Nixon than Senate Republican leader Scott, though his profile stirred
resentment among Scott loyalists. Reporters once asked Senator William
Saxbe, an ally of Scott, what he thought of Dole.

"He's a hatchet man," Saxbe said in a January 15, 1971, article in the
New York *Times*. "He couldn't sell beer on a troopship."

TOUGH GUYS, NOT BAD GUYS

In November of 1970 President Nixon nominated Rogers C. Morton, a bearish, friendly Republican National Committee chairman, to be his Secretary of the Department of Interior. At the same time Nixon chose George Bush, who had just lost a Senate contest in Texas to Senator Lloyd Bentsen, as the U.S. representative to the United Nations. A scramble then ensued for the Republican National Committee (RNC) chairmanship, coveted badge of power in Washington.

Close to Thanksgiving Bob Dole threw his hat into the ring. Mostly he wanted to see if he could handle the big leagues. In the Senate he was, and would remain for years, a junior member. Almost immediately Dole ran into opposition from Hugh Scott, the Republican leader from Pennsylvania, and Michigan's Bob Griffin, Senate whip, the number three Republican. The party chairmanship, Scott and Griffin asserted, required full devotion and was not for a senator with divided responsibilities. Undoubtedly they also remembered it was Dole a year earlier who had opposed Scott for the Senate leadership.

Dole had no close ties to Nixon's two top aides, domestic adviser John Ehrlichman and chief of staff H.R. "Bob" Haldeman. He did not know Ehrlichman and had clashed recently with Haldeman over protocol for announcement of a trip Nixon was planning to Kansas to give a speech.

On September 11 Haldeman had spent a "good part of afternoon on a huge flap with Bob Dole, who was incensed about screwup of announcement of our Kansas trip; Governor [Democrat Robert Docking] made it in Kansas, ahead of Dole or the university. After tracking it all back found it was Dole's fault," Haldeman wrote in *The Haldeman Diaries,* published posthumously in the spring of 1994 by Putnam's. In December, Haldeman wrote that Nixon had agreed to rule Dole out because he was an incumbent senator; Nixon wanted a full-time man. On December 11, Scott spoke to Haldeman "about his total disapproval of Dole for RNC," and mentioned he was "mobilizing senators to oppose the Dole possibility."

Closeted inside the White House, protected by a fiercely loyal palace guard, Nixon made it clear that he, not the party chairman, would run the 1972 reelection campaign. That made the RNC rather unalluring, but Dole still wanted it and with customary intensity campaigned for support from the party's committeemen and committeewomen, as well as from his Senate colleagues.

In December, twenty-eight Republican senators telegrammed their support of Dole to the White House. Perhaps as a test, Dole was ordered on December 22 to attack Ted Kennedy on the Senate floor about Kennedy's claims regarding a new list of American prisoners of war in Vietnam, which the White House already had in its possession, Haldeman wrote.

In early January, 1971, John Mitchell, the attorney general and a close Nixon confidant, called Dole, according to *The Doles: Unlimited Partners.* "You're going to be chairman when the vote is held in a few days," Mitchell told him. Pleased, Dole told colleagues on Capitol Hill and friends back home, and the word made it into the nation's press. On January 14, the night before Dole was to be formally selected, Haldeman telephoned Dole to say Nixon had changed his mind. The Senate's responsibilities would dilute the position and the president needed a chairman to give one hundred percent. Dole was not about to let Mitchell's pledge on the chairmanship be forgotten. He suspected there was more to the story; Dole said in an interview he felt Scott and Senator William Saxbe were "trying to do me in."

Dole immediately telephoned Bryce Harlow, who headed Nixon's office of congressional relations. "I threatened to quit the Senate," Dole recalled later. "I said, 'If the president says one thing one day and another the next day, I've lost my faith in this place.' " Harlow went to bat for Dole, setting off intense negotiations. Long after midnight, Harlow had a deal: Dole would become chairman, and Tom Evans, a Delaware businessman who had been Nixon's southern campaign coordinator in 1968—and who Nixon really wanted as chairman—would become his deputy.

Early the next morning Nixon telephoned Dole and welcomed him, in convincing enough tones, to his team. Yet as the Republican committeemen and committeewomen gathered later to vote, the White House played one final discouraging card. It proposed two separate elections for Dole and Evans, setting up the potential of a shared chairmanship. Dole's old friend, Huck Boyd, stepped in and, asserting his authority as the chair of the GOP's nominating committee, blocked the dual elections. Dole won the chairmanship and named Evans a deputy co-chairman along with Anne Armstrong of Texas.

"They thought I was too independent so they structured the committee where they thought they'd make the chairmanship, in effect, a nothing job," Dole remembered in an interview. "Tom Evans, who was put in there to sort of watch me, turned out to be a close friend and everybody else ended up in trouble."

To demonstrate his loyalty to the White House, Dole threw himself into the job. Several times a week he hopped aboard an airplane before dawn and flew across the country to make speeches, always with his edged humor, defending President Nixon and Nixon's agenda. He frequently challenged "liberals" in Congress, particularly Senator Ted Kennedy of Massachusetts. Once, Dole called Ramsey Clark, the former attorney general and well-known liberal, a "left-leaning marshmallow."

Dole's rhetoric prompted negative reviews in the media and among the party faithful. Lyn Nofziger, then deputy head of the RNC's communications department, took Dole aside, suggesting he tone himself down, and Dole attempted for perhaps the first time in his political career to soften his public image. "I want to be tough, but not too tough," he said, according to a Newhouse News Service story, June 22, 1971. "I don't want to invite sympathy for the people I take on; the problem is overkill." He wanted the RNC to be viewed as "tough guys, not bad guys. We want to gain respect, not ridicule for some stupid attack."

In August, Dole spoke out for Vice President Spiro T. Agnew, whom some Republicans wanted thrown off the presidential ticket before the 1972 elections. Only in Washington had Dole heard such opposition, not in the world beyond the capital. "Out there, where the people are, Spiro Agnew is admired as a straight talker, a straight shooter and a man of principle," Dole said on the Senate floor. "I need not point out that where the people are is where the votes are, too."

Through the first year of his chairmanship Dole made more than one hundred speeches. He supplemented his forays outside Washington by testing himself at the epicenter of public image shaping. He began appearing on television news shows such as "Meet the Press" and "Issues and Answers" and made a speech to the National Press Club.

"He always did well," said Mike Baroody, who wrote speeches for Dole during this period. "The press seemed to genuinely like him. They found his candor and his aggressive use of humor to be personally engaging, as well, and often it gave them a good lead on a story." Writing speeches was not unpleasant; Dole expected something timely and detailed on issues. A few times Baroody went to hear Dole deliver one of his speeches. Often Dole diverted dramatically from the text, a trait that would unnerve young speechwriters later in his career, but Baroody shrugged it off: "He's so good on his own, that's the way he chose to do it."

The White House increased its use of Dole as an outlet for scathing criticism of its opponents. Chuck Colson, Nixon's special counsel, sent over sharp-edged speeches for Dole to deliver and cartoons for the RNC publication *First Monday* to run. One showed Democratic Senator George McGovern of South Dakota, who would be Nixon's opponent in 1972, wearing a Viet Cong uniform and another hinted that Hubert H. Humphrey, a personal friend of Dole, was a drinker.

"There was always a little conflict between Bob and the *real* hatchet men in the White House," said Lyn Nofziger, who worked daily with Dole at the RNC. "They wanted him to do things he knew were—one—not politically smart and—two—not particularly helpful even for the president. He didn't mind standing up for the president but they were always pushing him to be a little tougher than he wanted to be, and sometimes he *was* tougher than he wanted to be. He began to resent the idea of being a hatchet man. He knew when things were counterproductive."

Mike Baroody recalled: "Dole put his foot down on more than one occasion. There were lines beyond which he wouldn't venture. Periodically they'd send something over, fairly insistent. They didn't always ask, 'Please.' Dole would scan the text and draw back from the page."

"We're not gonna do this," he would say.

Dole did attack Senator Edward M. Kennedy, the Massachusetts Democrat, over Kennedy's accusations that Nixon was dragging out the war to serve his political interests. "It's hard to conceive of this kind of gutter politics coming from a man whose own brother was president and who made many of the decisions that have led to the present situation in southeast Asia," Dole said in a June 1971 speech. He also criticized critics of Nixon's handling of the war, including Senators Edmund Muskie and

Humphrey, both possible presidential contenders. He chided Democratic Party Chairman Lawrence O'Brien for opposing policies pursued by Nixon that he had supported under President Johnson with "unrivaled vehemence."

Dole set no limits on the time he devoted to the White House. Neither did he shirk in his commitment to the Senate. Determined to keep his Senate voting record high, Dole developed a routine of boarding a plane early, flying as far as perhaps Nevada to give a speech, turning right around, flying back to Washington, arriving at midnight so he could vote the following morning. His planes stopped with remarkable regularity in Kansas for refueling, during which Dole would jump off to give a speech or shake a few hands with the home folks.

But the real home folks rarely saw him, Phyllis recalled in an interview. Driving himself to exhaustion for the Republican Party, Dole grew more distant from Phyllis and Robin. After he was elected to the Senate, the Doles bought a big brick home near Lake Barcroft in northern Virginia. It had a large living room, ideal for entertaining. And they did entertain, except Dole seemed distracted. About the only time he spent at home was to sleep a few hours at night and spend minutes in the morning sipping coffee that Phyllis had made.

Of course, Bob Dole had always worked hard, but once he became party chairman his hours soared. "A wife doesn't notice changes," Phyllis said. "It just grows and grows." Bob began to leave home at six o'clock in the morning, before Robin woke up, and would arrive home after eleven o'clock at night while Robin slept. He worked all weekend, Saturdays and Sundays. He rarely joined Phyllis and Robin for meals.

To keep busy, Phyllis had joined the Congressional Club, an association of members' wives on Capitol Hill, and became the group's vice-president. The partisanship and rancor on the Hill did not permeate the Club: wives of Republicans and wives of Democrats freely shared their views about schools, social activities, boy and girl scout duties, life in the Washington fishbowl, and recipes. Phyllis very much enjoyed the group. "We didn't talk about politics and we didn't care about politics," says Phyllis. Robin attended a public school. Phyllis knew their neighbors but did not share her loneliness with them.

At the Barcroft home, Dole took up residence in the basement, which had its own bed and bathroom. When Phyllis wanted to speak with him she would walk down to his basement office, where he would be reading, and grab a couple of seconds with him. Her own family life in New

Hampshire had not been idyllic. She wasn't sure where she was headed with Bob.

"We didn't have a close marriage," she said, "but if you don't know what a good marriage is, how would you know?"

One winter evening in 1971, Phyllis was sitting in the living room when Bob came upstairs.

"I want out," he said flatly. And walked back downstairs.

She was stunned. Christmas that year wasn't much of a celebration. Later, she looked at her calendar. She and Robin had had dinner together with him only twice that year, Easter and Christmas. She hoped to patch things up but he was always working, they didn't talk, she knew divorce was on his mind, and she became angry. She hired a lawyer, who learned Bob wanted her to appear at a hearing in Topeka on January 11, 1972, the day after Phyllis' birthday. She flew out, entered the Shawnee County courtroom, was taken into a judge's private chambers and signed papers for a divorce. Years later she contended she did not understand that at the moment she signed, she was divorced. She thought it took longer, perhaps sixty days, to be finalized. Dole had obtained an emergency divorce, effective immediately.

News of the divorce shocked many Kansans. The Doles' relationship had been built up in the media for years as a fairytale marriage between a wounded war veteran and the hospital occupational therapist who had nursed him back to vitality, which was not exactly the case. But that was the myth. Dole avoided questions from the media. In Washington it was viewed as a potential political liability; divorce was not common then among top politicians. Phyllis, on the other hand, spoke up. She told Joe Lastelic of the Kansas City *Star*: "I had no choice. It was at his urgent request. I didn't want to do it. I tried to stall. I wanted him to give me more time. I couldn't get anywhere with him. I had to do it."

In an interview Phyllis said she was "numb" for weeks afterward. "I made him promise he would explain it all to Robin," who was a senior in high school, and he did.

"After the announcement there was some publicity on it in the papers and my mom made sure I'd seen it," Robin Dole recalled. "While we were talking about it, the phone rang and it was my dad telling me about the stories. He wanted to talk about them too." Both parents, she said, helped her grow through the change; they did not want their differences to hurt her. She wrote a theme paper her first year in college about how divorce didn't have to be wrenching for a child. Phyllis remained in Virginia for another year before moving back to Kansas, where she still had friends, to find work and eventually remarry. Her second husband died in the early 1980s and she married again, happily, to Ben Macey, a former high school sweetheart from New Hampshire.

In the winter of 1972 Bob Dole moved into an apartment in the Watergate Hotel complex along the Potomac River, neighbor to the Kennedy Center for the Performing Arts. Robin spent summers there in 1972 and 1973 in the small apartment, enduring typical single-parent awkwardness. "He really couldn't figure out what there was to do until two o'clock in the morning and why I didn't get up at six in the morning," said Robin, adding he was not too difficult. Her average grades, which improved later, caused her to call Dole's longtime office secretary Betty Meyer for a "mood check" before telling her father. "He wasn't critical, but he wondered what I was doing in college." She earned a bachelor's degree in psychology from Virginia Polytechnic University that helped her to understand that her parents were happier apart.

After the divorce Dole spoke with President Nixon, neither mentioning Dole's domestic troubles. Nixon just told him he was doing a good job and asked, "Are you being tough enough?"

He certainly was trying to, particularly in defense of Nixon's goal of "peace with honor" in Vietnam. Meanwhile, protesters continued rallying against the war, staging sit-ins, burning ROTC buildings on campuses and demanding an immediate end to the mounting loss of American lives. In a speech to a Republican conference in Washington on January 21, 1972, Dole complained that Democrats in Congress were trying to saddle Nixon with full responsibility for the war, according to the Kansas City *Star*. Democrats were hiding "the sordid role their own party played in deliberately plunging us into the Vietnam quagmire," said Dole, who also had supported America's involvement in the war during the 1960s. "The fact that the Democrat party—traditionally this nation's war party—is responsible for a conflict which has cost the lives of over 55,000 Americans, is a source of some distress to the present crop of Democrat hopefuls, particularly since they are each, individually, so deeply implicated in the conflict." It was a theme to which Dole would return four years later.

The White House continued to turn to Dole. On April 12, 1972, according to Haldeman's diaries, Nixon ordered Attorney General John Mitchell to tell Dole to attack Ted Kennedy and Hubert Humphrey for undercutting Nixon on his strategy of intensifying American bombing of North Vietnam.

On June 17, 1972, five men were arrested in the Watergate office building adjoining Dole's hotel, at the headquarters of the Democratic National

Committee, a relatively quiet start to one of the twentieth century's biggest stories. One of the five burglars, James McCord, had been on the payroll of the Committee for the Re-election of the President (CREEP) at the time of the burglary. This led reporters to question Dole about his knowledge of the break-in. He was in Chicago June 17, and turned it into a joke: "It happened on my night off."

Dole attempted to divert scrutiny from the president. At the end of August, to counter accusations by the General Accounting Office of possible legal violations by Nixon's reelection team, Dole sent a letter to the congressional watchdog agency. He demanded the GAO review what appeared to be violations of campaign rules by Senator George McGovern's presidential campaign team. Democrats, Dole said, were bent on trying to implicate the president in Watergate, which was unwarranted. Like most of the nation, Dole at the time was unaware of the president's involvement in a cover-up and other crimes.

AFTER DOLE'S DIVORCE he settled into a solitary life in the austere apartment where he did little more than slept. The society pages occasionally mentioned him as an eligible bachelor on the Washington scene, but he seemed too busy with his work to pay attention to women. One day the picture changed.

In the spring of 1972 Elizabeth Hanford traveled from her office to the Hill on a mission. Thirty-five-year-old Elizabeth Hanford worked as deputy assistant for consumer affairs. She and co-deputy assistant Bill Walker went with her boss, Nixon-appointed Virginia Knauer, to request a consumer plank be included in the Republican platform at the Republican convention.

"Virginia said, 'We really need to talk to the Republican National Committee chairman. Let's go up and see him,' " Elizabeth said. "I had never met Bob Dole, really didn't know him at all. So we were taken into his office. I remember Virginia and Bill and me sitting across the table from his chair. And he was not there. He was on the Senate floor. Suddenly this side door opened to the left here and in came this man and I looked up and my first thought was: 'Gee, he's attractive.' "

They had a pleasant meeting, Bob was gracious. Elizabeth saw him again in the summer when he and Tricia Nixon opened the Republican campaign office near the White House. They exchanged hellos and cordialities.

That August Elizabeth traveled with Virginia Knauer to the Republican convention in Miami. Elizabeth had Virginia's daughter by the hand and was headed somewhere through a hallway when along came Bob Dole. "Again, we had a nice talk and all," she said. But that was it. At the time, Bob was flying across the country as chairman and was keeping long hours in the Senate. After the convention in the fall, he telephoned.

"We had a wonderful conversation," Elizabeth Dole said. "We talked for about forty minutes. We had all sorts of mutual friends and mutual interests, we talked about all kinds of things. And then . . . he hung up."

Not long after that Dole telephoned again for a slightly shorter talk. "I remember really enjoying talking to him, there was so much to share," Elizabeth said.

"Maybe we could have dinner sometime," he suggested.

"Well, that would be very nice," Elizabeth told him. "And he said, 'Good-bye.' "

During the third telephone conversation Dole finally asked Elizabeth Hanford out to dinner at a Washington restaurant. "There was something about *that* that really impressed me," she recalled. "I liked the fact that he was a little shy. That was very nice. And the fact that we had so much to talk about and really hit it off."

BEHIND THE SCENES that fall, however, Dole was frustrated. The Committee to Re-elect the President, CREEP, was running its own show for Nixon's reelection effort, draining money from the Republican National Committee. Irene Whitlock, the Hillsboro, Kansas, woman who had worked closely with Dole in his 1968 Senate race, was running CREEP's campaign operation in New Hampshire. Dole visited the state, angry at being out of the loop, she said.

CREEP kept enough of a lid on Watergate for Nixon to be easily reelected on November 7, 1972. Afterward Dole complained that Nixon's organization had done little to help congressional Republicans, prompting White House anger. Dole said that he had flown five hundred thousand miles as chairman from January 1971 to November 7, 1972, touching down in forty-six states for Nixon and congressional candidates. Knowing he would face a potentially challenging reelection bid of his own in 1974, Dole thought he would perhaps resign from the chairmanship position sometime in 1973.

Nixon apparently was no happier. Flying by helicopter to Camp David, the presidential retreat, he explained why to Haldeman. In *The Haldeman Diaries* the latter wrote, "The P feels that we need an analysis of the

Republican Party turnout. He wants to check to see if we really made the effort to get all the Republicans out, or did we rely too much on Dole and the National Committee. With only a 55 percent turnout, we should have won a big Republican vote, there must have been a weak Republican effort. "We should examine this ruthlessly."

On November 28, 1972, Dole climbed into a helicopter and flew to Camp David. Aboard the chopper with him was Attorney General Richard Kleindienst, looking grim, Dole recalled in an interview. It was Dole's first trip to Camp David, a cluster of woodsy cabins up in the Maryland Catoctin Mountains. Named for Dwight Eisenhower's grandson, the retreat was heavily forested with deciduous trees and located not far from the battlefield of Gettysburg in Pennsylvania, an hour's drive northwest of Washington.

Dole was not sure what Nixon wanted as he ushered him into Aspen Lodge. Nixon offered Dole a cup of coffee. The president then presented Dole with a map of America Nixon had autographed, showing the thousands of miles Dole had traveled as RNC chairman. Nixon then gave him a Camp David jacket.

"You've done a great job, Bob," Nixon told him. "What do you want to do next?"

"Well, I really hadn't thought about it," Dole said. "I'd like to hang around awhile and have a little fun."

Then Bob Haldeman walked into the room and Dole felt evicted. He understood now: they wanted him out. He told Nixon he would like to make a graceful exit from the job. As he left, Haldeman made sure a news photographer snapped a picture of Dole. The news was leaked and reporters quickly called to ask him if he planned to resign. Dole said he thought he'd stay on awhile, according to news stories published soon after.

Unknown to Dole at the time, his departure was carefully orchestrated. The story emerges from Haldeman's diaries that he dictated each night and notes kept by John Ehrlichman. Ehrlichman kept voluminous notes of every conversation he had with Nixon, writing them hastily on yellow legal pads. On November 14, Nixon gathered with Ehrlichman, Haldeman and others in Camp David's Aspen Lodge at 4:10 in the afternoon. Nixon wanted to reorganize leadership throughout the government, to get "good hacks" in departments as secretaries, loyalists accountable to him, not those who might have a mind of their own. Nixon said he could work better that way.

"Eliminate the politicians," Nixon said, according to Ehrlichman notes. "Except George Bush. He'd do anything for the cause."

On November 20, eight days before Dole's visit to Camp David, George Bush met with Nixon in the Aspen room with Ehrlichman present, taking notes. Nixon began their chat saying Bush had done a good job as U.S. Ambassador to the United Nations and he wanted to talk about his future. He was concerned about U.N. staffers who might be disloyal. Bush offered the name of a high-ranking staffer he thought was disloyal. Nixon asked Bush to write a letter about the issue directly to him, not to Secretary of State Henry Kissinger, offering "tough, political views" of the U.N. staff.

"Give us the names of loyalists," Nixon said, according to Ehrlichman. "Not brains, loyalty." The letter was to be sent to Ehrlichman, who would hand it to Nixon unopened. The discussion moved on to changes Nixon foresaw at Treasury. Then he mentioned the Republican National Committee, where he planned a "new concept" of moving politics out of the White House and setting up his own man to head the committee. The chairman would have two years to build the party. "Need full-time chairman," Ehrlichman wrote. "The RNC chairman will be Nixon's full-time adviser."

Nixon told Bush he wanted him for the job, it was a higher calling than the deputy treasury job in which Bush had expressed interest. Bush said his priorities were: "(1) deputy secretary of state, (2) under secretary of treasury, and (3) chairman of the Republican National Committee." Nixon said, "Will you let me decide?" Bush responded he wanted to "stay alive, stay visible."

Nixon continued to lean on Bush, noting the RNC job was "high risk" but also "high opportunity." He told Bush the "in clique" would be Ehrlichman, Haldeman, Kissinger, Roy Ash and Bush, "the political man," who could serve the president as a political adviser because Ehrlichman and Haldeman should stay out of that arena. "Do it for two years. Will then be some cabinet changes—could be very interesting ones," Nixon said. "Let me think about it," Bush said finally, according to Ehrlichman. "I'll do what you tell me. Not all that enthralled re RNC, but I'll do it." The meeting ended.

Two days later Nixon, Haldeman, Ehrlichman and another aide met in the Dogwood Lodge at 4:05 in the afternoon to talk about the reorganization plan, which bodies to move around. "Dole—he must go—in self-interest—need full-time man," Nixon said, according to Erlichman's notes, which elaborated why: "RNC chairman must be: (1) youth, (2) image, (3) build new majority, (4) center, (5) Midwest or South, (6) Bush?"

Perhaps Nixon wanted Dole out because Dole was viewed as a fire-and-brimstone type, more conservative than Bush. So five days later Dole was aboard a helicopter headed to a hanging: his own. When Dole arrived at Camp David, Haldeman wrote that Dole defended himself, even as Nixon suggested he resign, saying if it appeared he was being kicked out it might ruin him in Kansas. Nixon pledged to raise $300,000 toward Dole's reelection bid in 1974.

The machinery for his departure moved forward. At Mitchell's request Dole traveled in early December to New York to ask George Bush if he would consider the RNC post, apparently unaware of what had transpired before his Camp David visit. Bush was congenial but did not commit himself, Dole reported back. On December 7, the day the White House planned for Dole to announce his resignation, he told Haldeman he wasn't sure he would go along with it, that Dole had called Chuck Colson, "the only friend he had in the White House," and then "launched into a ten-minute tirade against me, followed by a statement that he was being forced out and screwed in the press. He wasn't going to stand for it," Haldeman wrote in his diaries. Over the next few days Dole finally relented and met with Nixon on Monday, December 11. "They agreed that Bush would stay on through the session [at the United Nations] and Dole would stay on at the RNC for the January meeting and [White House Press Secretary Ronald] Ziegler should shoot down the nonsense that Dole was pushed out," Haldeman wrote.

After the meeting Nixon called a surprised Huck Boyd in Kansas to tell him Dole was stepping down and Bush would become the new chairman. The debacle became a painful joke: Dole had gone to the mountaintop that November day—and was pushed off.

"I thought they treated him pretty shabbily in view of the fact he seemed to do everything he could to be helpful," said Senator McGovern. "In terms of the national chairman, I don't know anybody who was more dedicated to the Republican cause and the Nixon cause. It always struck me as rather brutal the way they treated him after the election."

This complex turn of events may have planted the seed of tensions between Bob Dole and George Bush, which would blossom into pitched battle in the 1988 presidential race. At the Republican party's annual winter meeting in mid-January 1973, where Dole was to formally pass the chairmanship to Bush, Bush showed up late.

"There he is now," Dole said, as Bush finally entered. "They're dragging him in."

Years later, Dole's assessment of how Bush got the RNC job still focused on Bush's connections, not his skills. "President Nixon said Bush wants to be number one somewhere and we can't do it at defense, we can't do it here or there," Dole said in an interview with the author. "I didn't know George Bush that well. He came to Congress, his father was a big-time senator, he got to be on Ways and Means as a freshman, which doesn't happen very often over there. But it always was who you are around here. All this created a mind-set that if this guy had been in my situation and I'da been George Bush, I'da been the one who had all those people taking care of me because he's somebody's son or whatever. So it was fairly tense there, but I don't remember it being the case when I left the chairmanship. I don't think he was too eager to take it either. He did it because he was asked and he did a good job, in fact raised a lot of questions about Watergate; as chairman he got a little too independent for them, too."

Yet if the warfare of the 1988 presidential primaries between Bush and Dole was rooted here, former President Bush apparently did not see it. "I am not sure what President Nixon talked to Bob about and when," Bush wrote in a letter to the author. "I do know that after the election all Cabinet-rank members of the administration were summoned one-by-one to Camp David. I was among the last to be summoned. There had been public speculation about President Nixon's wanting me to be RNC chairman. I do not know if the matter was discussed between Dole and RNC. Nixon told me that he knew George Schultz had asked me to be Deputy Secretary of Treasury under the new Super Cabinet plan Nixon planned to enact. He also told me that he would prefer I would head the RNC, something I told Barbara as I left for Camp David I hoped I would not be asked to do. I was sworn to secrecy on what was discussed at the Camp David meeting. I do not recall when Senator Dole and I talked about this for the first time. If this caused tension on Bob's part I must confess I never noticed that. Certainly, it was not cause for tension fifteen years later."

After leaving the RNC post in 1973, due to the strain of the dual schedules he had kept, Dole was worn down. Al Polzcinski, the political reporter for the Wichita *Eagle-Beacon,* was surprised at Dole's appearance at the annual Republican Kansas Day gathering on January 29, 1973, in Topeka. "I had never seen him so thin," Polzcinski said. But with only Senate duties to take up his time, Dole regained his strength. And it was needed, for Dole anticipated being challenged in 1974 by Democrat Robert Docking, a popular two-term Kansas governor.

That spring the Watergate story mushroomed after investigative spadework performed chiefly by Bob Woodward and Carl Bernstein in the

Washington *Post,* and others in the national media. Democrats, who controlled both Houses of Congress, set up a special select committee to investigate the White House's involvement and whether Nixon had authorized the break-in or was aware of it soon after and ordered a cover-up. After Nixon's two top aides, Ehrlichman and Haldeman, resigned, and Nixon fired counsel John Dean, the scandal only deepened. As the Watergate Committee dug into the morass, Americans kept up with the longest running political soap opera in the nation's history broadcast live on television that summer. It involved obstruction of justice, secret slush funds, unauthorized wiretaps on news reporters and political use of government agencies. Behind it all rang the questions: "What did the president know and when did he know it?" But Nixon had not yet been directly implicated in the cover-up.

Dole knew all Republicans would be tarred with Watergate in the 1974 elections and, as former party chairman, he would get one of the biggest brushes. In July's hearings, a White House aide disclosed a secret voice-activated tape-recording system Nixon had in the Oval Office, and a battle began in the courts for the tapes' release. On September 4 indictments were handed down for Ehrlichman; burglary mastermind G. Gordon Liddy; Egil Krogh, who headed the "plumbers" unit, a secret White House surveillance team; and David Young, a former aide to national security adviser Henry Kissinger, in connection with the burglary of the office of Daniel Ellsberg's psychiatrist. Ellsberg, a former Pentagon official, had leaked the Pentagon Papers to the New York *Times,* revealing an internal history of government lying about U.S. involvement in Vietnam.

On September 5, 1973, Dole introduced a resolution in the Senate to, in effect, pull the plug on the Watergate committee's live television broadcasts. The hearings distracted the nation from important foreign policy issues worldwide and the wavering U.S. economy. The people of Kansas, Dole said, were most concerned about inflation, the cost of food and "bailing wire and LP gas." Instead, they were being subjected to a ceaseless barrage from newspapers, radio stations and television broadcasts about Watergate.

"I am not questioning or quarreling with the Senate's legitimate and proper interest in conducting its investigation," Dole said in a lengthy speech. "First of all, it should be remembered that the purpose of the hearings is to serve legislative interests. It is not to try, convict and sentence Richard Nixon. Lives, reputations and careers can be hopelessly shattered by such exposure, and every citizen should be deeply concerned that every other individual's rights and freedoms are given the utmost protection."

Dole then delivered his punch line: "It is time to turn off the TV lights. It is time to move the Watergate investigation from the living rooms of America and put it where it belongs—behind the closed doors of the committee room and before the judge and jury in the courtroom. We must get on with the country's work. Time and the rest of the world will not stand still while America squeezes the last drop of anguish and printer's ink out of Watergate."

His amendment, which he said he offered "free and clear of any narrow partisanship," failed. The hearings continued, watched by America. They were the beginning of the end for Richard Nixon, and later trouble for Dole.

DOLE HAD OTHER non-Watergate thoughts on his mind in 1973. He began dating Elizabeth Hanford, though it was not easy to find time around both their busy schedules—his work in the Senate, hers in the consumer-protection office. Nonetheless, a relationship evolved over dinners at Washington restaurants, theater shows and movies. She enjoyed his candor, his straightforward approach to life, and his strength. "Which I think to some extent probably comes through adversity. You really get a sense that a person has been through a personal tragedy or has really suffered . . ." She paused. "I think it deepens your sensitivity, your concern for others."

After a time, Elizabeth invited Bob to spend time with her family, and he flew down to visit her parents in Salisbury, North Carolina. One morning, while Elizabeth's mother, Mary Hanford, was fixing breakfast in the kitchen, Bob walked in wearing pants and just a towel over his right shoulder.

"Mrs. Hanford, I think you should see my problem," he said, pulling off the towel.

"Bob, that's not a problem," Mary Hanford responded. "That's a badge of honor."

6

SKULL AND CROSSBONES

WHEN BETTY SEBELIUS visited Washington in early 1974 she made a point of stopping by Bob Dole's Senate office. Politics has strange ways of working out: After Dole vacated the First District congressional seat in 1968, her husband Keith Sebelius, whom Dole had defeated in 1960, won the job and the two men became friends and worked together on agriculture issues. Betty Sibelius came to warn Dole. Folks at home thought Bob was out of touch, Watergate infuriated them and his connection made them suspicious. "Bob, you need to listen to these people," she implored, according to her son Douglas. "You need to get back and listen to people at home. You are in trouble."

Dole knew that instinctively. It did not matter that two prominent and partisan Democrats, Senators George McGovern of South Dakota and Hubert Humphrey of Minnesota had publicly defended him, declaring it would be unfair to attack Dole for Watergate. Dole's defenses of President Nixon throughout 1973 and in 1974, followed by continued bombshell revelations concerning the scandal—eighteen potentially incriminating erased minutes on a June 20, 1972, White House tape, illegal intervention by the White House to steer federal agencies away from the case and the administration's apparent lying about a cover-up—had created a special problem for Dole. To turn on Nixon would be betrayal, but the president

76

was endangering Dole's re-election effort. His Senate campaign staff organized a series of fly-ins by party bigwigs, including former New York
Governor Nelson Rockefeller and Governor Ronald Reagan of California, to show support for Dole.

In the early spring, after former Governor Robert Docking—who most
thought could defeat Dole—withdrew from consideration, Dr. Bill Roy
filed to challenge Dole. The state Democratic party swung in behind Roy,
a moderate Democrat from Topeka, twice elected to the U.S. House. Roy
pledged not to throttle Dole about Watergate, choosing to stress their
different records.

Elected in 1970 by defeating an incumbent who rarely came home to
Kansas, Roy had gone on in 1972 to beat his Republican opponent,
winning 63 percent of the vote. At forty-nine, Roy, dark-haired, well-
spoken, was the only member of Congress who had both a law and a
medical degree. Life came relatively easy for Bill Roy; in a way, he was
above politics. Politics was something he got into in middle age, once he
had earned a comfortable living as a doctor. He thought he would stay in
Congress twenty years, retire and do something else. The politician's duty
of hugging babies was a natural to Roy. He had, after all, handled them for
years as a doctor, an obstetrician and had delivered hundreds of them.

For Bob Dole the baby obligation was one he tried to avoid. Dole was
not aloof. He was not coldhearted. He was not turned off by the way
politicians often seemed to pander to voters when they hefted a wide-eyed
infant. No, Bob Dole was afraid he would drop a baby. He would have to
catch one up with just his left arm, and he didn't always have a good grip
with his left hand.

In June Dole tried softening his defense of Nixon, and Republicans
rebuked him. Democrats challenged him to denounce Nixon or appear a
patsy. As he often did in tense times, Dole tried humor to let out some of
the emotional steam. Asked once by a reporter if he wanted Nixon to
campaign for him, Dole joked: "Maybe by plane. He could just fly over
Kansas in Air Force One. That would be fine."

During the spring and summer Nixon battled against release of his
secretly taped conversations from the period during and after the Watergate break-in. He had turned over transcripts and some tapes to the House
Judiciary Committee, refused to give up others. The ones he surrendered
dismayed many who heard Nixon bargain for survival and use countless
"expletive deleted" words.

On July 24 the Supreme Court rejected Nixon's argument that he had
absolute executive privilege as president to withhold evidence from the

Watergate special prosecutor and ordered him to turn over his tapes. Nixon stalled. On July 26 the House of Representatives opened debate on articles of impeachment against Nixon, approving charges that he obstructed justice and abused his presidential powers. Nixon continued to deny he was aware of the break-in initially and had not participated in a cover-up.

Bob Dole went on NBC's "Today" program July 25 as the House, now more fully aware of the breadth of the scandal than the year before, prepared for an impeachment debate. "He ought to put the cards on the table and discuss it with those of us who are loyal to the president," Dole said. "If the president's not involved, why not inform some of us? I think it's long past that we can say Watergate will just go away. I would guess that, with the exception of very few, Republicans in the Senate and Republicans in the House feel the tapes should be released."

The House adjourned July 30 for its summer break with the intention of returning in late August. Impeachment of President Nixon was considered certain. On August 5 Nixon announced he would release transcripts of conversations recorded on June 23, 1972, between himself and Bob Haldeman, his chief of staff. The sensational conversations revealed for the first time that just six days after the break-in Nixon ordered a cover-up by trying to block the Federal Bureau of Investigation's scrutiny of the Watergate break-in. Nixon's final Republican allies on the House Judiciary Committee bailed out, announcing they now favored impeachment.

On August 8 at 9 P.M. Nixon announced he would resign, the first president in the nation's history to quit the presidency. The morning of August 9 Nixon flung his hand overhead in one last victory sign and was helicoptered away from the White House grounds. Vice President Gerald Ford assumed the presidency with the statement, "Our long national nightmare is over."

One month later, on September 8, Ford issued a full pardon to Nixon for any wrongdoing associated with his years in the presidency. Dole reported that of six hundred telephone calls to his offices in Kansas and Washington, 20 to 1 were opposed to the pardon.

Not only had Ford pardoned Nixon, he also had imposed an embargo on shipping grain to the Soviet Union, creating further troubles for Dole in Kansas. By mid-September Dole's reelection bid looked precarious at best, even though at the end of June the Senate Watergate committee had issued a report clearing Dole of wrongdoing. "I don't think he was ever blemished in the slightest," Tennessee's Howard Baker said in an interview years later. "That's sort of remarkable, considering the party positions he held. He is absolutely free of that taint."

But voters were in a sour mood at Republicans generally over Watergate. Former Kansas Democratic party chairman Norbert Dreiling, a sharp attorney from Hays, twenty-five miles west of Dole's hometown of Russell, urged Bill Roy to attack Dole, now that momentum was building. "Knock him out now or he'll be there for life," Dreiling counseled. "And use Watergate."

Roy used it indirectly. "Dole knew or should have known about the Watergate affair in his capacity as party chairman," Roy frequently said. He criticized Dole on other issues, portraying himself as a clean outsider. Eight weeks before the November vote, polls showed Dole was twelve points behind Roy. Politics wasn't so hard, Roy decided, a sort of interesting intellectual exercise.

But politics was no hobby to Bob Dole. It was inherent in the drive that resurrected him after World War II tried to kill him, physically and psychologically. He had no other interests, no other highly marketable skill such as Bill Roy had. Dole was a lawyer but used his training to grind out laws in the corridors of the Capitol, where democracy lived and breathed. Dole realized he had to make things happen.

At the state fair in Hutchinson on September 21 Dole and Roy faced off in their first debate of the campaign. Dole had been reluctant to debate Roy, agreeing only after setting the place, the format—no moderator, just the two of them debating each other—and the topic, agriculture, Dole's specialty. Before the debate a poll of fair attendees by the Hutchinson *News* showed Roy leading Dole 49 to 43 percent. The Dole campaign caravanned in one thousand supporters from around the state in cars and vans to see the great four-time county attorney, former House member, Senator and past Republican National Committee chairman—a demi-god to Kansas Republicans—shred Bill Roy. Even though they were behind, they felt like a 12-0 team heading for the championship.

Roy spent the afternoon quietly. He took a nap and went to the fairgrounds determined to, in effect, stick it to Dole. A crowd of 4,000 gathered to hear the spectacle broadcast live statewide on radio. When it began about four o'clock Roy turned to Dole and asked him why he wanted to do away with the federal Department of Agriculture. "Roy hit him upside the head," one Dole supporter said. Dole of course did not support dismantling the agency, he had just supported a bill that would have reorganized various government agencies, folding agriculture responsibilities into other departments. He favored streamlining the department to make it work better for farmers. Except he didn't say that very well. He got flustered.

"You don't have to like Bob Dole," Dole responded later in the debate, according to the Hutchinson *News.* "You don't have to agree with Bob Dole on every issue. But you've got to recognize that being Number One of the Ag Committee on the Republican side in a Republican administration is a great asset to Kansas."

Roy counterattacked, noting he had been promised a seat on the agriculture committee by Senator Stuart Symington, a prominent Missourian who organized committee structures in the Senate. Roy slammed Dole on voting against increasing Social Security payments. As the debate unfolded, Roy and Dole argued back and forth, their exchanges punctuated by outbursts from their respective supporters. Dole grew angrier, his face clouded, dark. His supporters looked on, panicked.

The topic of abortion arose. Only the year before, the Supreme Court had issued its landmark *Roe* v. *Wade* decision legalizing abortion. Roy said he was generally opposed to abortions, though he thought they might be warranted under some circumstances. As a doctor he was one of the few, perhaps only, members of Congress who had actually performed an abortion. He had done about a dozen abortions in his career, in each case because of a pressing medical need or complication, he said in an interview.

Even though the debate was supposed to stick to agriculture, Dole realized he was losing on style. In the closing seconds, according to the Kansas City *Star,* he blurted out, "You heard him stand here today and say he's for abortion on demand." Dole added: "I want to know how many abortions you've done and where you stand on abortion." Astonished, the crowd booed for several seconds. Roy offered a lame reply. The hour-long debate ended. Dole rushed from the stage and the fairgrounds, leaving his supporters overwrought. "Everybody looked like they lost their closest friend," one later recalled.

Roy's supporters were jubilant. Albert Hunt, a *Wall Street Journal* Washington bureau reporter, caught up with Roy afterward, and Hunt declared, "This race is over."

"We had been hitting him on things that were very true," Roy said years later. "He voted against Medicare, he voted against increases in Social Security, he voted to do away with the Department of Agriculture. The things we were hitting him on were broad, but they were correct. And he wasn't doing a lot to very successfully counteract them. And then came this ad. Of course, television's such a powerful medium."

"This ad" was something Dave Owen got. Owen, a bright lawyer, handsome with carefully combed hair and a soothing country tone in his voice, was from prosperous Johnson County and had been working with Dole's campaign. At the time he was Kansas' lieutenant governor, a rising star in the state GOP and had a reputation as thorough, low key, a good organizer. Dole had been impressed with Owen's help in his 1968 Senate race. Owen had wired Johnson County for Dole, delivering an important primary win there over Republican former governor Bill Avery.

In the 1974 Senate race Dole's campaign had been using television advertisements produced by a Boston agency. Owen referred to them as "Casper Milquetoast" ads. One featured Dole standing in a cornfield on a blazing summer day talking, just chatting about why he wanted to be re-elected. Owen booked a local radio announcer, Richard Ward Fatherly, a conservative with a deep bass voice and the ability to look menacing, to sit before a movie camera on a stool, cigarette smoke curling around his somber face, and rip the hide off of Roy.

"Cornered by a question in Wichita, Senator Dole's opponent said he had voted for three anti-abortion amendments and against one," Fatherly said in the segment that apparently never ran. "The truth is he voted for one, against one and didn't even bother to show up for the other two he claimed he voted for and he misstated the intent of the amendment he voted for. Talk, double-talk, words and more words, fact or fiction. There's no way to be sure where he stands."

Owen called the Boston agency to tell them he would be using his home-made television advertisement, not their ads. They asked for twenty-four hours. A day later Owen received a package—the most famous campaign advertisement in Kansas political history: the Mudslinger Ad. As it began, the screen filled with a Dole campaign poster displaying Dole's head and shoulders. An announcer intoned, "Bill Roy says Bob Dole wants to do away with the Department of Agriculture." SPLAT! A gob of mud hit Dole's face. As the announcer listed item after item of supposed Dole transgressions—splat, splat, splat—Dole's face disappeared. Now he was covered with mud. Then the announcer's tone changed, became warmer, and he ticked off a list of the good things Dole had done on each of the issues raised by "Roy." With each one a mud pie flew backward off of Dole's face. By the end, the poster was clean again. The ad ended with the announcer declaring, "All of which makes Bob Dole look pretty good and makes Bill Roy look like a liar." Owen loved it, but the ending alarmed him. He telephoned Dole, pulling him off the Senate floor. Dole hit the roof when he heard the ending and advised a change. It was aired soon after with a new ending, ". . . all of which makes Bill Roy look like just another old mudslinger."

The ad created both furor and confusion. Kansans had never seen anything quite so harsh. Democrats railed at Roy for low-blow campaigning, mistaking it as his own ad. Dole's folks yelled at him for airing Roy's grievances in his own ad. Other Dole backers, thinking it was Roy's ad, complained that he did not immediately rebut the charges. No matter . . . it worked. Immediately, Dole's overnight tracking polls began to climb. The controversy made Dole nervous and soon he had Huck Boyd, his campaign chairman call Owen to suggest the advertisement was pretty tough stuff. Maybe Owen should pull it. Owen held out, then did. Dole's poll numbers turned south. So, a while later, Owen put the ads back on the air, Dole's poll numbers reversed, headed north.

At the same time Dole took drastic measures. He fired campaign manager Herb Williams. In the months he had run the campaign Williams managed to alienate most of Dole's campaign team and volunteers across the state with an argumentative field-general style. Dole defended Williams for his ideas, but to soothe his loyal troops he hired Dave Owen as his new campaign manager.

Owen moved into Dole's campaign headquarters in downtown Topeka and found disaster. Sorting through the mess in Williams' desk, Owen discovered two bombshells. The bad news was a pile of bills adding up to $100,000 in debts, soon due. Creditors had called. Out of money, Dole's campaign was on its last legs. Nothing was going to happen without money. That same day Owen telephoned Wichita businessmen he knew to hastily pull together a fund-raiser lunch at the upscale Petroleum Club. Owen walked out with more than $125,000.

The good news was the other thing Owen found in the desk: a one-page article from a publication for disabled persons that told Dole's life story in brisk prose. It discussed Dole's athletic youth; how he was injured in World War II; his two Purple Hearts and a Bronze Star; his thirty-nine-month recovery through paralysis and near death; his struggle to walk; surgeries by Dr. Kelikian, the Armenian who had worked on Dole; Dole's law training and his rise from the statehouse to the United States Senate. While Owen knew the basic biographical sketch, it was the first time he had read what happened to Dole on the battlefield and the grim aftermath. He saw it as a gold mine.

On a blank piece of paper Owen placed two photographs side by side, the one on the left showing just Dole's disabled hand, and the other showing a full-front portrait of Dole. Above that, Owen wrote a headline in large black letters: "You can sum up Senator Bob Dole with a 4-letter word: GUTS."

The Dole campaign made thousands of copies of the article and the cover sheet. A task force of volunteers drove all over the state in late September, music blaring from atop a motor home, handing out the flyers to people on the streets of small towns or sticking them under car and truck windshield wipers.

At the same time Owen arrived, Carol Wiebe, the Hillsboro business-woman and Marion County Republican party chair who had worked for Dole in 1968, kissed her husband and three sons good-by and moved to Topeka. She joined Owen and another young staffer, Bill Wohlford, to work around-the-clock from the campaign headquarters with the dozen other core campaign staff. Owen organized and raised money, Wohlford worked on policy for Dole, Wiebe did direct mail. But first Wiebe ordered one thousand red-and-white beret-style caps from K-Mart for the Dolls for Dole to wear when they went out campaigning.

Night after night, Wiebe sat on the floor stuffing envelopes with the GUTS flyer and requests for donations, and then mailed them to anyone she and the staff could think of who might vote for Dole. This was low-tech, seat-of-the-pants campaigning. The campaign had not one computer, nor any computerized list of possible supporters. Wiebe drew a matrix on a large piece of cardboard to record names and addresses and then looked them up in telephone books. She licked stamps and envelopes until after midnight each night. Wohlford slept on a cot in the headquarters. "Everybody was on edge, it was chaotic," Wiebe said. "It was like trying to win with a yellow lead pencil." To boost morale she made a large sign on white paper and hung it in the office: "YES, WE CAN!" She organized a reception at the Jayhawk Hotel and stacked Dole pineapple juice cans in an enormous pyramid along one wall. "Everyone," Wiebe said, "thought that was a kill . . . It didn't matter how corny, if you thought you could get a vote for Bob Dole, you did it."

Dole seemed to rebound, his spirits picked up. He was going to fight. At rallies and in speeches he forcefully challenged Roy. "We lit the match that struck the fire," said Wiebe. Dole caravans drove from town to town handing out campaign literature. Sisters Norma Jean and Gloria headed off to campaign for their brother. Daughter Robin boarded a motor home with her grandmother, Bina, and a campaign volunteer drove them to every corner of Kansas. Pulling into a town, their motor home blared the campaign theme song, "Let a Winner Lead the Way," over and over.

Robin and Bina would talk to people while handing out literature, then drive on to the next town.

"I don't think I had any idea how big Kansas was until that year," Robin said. She took time off from college, putting her life on hold, as she would in 1976, 1980 and 1988, requesting larger roles in each campaign as her confidence grew. "I don't think he's ever had to ask, 'Will you do this?' " Robin Dole said of her father. "Everybody just jumps in where they can."

In the closing weeks of the 1974 race Roy and his campaign team pounded Dole on issues and honesty. They placed advertisements in Kansas newspapers contending Dole's vote against an agricultural spending bill indicated Dole was against farmers. Dole countered he did not like provisions such as one offering food stamps for strikers.

Just as he had battled back those thirty-nine months in hospitals after the war, Dole refused to give up. He didn't know how. Besides, he was beginning to sense positive momentum. With Owen shouldering the burden for dozens of day-to-day details, the campaign smoothed out, Dole began to relax, his jokes returned.

On September 29 Dole and Roy showed up in Washington to debate each other a second time on CBS's Sunday morning "Face the Nation" program. Before it began, Dole and Owen agreed: Forget issues, let's psyche this thing out. Dole stepped over to chat with the panelists, all three journalists who personally knew him and who weren't acquainted with Roy beyond his résumé. Dole threw them a one-liner, then another. Soon he and the journalists were in a huddle, laughing and kidding, while Roy stood on the other side of the room, the color draining from his face.

On camera, Dole took charge: he smiled, he put Roy off balance by noting Roy was earning $250,000 a year as a doctor. He called the race "a classic contest between a known conservative, Bob Dole, and a known liberal, Bill Roy," according to the Associated Press Bill Roy was running on one issue, a "Watergate-style campaign," Dole jabbed. Sitting beside him, Roy felt miserable. The salary issue wasn't fair, he thought. He tried to deflect the Watergate charge by replying the race wasn't about Dole's involvement but about the question: "Which man do I trust more? Which one will do the most for Kansas?"

For Dole, the debate felt like a turnaround, even though a statewide poll a week earlier had showed Roy comfortably ahead, with 50 percent of the voters preferring him, 42 percent endorsing Dole and 8 percent undecided. The Dole army fought on, resorting more to its most volatile weapon, the abortion issue. Only the year before, the United States Supreme Court had delivered its *Roe* v. *Wade* decision that for the first time legalized abortion, polarizing anti-abortion activists against those who supported a woman's right to an abortion. Dole made it clear he supported a human life amendment, which if approved by Congress and ratified by the states could lead to a ban on abortions. The Right-to-Life groups in Kansas endorsed Dole, speaking out at meetings and rallies against Roy, "the abortionist."

The race became a media phenomena. National television and newspaper reporters swooped into Kansas to take the pulse of farmers and townspeople, interview the two combatants and hint that Dole was finished. The momentum had turned, except Roy did not realize it. The first two weeks of October he did not actively campaign; he remained in Washington to vote on legislation before the House. It was a critical oversight, he admitted later. He lost touch with the shifting mood in Kansas, and the issue upon which it had turned—abortion.

Roy told audiences in September and October that he was personally opposed to abortion, though he believed it should be curtailed by some means other than a constitutional ban as proposed by the human-life amendment. Furthermore, before when state laws outlawed abortions women found ways to obtain illegal abortions, sometimes endangering their health. He admitted he had performed abortions deemed medically necessary in consultation with another physician. The anti-abortion forces picketed him everywhere he spoke.

Dole declined to come out and explicitly say he opposed all abortions. He had voted against fetal tissue experimentation and co-sponsored an amendment in the Senate banning the use of federal funds for abortions or abortion referral services and opposed using U.S. foreign aid funds for family-planning ventures in foreign countries that offered abortions. According to the Kansas City *Times,* Dole appeared on October 5 at the Right-to-Life state convention in Hays and told the gathering, "If you want a human life amendment, then elect those who will support your position."

Dole traveled non-stop across Kansas, addressing rallies, speaking in churches and schools, shaking hands with people on the street, criticizing Roy on issues and at times mentioning abortion, according to reporters who covered the race.

Even the Emporia *Gazette,* headed for decades by Republican stalwart William Allen White, a friend of Dole, did not appreciate the tone of the campaign. One editorial warned: "In this year of Watergate, voters are looking for nice guys . . . The proper image for 1974 is Mr. Clean.

Congressman Roy projects this image naturally. He seems soft-spoken and reserved. Senator Dole is a witty, slashing campaigner whose barbs once made a hit with voters. Not anymore. His abrasive technique is out of style."

Bob Brock, the state Democratic chairman, got so disgruntled with the Dole campaign's rough style he held a press conference in October to say Dole represented the caveman philosophy of governing. A couple of days later, after letting their beards grow, two state senators and Dole backers, Wint Winter, Sr., and Rex Hoy, held their own press conference. They were big men. Winter had played college football at Kansas, Hoy at Nebraska. Dressed in leopard-print caveman outfits, carrying papier-mâché spears, they announced they were "Cavemen for Dole."

"Oh, people had a lot of fun with it," Winter chuckled. "And it helped build momentum in the campaign."

The two candidates debated again on October 20 in Wichita, a rough exchange in which each accused the other of mudslinging. Dole was giving it all he had. Roy's attacks began to backfire; some voters even felt sorry for Dole. One day, Dreiling suggested that the burglary tools for the Watergate break-in might have been stored in Dole's apartment, a ludicrous charge that Dole laughed off.

Despite the air of electricity and tension, Dole felt good about his prospects going into the final weekend. Then the contest exploded in controversy. On Sunday morning, Right-to-Life members fanned out across the state to place 50,000 flyers—with graphic pictures of dead fetuses in garbage cans and denunciations of Roy—on the windshields of cars outside of churches. Dole had tried to stop them from going out. Advertisements featuring a skull and crossbones ran in several newspapers in the last two days. Along one femur was the word "abortion" and on the other "euthanasia." No mention of Roy, it had lettering below: "Vote Dole." Dole got blamed for the flyers and ads. He said he had nothing to do with either of them. Roy couldn't figure out how to counter the negative publicity and did little. The state was in an uproar.

Reflecting back over the three decades he covered politics in Kansas for the Wichita *Eagle-Beacon*, Al Polzcinski said that Senate campaign ended on a spectacularly downbeat note. "It was the meanest-spirited race I've ever covered," Polzcinski said.

In the final days Dole looked deeply fatigued, yet wouldn't stop. He needed to tell a few more people how much he wanted to keep his job. "The *real* issue in this campaign, if there is one issue, is which candidate can best serve Kansas, which candidate can best produce for Kansas," Dole said in a campaign video. "I say that in the highest sense, I say that not as a Republican, but I believe I'm an independent thinker, an independent senator and one who loves his state and considers it a great honor to serve the people in the state."

On Election Day, November 5, Dole flew back from the northwest town of Norton, in the heart of his original House district. Even there the mood carried gloom. "Watergate was still hanging around, and I had been the [RNC] chairman and I hadn't paid enough attention to Kansas," was what Dole remembered people telling him. "I was prepared to lose, too. I told my folks that night, 'I don't know if it's going to happen or not.' "

Dole went to the Ramada Inn in Topeka to watch the vote returns. Roy lay on his bed in the Holiday Inn, slowly realizing the stream of voting was going the wrong way. By ten-thirty that night, he conceded. Over at the Ramada, Dole's supporters were elated and chanted for their hero to come downstairs and join in the victory celebration. Uneasy about the numbers, Dole would not. After midnight, he made Owen and several other staffers telephone the election officials in every one of the state's 105 counties, awakening some to get the results. Only then would he descend to acknowledge his win. "I wasn't going to go out there unless I really had it," Dole recalled.

The final tally showed that Bob Dole had won 403,983 votes to Roy's 390,451. He had beaten Roy by a scant 13,532 votes out of 794,434 cast. Years later, Roy would say that the abortion issue killed him. Without it he might have won by 50,000 votes. The traditionally Catholic strongholds around Topeka and in Atchison, where Roy did well in 1970 and 1972, voted for Dole.

"I've always said about that race, you need a little jolt like that now and then to bring you back to earth. Makes you a better senator," Dole said in an interview. "And you start taking a closer look at—lotta things. I've told Bill Roy to his face he made me a better senator."

Two years later, Pat Goodson, who was a member of Right-to-Life Affiliates of Kansas, said she had been in contact with Mike Baroody, a Dole aide, before the 1974 campaign seeking information on the senator's position on abortion. In 1976, she said she felt the Dole campaign was aware her organization would be placing the newspaper advertisements in 1974. They were placed by Esther Surs, a Johnson County woman, who said a Dole campaign staffer okayed the ad. And under state election laws in effect at the time, Dole in 1976 filed a campaign finance report acknowledging the newspaper ads as "in-kind" contributions because they benefited his campaign. The flyers were drawn up and paid for by a minister unconnected to Dole's campaign.

Also in 1976, R.W. "Johnny" Apple, Washington correspondent for the New York *Times,* recalled on CBS's "Face the Nation" that he had been in a high school where Dole spoke in 1974. "You said at the end of your little informal talk to the kids when Dr. Roy comes and—it was a Catholic high school I should add—that when Dr. Roy comes here you ought to ask him whether he's performed any abortions," Apple said to Dole.

"Right," Dole responded. "I think that's a good question if you're a doctor and I wasn't—I raised the question but we ended up disavowing the skull-and-crossbones ads . . ."

In an interview with the author, Dole said: "I'm not saying some Dole supporters weren't doing them, but it wasn't anything generated [by me]. I remember calling a lady in Johnson County and saying, 'Look, you're killing me running these ads. You think you're helping Bob Dole. You're killing me, I can tell from talking to people.' She didn't seem to care, she was getting her message out."

As it turned out, Roy might have held the antidote to the abortion controversy in his hand. Or it might have killed his own campaign. Roy's campaign team had prepared a final tough television advertisement linking Dole with former President Nixon and Watergate, a way to condemn Dole at the end with little time for Dole to respond. Nixon at the time was suffering from phlebitis. Roy and his campaign leaders feared Nixon would die on them and make them look heartless; they did not run the ad. Besides, Roy and his troops believed he was ahead. Roy's aides told him: "Act senatorial, you're a nice person, act like a nice person." Roy responded to that prompting; after all, his previous two winning races had not been confrontational.

In his heart, Roy was not a politician. He was a doctor, and doctors by nature are not instinctively confrontational. He returned to medicine.

"We were naïve," says Roy. "Bob Dole wanted it more than I did."

"DEMOCRAT WARS"

AFTER BOB DOLE'S victory party in Topeka that went deep into the night, he picked up the telephone to call Elizabeth Hanford in Washington. Excited, he told her he had won and announced they could celebrate together soon.

"I'll be back tomorrow," he said.

"Bob, don't you remember?" said Elizabeth, now a commissioner on the Federal Trade Commission. "I'm going to Japan."

Of course, he remembered *now*. She had mentioned Japan several weeks before in one of their nightly chats.

Through that grueling Senate campaign, he looked forward at the end of each day to talking with her, to unwind a bit. As he always would do when on the road, Dole campaigned through the days then traveled ahead at night to sleep where he had his first appearance or speech the following morning. That fall, driving across Kansas, he called her quite late, often around midnight.

"So I figured, 'Okay, that's my contribution to the campaign,'" she would recall. "Whatever time he wants to call, I'm available for a quick chat or a forty-minute conversation. We both enjoyed that. And he still does that. If I'm on the road he calls at least once a day. He checks into this office once a day. That's something that's been there through all the years."

He had endorsed the Japan trip. He had thought it was a fine opportunity for her to study the Japanese government, but the date skipped his mind until he made his election night call. Elizabeth went. In part, that was what attracted him to her; she was a professional woman, beautiful, smart, full of as much ambition as he possessed. She had a law degree from Harvard Law School and had studied at Oxford, impressive credentials to a guy from Kansas. She was upbeat, possessed with warm southern charm. Officially an independent, Elizabeth got her first job in government in the Johnson administration.

When Elizabeth returned, Bob presented her with a dozen red roses and began "talking about 'when now, are we going to get married?' " she recalled. The two lived in apartments at opposite ends of the Watergate hotel complex for another year, continuing to date, conducting a quiet courtship.

On December 6, 1975, Bob Dole and Elizabeth Hanford were married in the Bethlehem Chapel of the Washington Cathedral. He was fifty-two, she was thirty-nine and had not been married before. Robert Ellsworth was his best man. Her sister-in-law was the matron of honor, and seventy relatives, friends and family joined the Doles for a wedding breakfast and a ceremony later in the afternoon. According to the Doles' 1988 book *Unlimited Partners,* Elizabeth studied her marriage vows while Bob decided to wing it. The music played and stopped, Dr. Elson, the presiding Senate chaplain, began the vows. At the first pause Bob jumped the gun. "I do," he boomed.

They flew to the Virgin Islands for a honeymoon.

The following day, seventy-five-year-old Doran Dole, resting for the trip back to Kansas, had a sudden heart attack in Dole's Watergate apartment and died, and the newlyweds cut short their honeymoon to return home.

EIGHT MONTHS LATER an old-fashioned nomination showdown took place in August 1976, at the Republican National Convention in Kemper Arena, a big white wedding box stuck in a gray industrial alley of Kansas City, Missouri, just across the river from Bob Dole's home state. President Gerald R. Ford was battling to win the Republican nomination over a strong challenge from former California Governor Ronald Reagan.

Meanwhile Jimmy Carter, the sunny former governor from Georgia, won his own battle for the Democratic nomination as an outsider to Washington's power structure. In July, he and running mate Minnesota Senator Walter "Fritz" Mondale had rocketed out of the Democratic convention with polls showing them as much as 33 points ahead of Ford. Many voters disapproved of Ford pardoning President Nixon in 1974.

Not only did Ford have to secure the nomination, he would need a new vice-presidential running mate. Nelson Rockefeller, the former New York governor, had agreed to take the vice-presidency under Ford in 1974 but rapidly lost popularity and announced in November of 1975 he would not run again with Ford.

The convention battle between a relatively stiff Jerry Ford and former Hollywood actor Ronald Reagan came down to a wild floor fight over Rule 16C, requiring each candidate to name a vice-presidential running mate before the vote on the presidential nomination. Reagan's people reasoned that if Rule 16C passed, Ford's choice would probably alienate a faction of his support in some areas of the country, thereby enabling Reagan to steal delegates and win the nomination.

When the final tally on Rule 16C was taken in a sweaty, white-knuckle vote, Ford's team held its delegates and defeated the rule. Ford won the nomination after midnight August 19 by a slim margin—1,187 delegates for Ford, 1,070 for Reagan. After the vote Reagan and Ford met uncomfortably in Reagan's hotel room in the Alameda Plaza Hotel. Reagan congratulated Ford, who then told Reagan the six people he was considering for vice-president. Reagan was not on the list.

Still up at three in the morning, Ford and nine top aides gathered in a hotel suite to discuss his running mate. The six contenders, according to news stories, were Treasury Secretary William Simon; Howard Baker, the Tennessee senator who played a lead role in the Senate Watergate Committee hearings; former deputy attorney general William Ruckelshaus; Anne Armstrong, U.S. ambassador to Great Britain; John Connally, the former Texas governor; and Bob Dole.

Earlier that week, Dole had telephoned friend Lyn Nofziger, Reagan's press secretary from the California days, who was again advising Reagan for 1976. As usual, the exchange was jocular. When the talk turned to the vice-presidency, Nofziger detected something in Dole's tone.

"Do you really want to be vice-president?" Nofziger asked Dole.

"Yeah," said Dole.

"Well, what do you want me to do?" said Nofziger.

"I want you to talk to Reagan," Dole said, "and if Ford asks him about me, have him say something nice about me, or at least don't have him say anything bad."

Nofziger said, "Sure. That's no problem."

He later told Reagan, "If Ford asks you about Bob Dole as vice-president, try to say something nice about him." Reagan agreed. He also let Reagan know that if he managed to win the nomination, Dole would welcome being Reagan's vice-presidential nominee, too.

In the pre-dawn August 19 meeting convened by Ford, a winnowing process began. Simon was viewed as a Washington insider. Baker and Ruckelshaus, who had been fired for refusing to fire Watergate Special Prosecutor Archibald Cox, were both eliminated on the feeling that dredging up further memories of Watergate could backfire. Connally, linked to a milk-fund scandal, had high poll-negatives. Armstrong was ruled out; some GOP women raised questions whether the country was ready for a woman.

When Dole's name came up, the Ford group remembered that Reagan had seemed supportive. Ford's aides ticked off Dole's liabilities—his sharp tongue, his divorce, the fact that he and Ford both were from the Midwest, providing no geographical diversity to counter a Democratic ticket from the South and Midwest. On the other hand, Dole would bring party loyalty, a proven track record as an aggressive fighter and a clear appeal in the Farm Belt, where, indeed, Ford was in trouble. Further, Elizabeth was from North Carolina, which might help pull in southerners, another Ford weak spot. Ford asked everyone to sleep on it and the group broke up.

Bob and Elizabeth Dole had stayed awake about half the night in their room at the historic Muehlbach Hotel, keeping an eye on Connally's room next door because they, and Connally, believed Connally would be the nominee. Rumors that night had Ruckelshaus flying in to accept the nomination.

At 6 A.M. August 19, the telephone rang in the Doles' room.

"Well, congratulations!" Bob Clark, an ABC correspondent, told Dole.

"For what?" said Dole.

Clark told him he'd been tipped off by a source close to Ford that Dole was Ford's choice. Dole responded that he hadn't been called by the president or his staff.

Ford reconvened his staff at 9:30 A.M. and soon announced he had reached his decision.

"Let's get Bob Dole on the phone," he said. Around ten, the telephone rang again in the Doles' hotel room.

"Bob, I want you to be on the ticket," Ford declared.

Dole responded, "If you think I can help, certainly." In a second conversation Dole said, "Mr. President, will you come to Russell tomorrow?" And Ford agreed.

Pandemonium erupted among the Dole family and his supporters. Delegates were wide-eyed with surprise. The one bit of advice Ford had given Dole was, "You'll have to be careful with what you say. " Dole responded, "I'll do my best." That evening Ford and Dole stood before the cheering throng to deliver their nomination acceptance speeches. Despite infighting and his woeful lag behind Carter and Mondale, Ford promised to attack the Democrats and challenged Carter to the first televised presidential debates since the 1960 Kennedy–Nixon debates.

"We will wage a winning campaign in every region of this country— from the snowy banks of Minnesota to the sandy plains of Georgia, we concede not one single state. We concede not one single vote," said Ford. "Yes, we have all seen the polls and the pundits who say our party is dead. I'll tell you what I think: the only polls that count are the polls the American people go to on November 2. Right now, I predict that the American people are going to say that night—'Jerry, you've done a good job. Keep right on doing it!' "

In Dole's acceptance speech, his first address as a national candidate, he thanked Ford for choosing him, was "humbled by this new opportunity" and criticized Carter for suggesting the nation tighten its belt and lower its expectations.

"America wasn't built by men and women with limited vision and small hopes and low expectations," said Dole, his voice echoing through the arena. "It was built by men and women with tomorrow on their minds."

Out in Russell, in preparation for their moment in the national spotlight the next day, everyone was working as hard as Bob Dole. Russell Townsley, publisher of the Russell *Daily News,* got a telephone call about noon on August 19 from the White House seeking a half-page advertisement in the paper for the Ford–Dole ticket, and another call soon after, basically asking, "What is out there and what can you do?" "What do you want?" Townsley said. A lot. All White Houses asked a lot. Townsley and others rounded up dozens of volunteers for nineteen frenzied hours of work.

Late that afternoon a planeload of Secret Service agents and advance people invaded the town and eventually chose their rally site on the lawn of the Russell County Courthouse, where twenty years before Bob Dole had served as county attorney. Scouring the town, the Secret Service agents checked out roofs of buildings, finding potential trouble spots at which to position law officers. They visited the local hospital, just in case.

Bleachers from the fairgrounds were dismantled and hauled to the court-house, and a stage for Ford and the Doles was hammered together. Yards of telephone lines were strung and nailed to trees for the national press.

Surveying the scene, the White House advance people declared it wasn't "rural" enough, Townsley recalled. Volunteers rounded up large grills and scrambled to grocery stores for miles around Russell, buying thousands of hot dogs and buns. Horse-watering tanks were comman-deered and brought to the courthouse to be filled with ice and studded with thousands of cans of soft drinks.

The next morning volunteers tacked red, white and blue bunting onto the stage and draped it along the bleachers. Dozens of American flags were hung along the route the presidential motorcade would take. At ten, eleven unsmiling men in trench coats, all dark-haired but one, with ear-phones and wires running through their jacket sleeves, showed up and took up positions around the courthouse. President Ford and the Doles flew to Salina in a jet, then were helicoptered to Russell. Riding in a presidential motorcade, Ford and Bob and Elizabeth Dole stood up in the back of their limousine to wave at the crowd lined along Main Street the last dozen blocks to the courthouse.

With the all-American smell of grilled hot dogs wafting through the crowd, Ford and the Doles mounted the stage in front of the courthouse. After the introductions Bob Dole rose to speak, facing the crowd of ten thousand. "I never really believed I would ever be in this position, believe me, when I was county attorney of Russell County, or the state legislature before that. I never believed it when I got to Congress after drowning Keith Sebelius in Dole pineapple juice," Dole began, looking out and catching the face of a friend here, a friend there. "I never believed it when I went to the Senate and I don't really believe it yet today. But it shows you can come from a small town in America and you don't need all the wealth and the material things in this world to succeed, if I've succeeded, though some might quarrel with that. I want to re-emphasize: if I've done anything it's because of people I've known up and down Main Street. And I can recall the time when I needed help, the people of Russell helped. And I think . . ."

Dole stopped mid-sentence, his left hand jerked up to cover his face. Silence engulfed the crowd.

"When a large crowd suddenly becomes silent you know something is very, very wrong," said Townsley, who was standing nearby. "And as a newspaperman, you'd better find out what it is, fast."

Bob Dole was crying. His shoulders shook. Claps and cheers arose from the crowd. Elizabeth and Robin sat frozen in their seats. Finally, President Ford stood up, looking sympathetic, and led the audience in applause. It built to a roar, punctuated by shouts and whistles. It went on for half a minute.

"That was a long time ago," Dole finally said, recovering his composure, "and I thank you for it again."

Dole introduced the president, who trumpeted Kansas' wheat and cattle industries and well-known state politicians.

"What I am really saying is you not only produce cattle and wheat and energy," Ford said, "but doggone it, you produce great people."

Ford praised his running mate's legislative experience and ability to connect with people, and spoke of his own commitment to insuring that farmers received fair prices for their goods.

When the event ended, the presidential motorcade rolled through the neighborhoods to drop Bina Dole off at her home on Maple Street. The motorcade stopped, Ford and the Dole clan got out.

"I was born down there, where that pile of dirt is," Bob Dole said, according to a press pool report, gesturing down the street where the family's first wood frame home had stood until demolished.

Someone in the press pool asked Bina how she felt about her son. "I'm just so excited. I'm happy for him," she said. Would he win? "Sure, he always wins," she said. Dole looked over to the press group, cupped his hands and *sotto voce* said, "I think she's a little biased." Beaming, Ford joined in with, "I haven't lost an election, either."

At the porch Bina reached into the mailbox for the key, not finding it. She walked over to a ledge nearby, shielded behind a green shrub, to feel for her key. Not there either. The group fidgeted while Robin Dole, Bob's daughter, walked back over to the car and returned empty-handed. Finally, Elizabeth saved the day. She checked behind a drainpipe and found the key, which had "slipped down" from its usual place. The group went inside, stayed five minutes, ate cookies and drank milk and juice, and came out to head for the airport. As Ford left Dole on the tarmac Ford said, "We'll see you next week."

FORD WOULD ADOPT a Rose Garden strategy, holed up in the White House to look presidential while Dole dove into the briar patch to go after Carter. Dole, pretty much on his own, flew with a couple of staff people on a commercial jet to Seattle to speak to an American Legion convention. Ford's people wanted to play up Dole's war-veteran status to match

Carter's record in the U.S. Navy. The speech went all right, but Dole's small entourage—himself, Elizabeth, Dave Owen, Larry Speakes, whom the Ford campaign sent over as Dole's campaign press secretary, and Noel Koch, a speechwriter—stumbled along in the following days. "It was a ragtag operation for about three weeks," Dole said in an interview.

Dole and the Ford campaign persuaded Nofziger to join Dole on the campaign trail. Nofziger and Charlie Black, a North Carolinian who had worked on conservative Republican Senator Jesse Helms's staff for several years, would be the two political advisers who would take turns flying around the country with Dole, helping Dole sharpen his message, organize his schedule and focus on criticizing Jimmy Carter's record.

When Nofziger came aboard with Dole he noticed right away that the Ford team was paying practically no attention to Dole's campaign. He and Black instituted a systematic schedule and tried to get Dole to be consistent in his statements. The Dole campaign barnstormed the country, homing in on Ohio and other farm-belt states. The two political advisers contended they kept the White House informed and received enough direction from the Ford group to believe they were doing what was expected.

"The fact is, what Bob Dole did was exactly what the leadership in the Ford campaign asked him to do," said Black. "It was definitely not Bob Dole out acting like the Lone Ranger."

As Republican National Committee chairman four years before, Dole had jetted around America defending Richard Nixon, but that was a relatively small affair. He had never been in a national campaign and now he was the guy in charge of one: plane, staff, messages, schedules, pressure, media and all. On the campaign trail Dole was tireless. He pushed his team hard and his assessments of their efforts could be withering. Sometimes he would take a speech, glance at it five seconds and pass it back, "Here . . . you go out and give this. I'm not going to," he would say jokingly, meaning go rewrite it—now. Black learned what it took to meet Dole's expectations.

"If he asks you to call twenty people, he doesn't want you to call eighteen and let the other two slide," said Black. "He wants you to call all twenty. If you can't get two because they are unreachable or out of the country he wants to hear that, but he'll be satisfied. He doesn't want you to come up there without knowing what you're talking about and having your arguments marshaled. He works harder than anybody. There will never be anybody who works for Bob Dole who'll be asked to work harder than he does."

Under direction from Nofziger and Black, Dole's appearances smoothed out. He spoke more often before generally sympathetic audiences and frequently made news. Dole's speeches focused on Ford's plan to improve the economy, and the president's opposition to granting amnesty for Vietnam war draft evaders. He criticized Carter and Mondale for proposing deep cuts in defense spending and for appearing to favor tax hikes.

As the Dole team soared around on the jet stream, voters who heard Dole speak remembered the jokes and wicked barbs aimed at his opponents. "Just remember pineapple juice doesn't stick to the roof of your mouth like peanut butter," Dole reminded audiences. Often Dole said he and Mondale were ideal senators to run as party vice-presidential nominees. "When he votes yes, I vote no. When I vote yes, he votes no," Dole said according to Newsweek magazine, October 26, 1976. "We will never be missed, for we are two senators who can be absent without changing a single thing."

He noted Carter's links with AFL-CIO chief George Meany, whose longshoremen had the year before held up ships of grain bound for the Soviet Union, pressuring Ford into imposing a grain-shipment embargo. The negative fallout from the grain embargo was one reason Ford chose Dole, to help him win back voters in the farm belt. "Someone asked Meany why he didn't run for president," Dole joked, "and he said, 'Why step down?' "

In early September, Playboy magazine published an interview with Carter. In the magazine Carter, who drew support because of his Christian faith, admitted he had "looked on a lot of women with lust. I've committed adultery in my heart many times." He also said, "I don't think I would ever take on the same frame of mind that [presidents] Nixon or Johnson did—lying, cheating and distorting the truth." He later apologized to Lady Bird Johnson, the president's widow, and conceded he was wrong ever to have granted the interview. Dole jumped on the controversy; a typical campaign-trail line went: "Carter has given lots of interviews lately. Some are in black and white. Some are in color. Some are without pictures. Some are with pictures. Some people say a picture is worth a thousand words."

Watergate came back to plague Dole in September. On September 6, Claude Wild, Jr., a former lobbyist for Gulf Oil Corporation, which had handed out four million dollars in illegal contributions to Republicans in the early 1970s, said in the New York *Times* that he remembered giving $2,000 in cash to Dole in 1970 to pass on to Republicans. Dole denied receiving the money but disclosed he had been questioned about it earlier in 1976 by a grand jury investigating Watergate. Dole said he told the grand jury then he had not received any money from Gulf Oil. Hastily the next day Wild apologized; his memory was incorrect, he said, and he had done a "serious disservice to Senator Dole."

Three weeks later Dole disclosed that two pages had been removed from a ledger of his 1973-74 campaign finance report, potentially covering an accounting of the time Wild spoke of. Dole explained that his personal secretary Jo-Anne Coe kept the records. Coe said at the time she wrote on the ledger's inside cover that cash receipts were entered beginning on page nine, made a mistake on that page, tore it out and began on page eleven. The story died.

Dole campaigned relentlessly through September; polls showed that the Republicans were closing the gap with the Democrats. Then Ford matched Carter's Playboy gaffe in the second presidential debate on October 6 in San Francisco. He said, "There is no Soviet domination of eastern Europe," a statement he was forced to recant a few days later under heavy pressure from Carter and American immigrants from eastern European countries. A Gallup poll taken before the debate showed Carter barely ahead, 47 to 45, within the margin of polling error, but in one taken following the debate Carter led Ford 48 to 42 percent.

Dole's only personal contact with Ford was an occasional talk on the telephone in which the president always told him he was doing a good job, Dole said later. Ford offered no strategy for answering a question that came up in early October: If he became vice-president what would Dole do? He tried deflecting the question, saying, considering their poll standings, he was too busy trying to *get* to be vice-president to have time to contemplate what he'd do with the office. He wanted the job, he kidded, because "it's indoor work and no heavy lifting."

Dole's aides felt he simply was being pragmatic about the limited role of the job, in which the occupier's sole constitutional responsibility was to be breathing if the president *stopped*. Dole felt like his job description that fall was clearly defined: challenge Carter. Beyond that, he didn't have time to speculate about his role as vice-president.

In Pittsburgh in mid-October Dole was asked what he would do in his first hundred days as vice-president, according to an article in the Washington *Post*. "I think anybody running for vice-president (with) a plan for the first hundred days is kidding himself," Dole said. "I may not do anything in the first hundred days and I may not in the second hundred days. I've known vice-presidents who've been there four years and haven't done anything. If I'm asked any policy decisions I'll plead the Fifth Amendment."

The poll slippage put pressure on Dole as he headed to Houston for an October 15 vice-presidential debate with Mondale. Dole's mission that night was to raise questions about Jimmy Carter's firmness on political positions and portray Ford as a leader able to make tough decisions amid political adversity. It was a big test for Bob Dole: a live national debate.

Dole and Mondale met at eight-thirty Friday night on a stage in the Alley Theatre in Houston before an estimated radio and television audience of eighty-five million people in America and overseas. By a coin toss Dole won the opening statement, beginning as he did most addresses with a joke. "I think tonight may be sort of a fun evening. It's a very historic evening. But I've known my counterpart for some time, and we've been friends, and we'll be friends when the election is over and . . . he'll still be in the Senate." Dole then got right down to business, praising Ford and calling Mondale "the most liberal senator" in the entire Senate. "My opponent has a record of voting for every inflationary spending program, except in defense, where he votes for every cut," said Dole.

Mondale sidestepped Dole's jabs and turned to the economy. It was in bad shape, with "the highest unemployment since the Great Depression, fifty percent higher than when Mr. Ford took office." Republicans had had eight years to solve problems of health, education and housing, and had failed. The nation needed new leadership, he said.

Mondale stood facing squarely toward the moderator, while Dole leaned on the podium with his left shoulder, a casual pose, as he tossed off acerbic observations. Dole answered questions with criticism of Carter and catchy turns of phrase: "Some of those who lust for power are not really concerned about people." Meanwhile, Mondale fought back in defense with attacks of Ford's and Dole's records. He spoke in platitudes about how Carter planned to improve the lives of Americans.

Both candidates were asked what they would do as vice-president. This time Dole had an answer: He had talked it over with Ford and expected he would have "some role" in increasing agricultural exports. Because of his association with families who had relatives missing in action and prisoners of war in southeast Asia he would serve as Ford's representative in seeking news of those unaccounted for.

Mondale envisioned a bigger responsibility. As vice-president he would have a "substantial role in both domestic and foreign policy," he said, and would work with Carter to restructure and reorganize the federal government. He said he would head a task force on crime, work on economic problems, fight inflation and establish an "interdepartmental agency under the chairmanship of the vice-president."

They traded more punches. Mondale criticized Dole's vote against Medicare. Dole responded by saying the Medicare bill provided benefits to all whether a recipient needed them or not. He charged Democrats had trimmed unemployment in the 1960s because "they had a full-grown war in southeast Asia. That's not the way we tried to end unemployment in the Republican party."

Mondale complained Dole "has probably the worst record in favor of loopholes of any senator in the United States Senate. And Mr. Ford has one of the worst records in favor of tax loopholes in the history of the House of Representatives."

Dole responded, "I think Senator Mondale's a little nervous." President Carter's tax return showed he had a tax liability of $58,000, took off $41,000 as an investment tax credit for machinery, a tax loophole for the rich he himself used.

At other moments Dole spoke of "the war we inherited from another Democratic administration in southeast Asia," and "Democrat" agreements at Yalta and Potsdam during World War II that enslaved Eastern Europe. He also expressed negative feelings about the leadership of President Roosevelt. "I think about that every day, because of a personal experience in World War II," he said.

But what many Americans remember about the debate came in an exchange in the last moments. It began when Mondale raked Dole for defending President Nixon to the end of his presidency and complained about the Ford administration's efforts to oppose Watergate legislative reforms. Dole said Watergate was the Republicans' great burden, but noted Democrats were forever bringing the issue up to exploit it politically.

Associated Press Special Correspondent Walter Mears, a debate panelist, had a question. He noted that when Dole ran for Senate re-election two years earlier in Kansas he had openly said that Ford's pardon of Nixon had been premature. Mears asked if the issue was fair game to discuss in Kansas then, why not now?

Dole then spoke perhaps the most memorable—some would say most partisan—words of his political career. "Well, it, uh, it is an appropriate topic, I guess, but it's not a very good issue, any more than the war in Vietnam would be, or World War II, or World War I, or the war in Korea. All Democrat wars. All in this century. I figured up the other day, if we added up all the killed and wounded in Democrat wars in this century, it would be about 1.6 million Americans, enough to fill the city of Detroit."

Mondale took his cue. "I think, uh, Senator Dole has richly earned his reputation as a hatchet man tonight, by implying, *stating,* that World War II and the Korean War were Democrat wars," Mondale said. "Does he really mean to suggest to the American people that there was a partisan difference over our involvement in the war to fight Nazi Germany? I don't think any reasonable American would accept that. Does he really mean to suggest that it was only partisanship that got us into the war in Korea?"

President Ford called immediately after the debate. "You hit hard but fair," Dole later recalled him saying. The first poll showed Dole winning, but after the "Democrat wars" comment and other attacks were aired in the following days, the national press declared that Mondale had walked away with the debate. Democratic National Chairman Robert Strauss, who years later would become a close friend of Dole, said Dole "did the president and the Republican party a great disservice." Conservative columnist George Will said Dole needed a history lesson about the origins of wars. "People who lie about history deserve to be forgotten by it," Will wrote of Dole. On the campaign trail people waved anti-Dole signs: "Fritz Dulled Dole's Hatchet," and "Ford Needs to Pardon Dole Now."

More than anything else Bob Dole said that fall, the phrase "Democrat wars" became lodged in the collective memory of millions of American voters, and it would endure to haunt him for years.

Despite the spate of bad press, Ford and Dole crisscrossed the country in the final two weeks, and Ford's internal polling showed a big gain. In one of the final days, Ford called Dole:

"Boy, this thing is moving just right!" Dole remembered Ford telling him. "Just keep on working. You're doing a great job. We're going to win! We're going to show them."

When Americans went to vote on November 2, the final campaign polls suggested the race was a dead heat. Bob Dole finished his nine-week odyssey by voting in Russell, Kansas, nibbling on cake made by his mother and taking a foil-wrapped dish with fried chicken for the plane ride back to Washington.

On election night he and Elizabeth were driven to the White House to watch returns with Jerry and Betty Ford. Ford and Dole then realized the tide had moved against them; the Doles went home. Late that night it was official: Jimmy Carter narrowly beat Jerry Ford, 51 percent to 48 percent.

The next day Bob Dole was sick. The marathon left him fighting a virus and deep fatigue. He sipped milk in his Watergate apartment. Barbara Walters asked Dole in a television interview if he thought his aggressive style had cost Ford the election. "I thought it was kind of a low blow,"

Dole would say. "What was I supposed to have done different?" Others in the media soon blamed Dole for Ford's loss. Some of Ford's own team anonymously complained to the media that Dole cost Ford the final two points, the difference between loss and victory. But Ford did win most of the farm belt, a key reason Dole had been selected as his running mate. Dole himself said he did not regret the "Democrat wars" phrase, though he acknowledged it may have "sounded partisan."

Looking back years later, Charlie Black felt that Dole's style may have seemed abrasive, but that it still helped Ford. "The plan damn near worked," said Black in an interview. "If that election had been on Thursday instead of Tuesday, Ford would have won. Which is another reason I don't like this whole revisionist thing that Bob Dole cost Jerry Ford the election. My recollection is Ford was thirty points down when he put Dole on the ticket and he lost by two. Sure, there's a few unfortunate lines, like 'Democrat wars' and stuff, but I don't know of any candidate who goes through a national campaign without saying a couple things you wish you hadn't."

James Baker III, who was a top strategist for Ford, said various political observers suggested after the race that if Ford had kept Nelson Rockefeller as his vice-president Ford would have won re-election. "There are others who have suggested that if he had offered it to Reagan, Reagan would have had to take it out of a sense of duty and Ford would have won the election," Baker said. "But having said all that, that's all speculative and surmise. I don't think you can say that Bob did anything but *help* the ticket. He was an indefatigable campaigner. And he certainly did everything the president and the campaign asked of him."

Despite the hazing he endured in the media after the election, Bob Dole felt—nearly two decades later—that Ford approved of the job he did for him in the fall of 1976: "Whenever I see Ford now, he says, 'We were a great team! We were a great team!'"

Ford himself said as much in an interview: "It was a good decision and proper decision the time it was made. In hindsight I have no regrets. I knew Bob as an able, intelligent, qualified person. From a political point of view it was very pragmatic. We knew that Jimmy Carter would carry the South. In order to offset the loss of the South, we had to carry the agricultural western states from the Mississippi out to the Pacific, and Bob Dole was the ideal candidate for that purpose. And it was successful. The only two states we lost west of the Mississippi were Minnesota with Mondale and Texas.

"The fundamental reason [we lost] was we got bad economic news in

October," Ford continued, "which indicated that our economic recovery was stalling. And four weeks later, when the November economic news came out, it showed that was just a hiatus and we were moving very strongly to an economic recovery. In that close an election, you can't really pinpoint any factor. I think Bob's contribution was positive."

THE NEW BOB DOLE

THE PUZZLING QUESTION facing Bob Dole after the 1976 presidential campaign was how to escape the on going public perception that he was the GOP's hatchet man. Dole liked his first rough ride on a national political campaign, despite the bad reviews meted out by what he called the liberal press. The Doles borrowed tapes of evening newscasts that had highlighted his campaigning. Their studied assessment: he was not that rough. They thought the media spin afterward was inaccurate. But Dole decided to work on his public image and speaking style.

He went, in effect, to charm up for a session with school, signing Dorothy Sarnoff, a speech dynamics consultant in New York City. Sarnoff, a former actress and author of public-speaking books, would later work with Israeli Prime Minister Menachem Begin, who had angrily exploded in an interview that damaged his reputation in Israel. Sarnoff would fly to Israel at Begin's request, push past Begin's wife ("What are you going to do to my husband! He made Prime Minister without you!") to buy Begin new shirts that fit, so his neck didn't swim around inside them, and help him rehearse his speaking style to come across more clearly with enthusiasm and authority.

Elizabeth Dole had gone to Sarnoff first, seeking help before an appearance on television. "She had a lot of vitality," Sarnoff recalled. "She was very articulate, she had animation, you felt that she had passion." Elizabeth Dole absorbed and projected Sarnoff's five maxims for putting a best foot forward on television: joy of being there; enthusiasm; concern; credibility or sincerity; and command, being in control.

When Dole arrived for his session he was "very, very withdrawn," Sarnoff said. He had overcome butterflies decades ago in Kansas by sheer willpower, not with the aid of an image-shaper. He stood before Sarnoff and delivered a little speech he had prepared to start their four-hour session. Despite his reputation, Dole's tone was nearly timid, his voice scraped low in a monotone. Worse, he leaned on his left arm, just as he had done in the 1976 vice-presidential debate with Walter Mondale, which hid his disabled right arm but had the effect of diminishing his presence. Sarnoff told him to keep the tips of his fingers touching the edge of the lectern and to carry himself straight forward, to project authority. She told him to boost his energy and put animation in his face so that "you don't look mad." Enthusiasm worked like an embrace, it persuaded people, Sarnoff preached. She recommended he wear more dark suits for a more senatorial look.

Dole's humor, which had often been used to criticize opponents with a smile, underwent a metamorphosis. He became softer on his adversaries and more self-deprecating about himself. At the 1978 Gridiron Dinner in Washington, an event at which politicians get roasted by the media and vice versa, Dole made fun of his 1976 debate performance. "I'll never forget the Dole–Mondale debate, and don't think I haven't tried," Dole said, cracking a rueful smile. "I won't say how we did, but halfway through the debate, three empty chairs got up and walked out. If you remember those debates, President Ford was supposed to take the high road and I was supposed to go for the jugular. And I did—my own!"

During this period he gained a reputation for moderate views in two linked areas: farm policy and nutrition. In the early 1970s he had joined and subsequently became ranking Republican on a Senate select committee on nutrition and human needs, chaired by South Dakota Senator George McGovern, the 1972 Democratic presidential nominee Dole had chided as chairman of the Republican National Committee.

"He had been under the impression I was using that committee simply for political purposes," McGovern recalled. "And he was startled, I think, to discover I had a genuine commitment to hungry people and doing something about the American diet. He got really caught up in that committee and he and I started working closely together on strategy for how to get legislation passed. For about eight years we kind of dominated the whole field of nutrition. It wasn't simply doubling the money for food stamps, it was a major expansion of the school lunch program and creation of the Women, Infants and Children program, which Dole and I pushed through the committee and onto the Senate floor for passage in 1974. We conducted field hearings all over the country," McGovern continued. "We saw genuinely hungry people and undernourished kids, malnourished mothers and nursing mothers and pregnant mothers, and we saw the ramifications for that in underweight children and for the learning process. There weren't too many hungry people in Kansas or South Dakota. But there certainly were in places like south Florida and West Virginia."

Dole underwent a transformation. In the 1960s he had opposed food stamps, now he became a strong advocate. McGovern said he and Dole also wrote virtually all of the agricultural legislation in the 1970s covering feed grains, which helped farmers in their home region. They developed a good political and professional relationship. "I discovered in that period Dole was not a hard-edged person when it came to anybody who's handicapped, or vulnerable children, or vulnerable young mothers, or people with physical or mental handicaps," McGovern asserted. "He has a real compassion for people that need help from government. The notion he's a hard-edged scrooge just doesn't hold up for the people that really need help." His grandparents, who once received welfare checks he signed as county attorney, needed help, and so did others, Dole learned.

Dole's image enhancement and emphasis on moderate issues dovetailed well with his new ambition: to run for the presidency himself in 1980. Soon after Jimmy Carter assumed the presidency, Dole challenged Carter's policies, criticizing him for declining farm income, for his tax on energy and proposals for welfare and social security reforms. The Kansas senator also spoke out on foreign policy matters, pushing his own profile in an area presidents were expected to master, opposing aid to Vietnam and normalization of relations with Cuba. He drew the most attention for staking out a moderate Republican line concerning the Panama Canal treaty Carter was negotiating. The treaty required the United States to relinquish control of the shipping lane between the Caribbean Sea and the Pacific Ocean in the year 2000 when eventually signed. Dole won inclusion of a provision giving the U.S. rights to navigate through the canal during wartime. In other ways Dole also sounded conservative themes to try to corner some of the market Ronald Reagan seemed to have locked up.

Throughout 1977 Dole flew around the country hitting the GOP banquet circuit, delivering more than one hundred fifty speeches to shore up the GOP faithful, particularly those in Iowa and New Hampshire, home of

the first precinct caucus and primary. Dole borrowed the strategy used by
Richard M. Nixon in the years leading up to 1968, seeking to build a
national web of supporters and those who would owe favors to him.
Unlike Nixon, Dole would not be the assumed front runner. Besides
former California Governor Ronald Reagan, others were actively mentioned as potentials for the Republican party's nomination.

"Everybody disclaims any interest in the nomination," Dole joked dryly
in an Associated Press interview in October 1977, "while they're boarding
the plane for the speaking engagement."

In November 1978 Dole became alarmed when more than nine hundred followers of the Reverend Jim Jones were found dead and bloated at
their religious camp in remote Jonestown, Guyana. Acolytes from Jones'
People's Temple had killed Representative Leo Ryan of California, who
had come to investigate their religious cult. Later, all the men, women and
children drank poison-laced Kool-Aid. Reading news accounts, Dole disagreed with the tax-exempt status granted to those religious organizations
that might brainwash young people, forcing them to surrender all posses-
sions and forsake their families. In particular, he raised questions about the
Unification Church led by the Reverend Sun Myung Moon.

In early February 1979 Dole convened a Senate hearing on the tax-
exempt status of religious groups, that backfired when he received threats
and was accused of leading a witch-hunt to infringe on religious freedoms
in hopes of exploiting the publicity to run for president. Dole was concerned about the civil liberties issues, but proceeded with the hearing to
try to divine a course of leadership in addressing religious cults. He
dropped the subject after the daylong hearing.

As the spring of 1979 greened, the Doles prepared to launch a presidential quest. The decision was difficult for Elizabeth Dole. In 1976 she had
taken a nine-week leave of absence from her job as a commissioner on the
Federal Trade Commission to campaign for the Ford–Dole ticket. Again
Elizabeth felt torn between her professional ambitions and her wish to help
her husband fulfill his own. Despite misgivings of friends who thought she
should not put his career ahead of hers, she announced her resignation in
February, and in March left her position on the trade commission. Packing
boxes in the large paneled office in the commission, she told the Kansas
City *Times*: "We'll be doing this together. But I'll miss this, I really will."

On May 14, 1979, Bob, Elizabeth, Robin and about 5,000 people
gathered in a tight hemisphere at 8th and Maple streets in front of City
Hall in Russell for Bob's official announcement. Nearly all of his extended
family was on hand that sunny spring Saturday. As he spoke, Dole was

trying to, as the press would later write, "bury the hatchet," and project a modified image of himself: man of compassion.

"In government we have institutionalized compassion, forgetting that compassion is a human virtue that comes from the heart, and that institutions lack these attributes, and so they fail in doing the compassionate thing—in helping to see that children are adequately clothed and fed and educated, in assuring the elderly are cared for and loved rather than warehoused and tolerated, in seeing that the needy are helped to provide for themselves," Dole, now fifty-five, told his townspeople and the assembled state and national media.

Outlining his candidacy, Dole promised to run a positive campaign, attacking neither Carter nor his own Republican opponents; his adversary instead would be a federal government grown too large, too expensive and too institutionalized. "It's going to be a hard campaign; we are not going to try to mow down the opponents," Dole said at a press conference afterward, according to the Washington *Post* held in the Russell Volunteer Fire Department, where his father served for a half century. He would challenge Americans to look beyond narrow single-issue constituencies to seize their own lives and the soul of the nation—to "let America be America again."

He pledged to seek out both Democrats and Republicans, because no political party has a "corner on wisdom," and work with people of different ethnic and racial backgrounds, labor groups and big business executives, the young, the old. Evoking Harry Truman, a president Dole admired for his frankness, Dole said, "Above all, I mean to say what I stand for and speak plainly."

That afternoon, Dole flew to Des Moines, Iowa, and then on to New Hampshire, making similar announcements. The strategy was lean; he would hit Iowa and New Hampshire hard, where he hoped his agricultural background and conservative fiscal record would build enough momentum to carry him on through later primaries. Dole had already visited New Hampshire fifteen times by the day he arrived as an official presidential candidate. He surprised people with his lack of sharp-tongued rhetoric, his positive themes, his humor. One standing line: Dole said he had come to the state to help President Carter *out*. It was so soft—think of that, Bob Dole too subtle—not everyone got it.

As summer heated up, President Carter's poll ratings declined, driven by his handling of the economy, double-digit inflation and foreign policy stumbles. Dole quietly hoped that Senator Edward M. Kennedy of Massachusetts would successfully challenge Carter the following year for the

Democratic nomination. It would be easier to take on a senator rather than an incumbent president, and he could label Kennedy a far-left liberal.

On the Republican side, the presumptive front runner was Ronald Reagan. Dole theorized that if Reagan and George Bush canceled each other out, and the same happened between Howard Baker and former Texas Governor John Connally, Dole would be *the* one left. He also privately told at least one confidant that if Reagan withdrew—for any of the myriad reasons a candidate occasionally flared out, illness, money, defection, scandal or voter rejection—he thought himself as good as any on the B Team, better than most.

By August, Dole realized the man of compassion was not catching on. Some voters still viewed him through the 1976 prism as a gunslinging partisan. He spoke of himself often as a "survivor," both of injuries in World War II and of political wars. In political appearances that summer people asked Bob and Elizabeth about the "New Bob Dole." They remembered well the old one, and so did political donors who were lukewarm to Dole.

He made news briefly then, the kind a political candidate dislikes. Dole fired his presidential campaign manager, Tom Bell, starting a tremor that would have larger meaning later in his campaign. Bell told the press Dole was nearly out of money and without money there would be no campaign. Dole's fund-raising objectives were not being met, he lagged far behind Reagan and trailed Baker and Connally. "John Connally comes through with a vacuum cleaner, sweeping up all the big money," Dole observed in the Wall Street *Journal.* "I come along later with a whisk broom."

He tried a gimmick or two to commandeer the national spotlight. On vacation in August, President Carter swatted at a supposedly rabid rabbit swimming toward his canoe, creating an international sensation. A photograph of Carter, a somewhat crazed look on his face, canoe paddle cocked over his head, made millions laugh. On August 31, Dole issued a memorable press release, urging Carter to apologize for "bashing a Georgia bunny." Straight-faced, Dole observed that he had sponsored legislation outlawing the use of live rabbits at greyhound dog racing tracks. "I'm sure the rabbit intended the president no harm," Dole said. "In fact, the poor thing was doing something a little unusual these days—trying to get aboard the president's boat. Everyone else seems to be jumping ship." Lest America had forgotten, Dole made a reference to Carter's Playboy interview. "This isn't the first time President Carter has gotten into trouble with bunnies. It seems to me he had a problem back in the fall of 1976 as well."

But Dole's own presidential boat remained pretty empty that autumn.

In campaign spending reports he had one of the smallest war chests of the candidates. He kept his presidential quest alive in December with an infusion of federal matching campaign money, garnered in part by a $50,000 loan to his campaign from his wife. That loan later drew an investigation by the Federal Election Commission into whether the money had been a loan or a donation. A donation of that size would exceed federal limits. The investigation was dropped when the election commission agreed, as the Doles had argued, that her money was his money.

Late autumn, Bob Dole dispatched to New Hampshire his trusted advisers: Dave Owen, now chairman of the unannounced Dole 1980 Senate re-election campaign; Tully Plesser, a New York pollster from the 1976 vice-presidential campaign team; Jo-Anne Coe from his Senate office and Kim Wells, a rising Kansas political operative and son of Bob Wells, treasurer of Dole's 1974 Senate race and a broadcast executive in Kansas.

The verdict: New Hampshire didn't look good.

"Okaayy," Dole said, "I'm gonna have to go."

That fall, Bob Dole was bollixed by twin allegiances, his duties as a senator and his aspirations as a presidential candidate. For four months beginning in October, the Senate engaged in a stormy debate over raising the windfall profits tax on newly discovered oil. As the bill manager for the Republicans in opposition to the hike, Dole was kept on the Senate floor. He would spend all day on the floor, fly to New Hampshire for a political event that night, turn around the next morning and be on the floor when the Senate went back into session. His most extensive campaigning was on weekends and during congressional recesses. Other candidates spent whole weeks in Iowa and New Hampshire. Bush and Reagan campaigned nearly full-time through 1979. Dole's style led political observers to conclude he really did not want to be president. He tried to spin it: "I am the working candidate," he told audiences in New Hampshire, according to the Associated Press. "I am employed, which makes a difference."

That was his asset, he thought. He had maintained a 95 percent voting record in the Senate. He was a candidate of experience on real issues, social and fiscal matters that affected everyone in the nation, not just those living in California or those spooking around the Central Intelligence Agency. Dole's campaign handed out a 50-page summary of his views on issues—agriculture, crime, civil rights, gasohol (an automobile fuel blending gasoline and corn-distilled alcohol), government regulation, nuclear power and the range of foreign countries of concern at the time: Iran, Cuba, Turkey, Korea, Vietnam and the Soviet Union. Painfully that winter, the issue candidate was a non-issue. News stories centered on the horse-race aspects of the presidential campaign, who was up or down in polls, where they stood in fund-raising and what the important political pundits were saying about the candidates. When Dole was mentioned he got no more than a couple of paragraphs in general campaign stories.

Internally, Dole's campaign was falling apart. By December he had hired and fired several dozen campaign managers, press aides, political directors and fund-raisers, replacing each team with one of less experience. As some left, they complained Dole was difficult to work for, mercurial, impossible to schedule and unwilling to delegate responsibility to his professional staff. Dole brushed off the departees. When Bell left in the summer, Dole noted he could pay more attention to primary states with fewer staff in Washington.

The December departures were: "a sign of progress. I hadn't been particularly satisfied with what had been happening, so now I feel relieved in many ways. The people who left, a driver and secretary in New Hampshire and the office manager and a young girl here in Washington, have not been any serious losses," he said, according to a news wire story. The "driver" was hurt by that comment; news stories said that Gordon Bartlett had been an official in the New Hampshire Republican party before he joined Dole's team.

The downward trend on professional campaign experience robbed his organization of cohesion and morale. Bob and Elizabeth Dole were now virtually in charge of the campaign enterprise, running most decision-making, planning, scheduling and all but flying their near-empty campaign plane.

In early January, 1980 Tom Bell's firm, Response Marketing Group, filed suit in Alexandria, Virginia, against Dole, seeking $237,000 for bills he felt his firm was owed but Dole had refused to pay. Joining Bell in the suit was William Russo, who had worked with Bell but stayed on as a part-time adviser to Dole when Bell left. When Dole's aides had learned Russo still worked at a desk in Response Marketing's offices in September, he was ordered off the campaign team.

Dole counterattacked that he had fired Response Marketing, referring to it as "Ripoff Marketing," for unauthorized spending. The Dole for President Committee filed a countersuit at the end of January against Response Marketing, alleging breach of contract, negligence and fraud. The suit contended that Bell and others, without authorization from Dole, had accepted fifteen corporate campaign contributions in violation of federal campaign laws, which had prompted the Federal Election Commission to consider charging Dole's campaign with campaign violations. The suit also accused Bell of diverting money into his accounts and spending lavishly for campaign travel, lodging and office expenses. None of this, of course, was helpful to Dole's campaign. Dole later agreed to a $100,000 settlement.

Driven by a stubborn hope the campaign would change, Dole pressed on in Iowa. His strategy for the January 21 caucuses was to combine three seemingly natural constituencies—the farmer, the veteran and the disabled —into a coalition that could give him a solid showing. He still had not found his voice as a candidate. Voters weren't sure what Bob Dole wanted to do with the nation, and his Iowa campaign was disorganized. The entourage of reporters following him withered to mostly local reporters and occasional ones from his home state.

When the precinct caucuses were held on January 21 in Iowa, Dole came in last, far behind Reagan and Bush: 1,576 votes of 106,000 cast. The big news out of Iowa was not Bob Dole, it was George Bush's surprising upset over Reagan. Dole flew to New Hampshire, now even more of a long shot in what had become essentially a two-man race—Reagan and Bush.

"I've just been campaigning in Iowa," Dole told audiences in New Hampshire, with a comedian's pause. "For no apparent reason."

New Hampshire became Bob Dole's Little Big Horn. All but a handful of staffers were dispatched there for the February 26 primary to try to build support, emptying his large campaign headquarters in Alexandria, Virginia.

Dole flew into the Granite State and frenetically worked his way through towns and meetings. Elizabeth had already campaigned across the state for an entire month. Even so, polls showed that Bob Dole had less than .5 percent of voter support. At the last minute, he tried to withdraw from the primary in Puerto Rico held just before the New Hampshire primary. If he lost badly in both primaries, the Federal Election Commission would decertify his campaign, cutting off further flow of federal campaign funds.

Meanwhile, Dave Owen worried about the impact of Dole's wobbly presidential campaign upon Dole's probable bid for re-election to the Senate in Kansas. Owen was concerned that if Dole withdrew from the presidential race before April 1, his name would still be on the presidential primary ballot in Kansas and he might lose his own state, creating a boomlet of embarrassing news. In late January Dole told Owen to contact campaign directors of the other major contenders—Reagan, Bush, U.S. Representative John Anderson, Connally and Baker—to plead that they not file. They ignored the request and signed their candidates up for the Kansas primary. Kansas Republicans and Democrats alike reacted negatively to Dole's holdout, complaining it might damage chances the state legislature would approve future presidential primaries. Dole let the filing date February 12 pass without putting his name on the presidential primary ballot in his own home state.

On February 20 in Manchester, New Hampshire, the seven Republican presidential hopefuls gathered for a nationally televised debate in a high school auditorium. They made little news, and polls showed Reagan the narrow winner of the event. Bobbling a few answers, Reagan nonetheless showed himself to be alert, reasonably informed and human. Dole served up humor, offering a jibe at Reagan's momentum overshadowing Bush's, "Big Mo and Little Mo." He urged viewers to listen closely: "You know, somebody here may get elected."

What happened next had a big impact on both Dole's and Reagan's campaigns. Reagan had proposed a two-man debate between Bush and himself after the Manchester event. Reagan's campaign team had obtained sponsorship for a debate in Nashua, New Hampshire, by the Nashua *Telegraph*. Dole filed a complaint with the Federal Election Commission, arguing that the sponsorship amounted to an illegal campaign contribution to Bush and Reagan by excluding the other Republicans, according to Lou Cannon in his biography *Reagan*. The election commission sided with Dole, so the Reagan camp then proposed that the Bush and Reagan campaigns simply pay all the costs, allowing them to exclude the others. Bush's campaign refused, Reagan's team agreed to pay for the debate alone, but having done that, Reagan's team then called Dole and the others, suggesting they come to the debate.

As they met in the Nashua High School gymnasium before the debate, Reagan's campaign team pressed to open up the debate to the four others —Dole, Baker, Anderson and Representative Phil Crane, who were standing testily by. Bush's team flatly refused. When the debate was to begin, Reagan marched the four into the gymnasium, took his seat, and the quartet stood behind him. Jon Breen, editor of the *Telegraph,* told the technicians to turn off Reagan's microphone. Furious, Reagan said, "I paid for this microphone, Mr. Green!" getting the name wrong, but that didn't matter, Cannon wrote. Bush sat stunned as Reagan shouted for the debate to be opened to the others. Reagan had whomped Bush on style; he came out looking like a maverick champion of free speech while Bush looked like an uptight east coast preppie.

The debate outcome was great news for Reagan, launching him inexorably toward a defeat of Bush. For Bob Dole it was another dismal event; once again he was upstaged. On February 26 New Hampshire offered its view of Dole. He got just 607 votes of more than 145,000 cast, barely .4 percent of the popular support. He finished last behind Reagan, Bush, Baker, Anderson, Crane—*two House guys, from the Lower Body*—and Connally, even behind "write-ins," who got 1,310 votes. The dispiriting loss was the final signal to the national press that Bob Dole's campaign was dead.

Dole disbanded his campaign staff, ceased campaigning in South Carolina, withdrew from the February 28 debate there, took his name off primary ballots in other states and formally ended his campaign on March 15 in Lawrence, Kansas. He told supporters and onlookers he had known for weeks he lacked the fundamentals of all successful political campaigns, the Five M's: money, manpower, management, media and momentum. "What I considered my greatest asset in the presidential campaign—a record of experience and performance in the Senate—actually turned into my greatest liability," Dole said. He pledged to work with whomever won the party's nomination to insure their election that fall, and later signed on with Reagan.

"1980 really was Ronald Reagan's year," Elizabeth Dole recalled. "I can even remember my dad saying, 'This looks like Reagan's time.' And we had a lot to learn about running a national campaign, earning credibility, building an organization. For Reagan, it was the culmination of a drive for the White House that began in '64. In contrast, for Bob, it was kind of the beginning of his drive for the White House."

In his own heart, Dole's disappointment was acute as he returned to his Watergate apartment in Washington. For the first time he seriously contemplated retiring from the Senate to head off into one of the dozen or so high-salary law firms in Washington that would eagerly welcome the prestige and contacts of a nineteen-year veteran of Capitol Hill.

Dole delayed his announcement for weeks, a move that sent jitters through the Kansas Republican party. The organization Dave Owen had set up more than a year before, with a Dole chairman in each of the 105 counties, continued fund-raising and planning. While Dole had not caught on with voters in presidential primary states, the national race did enhance his stature for a Senate re-election bid in Kansas, Owen found. He had raised more than $1 million for Dole without breaking a sweat.

Anxiety mounted. State reporters began a drumbeat about his indecision. Finally, Dole scheduled a press conference on May 24 to announce his plans. "Throughout my career I've never forgotten the question with which I launched it thirty years ago: what could I do to serve the people of Kansas?" Dole said. "I've pondered it often these last few weeks, even while thinking about the attractions of private life. And in the end the answer remains the same: I am pleased to announce I am a candidate for re-election to the United States Senate."

His Democratic opponent John Simpson had been flailing at Dole for months, and continued to do so, without landing a solid punch. That summer and fall, Dole's troops poured on their grassroots efforts. On November 4, 1980, Dole easily won re-election to a third term in the Senate.

ALTHOUGH DOLE'S TWELFTH victory in his long political career was universally expected, it capped a stomach-churning decade for Dole, and it marked a meaningful turning point. In the 1970s, Bob Dole championed President Nixon; divorced his first wife Phyllis; vigorously headed the Republican National Committee; was, in effect, kicked off the RNC; watched his president be driven from office; battled himself against Watergate; barely won re-election to the Senate in 1974; remarried, to Elizabeth Hanford in 1975; lost his father; ran as a hell-for-leather vice-presidential nominee; and then lost a presidential contest of his own.

In Washington on election night Howard Baker, the Senate minority leader from Tennessee, nervously watched returns from Senate races around the country. Baker and Senator John Heinz of Pennsylvania, chairman of the National Republican Senatorial Committee who would die in a 1992 plane crash, had a big tote board on which they tallied the outcome. Republicans, who held 41 seats to the Democrats' 59, had expected to make gains in the Senate. The evening brought some surprising Democratic losses. The board shifted from 47 Republican seats to 48, to 49, to 50, to 51, and eventually would end with 53.

Helped by Ronald Reagan's landslide win, a new Republican majority would rule the 100-member Senate, the first time since 1954. Howard Baker would become the majority leader, switching places with Democratic Senator Robert Byrd of West Virginia. Baker congratulated Republicans roaming by, exhilarated by the prospect of becoming chairmen of their committees instead of ranking members of the minority party.

Baker telephoned Dole in Kansas. "Bob, just think, you're going to be chairman of the Finance Committee," Baker told him, referring to the principal committee that handles taxes and Social Security, which was headed by the powerful Louisiana Democrat Russell Long for fourteen years.

"That's great, Howard," said Dole, then paused. "Who's going to tell Russell?"

MR. CHAIRMAN

IN EARLY JANUARY 1981, inside the stately wood-paneled Senate Finance Committee hearing room in the Dirksen Office Building, there took place a symbolic transfer of authority. Russell Long, a Louisiana Democrat known as the "most powerful man in the Senate," now after fourteen years' tenure vacated the leather swivel chair bearing on its back the nameplate "Mr. Chairman." In the horseshoe of twenty chairs, Long moved one left, reserved for the highest ranking minority member. Kansas Republican Senator Bob Dole now occupied the post at the apex. Though it took some getting used to, Long and Dole managed a smooth transition.

Elizabeth Dole also was adjusting to new tasks. James Baker III, who helped Ronald Reagan assemble his White House staff, had telephoned at the end of the year proposing she head the White House office of public liaison, and she accepted. That put her in frequent contact with the new president, who sought contact with the business public.

In one of the first Finance Committee meetings, committee staff director Robert Lighthizer called the roll for a vote on a minor matter. By tradition, he would call members of the majority party by seniority, then the minority party similarly, ending with the chairman. When he called the Democrats' highest ranking member, Russell Long voted. Reaching the end of the roll Lighthizer said, "Mr. Chairman?" And Long voted again. Everyone chuckled. "He'd been doing it for fourteen years, voting last, so he voted twice," Lighthizer said, smiling.

Long and Dole had worked compatibly together in the 1970s, and would continue to do so. "Even in Dole's most private moment with me there was never a hint of 'who-does-he-think-he-is?' " said Lighthizer. "The extent to which people are friends in the Senate is kind of a funny thing. You have to make your own judgments about it. Dole and Long had what I considered a pretty close relationship. I never, as Dole's principal staff person, looked upon Long as an adversary." The year before Dole became chairman he and Senator Daniel Patrick Moynihan, the New York Democrat and another prominent member on the Finance Committee, appeared in a campaign advertising commercial for Long, supporting his re-election bid in Louisiana.

"We just had a little meetin' in my little hideaway in the Capitol building and shot some things. And both of them said some nice things about what Russell Long had managed to do for Louisiana, which I 'preciate very much," Long recalled in his dense bayou accent. "I suppose I'd ought to be forever indebted to Bob Dole because it didn't hurt a bit to have a highly regarded Republican say some nice things about me. During those years when he was chairman, it seems to me, he was about the best friend I had in the Senate because he was very considerate, very helpful to my problems."

Long's deference was both a southernism and a protocol of the Gentleman's Club to which he belonged for thirty-nine years. The chumminess of the Senate was more pronounced in the rarified air of the Finance Committee, where senators often shelved their partisanship to work on the truly towering issues facing America.

The issue that landed there in early 1981 was called the Reagan revolution by admirers, the death of President Roosevelt's New Deal by detractors and, finally, Reaganomics. Adhering to a theory called supply-side economics, President Reagan promised to chop the $80 billion federal deficit, boost defense spending and slash income taxes, bringing security and prosperity to America. He would do all that, *and* balance the federal budget by 1984. The heart of his agenda was a three-year, thirty percent cut in individual income taxes and faster write-offs for business capital investment. In simplest form, it took money the government collected and gave it back to individuals. The theory was that the new money would trickle down into the economy from thousands of sources rather than from a sole source, the federal government. Congress initially embraced Reagan's bold agenda because of his commanding election victory and, simply, because it had not been tried.

In February, Bob Dole spent twenty-two days in Walter Reed Army Medical Hospital undergoing major surgery to remove a kidney stone. To pay respects, Reagan dropped by to visit Dole in the hospital and brought him a book, George Gilder's *Wealth and Poverty*, a manifesto on supply-side economics. Once he recovered from surgery, Dole pledged to be Reagan's "ball carrier," but warned he might veer on his own course running down the field.

Bob Dole veered first in April. He told the White House his committee would not approve a full thirty percent income-tax cut. Members feared the revenue loss would ignite inflation. Not only was there trepidation in the Republican-controlled Senate, but many in the Democratic-controlled House were alarmed over the potential impact on the federal budget from a loss of $54 billion Reagan sought in tax relief.

Treasury Secretary Donald T. Regan testified in early May that the White House was sticking with its three-year plan, called 10-10-10. On May 17 Dole said on CBS's "Face the Nation" that he had warned Regan. "I told him there were two other 10s," Dole said. "They are 10 for and 10 against in the [Finance] Committee. And that would be on a *good* day . . . I am very willing to support my president, but I am also the chairman of the committee, and I've got to have enough flexibility to convince Democrats and Republicans on my committee and on the Senate floor that this is a bill we can pass."

Dole and his staff worked up two proposals of their own. First, they proposed to cut $22 billion in federal spending for government programs in the following two years, slightly *more* than the president had proposed in his own separate spending cut bill. Then, in late May, Dole unveiled a proposal for a twenty-five percent reduction in individual income-tax rates over two and a half years.

The Finance Committee took up the matter, and after an all-day negotiating session agreed to add just two small amendments, modified slightly to earn blessing for the entire package from the White House. The committee approved the measure on a 19-1 vote. The full Senate followed suit.

In July the House stalled, signaling danger to Reagan's first substantive initiative. House Democrats called the Senate plan unworkable: It would bankrupt the government with reductions in revenues collected by the Treasury, it favored the rich with its tax cuts for the wealthy and it would not measurably curtail the federal deficit.

In a July 10, 1981, op-ed article in the Washington *Star,* Dole argued otherwise, contending the new Reagan plan would reverse the steady trend of higher taxation tied to inflation—bracket creep—and would fulfill one of Reagan's popular campaign pledges. "The president is doing exactly what he vowed to do last fall: putting more dollars into more pockets," Dole wrote. "He is refurbishing old ideas like incentive and profit. He is redefining the role of government. Those opposing the Reagan tax cut aren't merely out in left field. They haven't found their way to the ballpark."

Reagan's popularity soared after his recovering from a gunshot wound resulting from John Hinckley, Jr.'s attempted assassination in early spring. He parlayed that goodwill and personally lobbied members of Congress for a tax cut. He had good reason: Representative Dan Rostenkowski, the new House Ways and Means Committee chairman. The burly Chicagoan, schooled in the Windy City's tradition of machine politics, had his own plan. On July 27 Reagan went on the offensive, making a nationally televised appeal for public support. The public responded, enabling the White House to steamroll Rostenkowski. On the 29th, the House approved the administration's plan, and a House and Senate conference committee worked out differences on a bill with special-interest tax breaks included to win votes.

Handing a triumph to Reagan, Congress had approved a bill providing modest accelerated depreciation on business investment and a twenty-two percent income-tax reduction over three years. The Economic Recovery Tax Act of 1981 was the largest tax cut bill in the nation's history.

Despite his support, Dole had doubts about supply-side economics. Dole believed you always spent a little less than you made. That was how Doran Dole operated through the years he ran his cafe, cream station and grain company in Russell, Kansas. Doran Dole always saved nickels and dimes, and was responsible, so when the bills rolled in he had enough money to keep his family financially afloat. Yet Dole, the pragmatist, realized Reagan had won the election in a landslide.

What did Bob Dole really think of the idea? Bob Lighthizer said Dole's view was best explained in an oft-repeated joke on the matter that Dole attributes a professor at the Wharton School of Economics.

"The good news is a busload of supply-siders went over a cliff," Dole would say. "The bad news is there were three empty seats."

Earlier that spring Dole showed another streak of independence from the White House, this time over food for the poor. Dole teamed up with liberal Democratic Senator Patrick Leahy of Vermont to fight one of his own colleagues, Republican Senator Jesse Helms of North Carolina.

Helms, chairman of the Senate Agriculture Committee, was trying to help the Reagan White House slash subsidies for all agricultural spending in the next five-year farm bill. This included large cutbacks for food stamps for the poor. Dole believed that many food stamp recipients were honest, hungry people. It did not hurt that food stamps boosted demand for agricultural products and were popular with farmers in Kansas. Dole shuttled back and forth between the Finance Committee and the Agriculture Committee to win moderation of Reagan's food stamp cuts.

In the fall of 1981 Helms again ran up against Dole on the farm bill. Helms was in charge of overseeing cutbacks in subsidies to various farm products to meet overall caps. But his colleagues became outraged when they realized he aimed to spare the tobacco and the peanut programs, two vital crops in his home state, at the expense of subsidies to other crops. Dole took control of the bill on the Senate floor, preserving balanced cuts that affected all in a similar fashion.

As other issues arose Dole gained a new reputation. He was not the partisan firebrand of the 1970s; he was a legislative pragmatist, on the lookout for the compromise that would move legislation forward. "When I was working for Dole it always occurred to me that he loves to just solve problems," Lighthizer, the Finance Committee staff director, said. "I can remember sitting with him and he'd say, 'Let's deal with this! Let's deal with the amendments!' I used to say, 'Senator, we can deal with all these amendments, but there's an infinite number of them. If you have a week and you deal with all of them on the first day, there'll be more of them. It's not like washing windows or milking cows. There'll always be someone on the other end making up more of them. What's the point?' But he never bought that. He wanted to deal with them, get them done. He was in a position to do a lot of it because he had real power."

AUTUMN BROUGHT BAD economic news. Between the time the tax cut bill was passed in July and when Congress returned from its summer recess, the recession had deepened. "Dole joked that they just shouldn't have gone on vacation," said Lighthizer. Reagan maintained the Economic Recovery Tax Act had not had time to work, but unemployment rose in the fall and winter, soup kitchens opened, voters became angry, the federal deficit, instead of shrinking as planned, fattened by $20 billion. Meanwhile, at 1600 Pennsylvania Avenue the era in which Jimmy Carter carried his own suitbags, wore sweaters and preached economizing had clearly passed. The

Reagans' lifestyle was noted for lavish parties, borrowed designer dresses, wealthy friends and glitzy Hollywood chums.

In May 1982 the extension of the Voting Rights Act of 1965 guaranteeing blacks and other minorities the vote brought Dole together with an old adversary, Senator Ted Kennedy. For weeks, the liberal Massachusetts Democrat had fought the White House to strengthen the act. Dole believed Republicans, from the party of the great emancipator, Abraham Lincoln, had an obligation to better address civil rights issues to reach out to minorities. Working with the Leadership Council on Civil Rights, a leading civil rights organization, he found a middle ground that Kennedy and the White House could accept. Dole's proposal addressed what standard of proof should apply in proving discrimination against minorities. Dole favored an analysis based on the results of actions rather than a Supreme Court test, which asserted that voting rights were violated only when officials knowingly sought to discriminate. His bill would base proof of discrimination on the effects of government action and would not require proof that discrimination was intentional. It also would set damage limits if discrimination was found. Joseph Rauh, a noted liberal civil rights advocate, said of Dole: "He was superb. He got us the perfect bill."

A year after carrying Reagan's income-tax-slashing ball through Congress, Bob Dole came back, with his *own* ball. His goal: to dramatically curtail the federal deficit. Working with his staff, Dole fashioned a laundry list of ways to close dozens of tax loopholes. Now it needed a catchy, positive name, one of those inside-the-Beltway phrases that trip off the tongues of politicians, pundits and Hill staffers: The Acronym. More than any other place on the planet, Washington worships acronyms, for they bespeak of vitally important laws, and those who master them are vitally important players. One afternoon, Rod DeArment, Dole's number two Finance Committee staffer, wrote a list of possible names. Dole ambled in.

"Hey, what's goin' on?" said Dole.

"Trying to choose a name," said DeArment, showing Dole the list.

"I like that one," said Dole pointing to TEFRA, the Tax Equity and Fiscal Responsibility Act.

It soon joined the pantheon of other acronyms: ERTA, FIFRA, RCRA, NEPA. They pronounced TEFRA "teh-frah," but everyone told them they should have called it "tea-frah," so that if they returned another year with a follow-up they could have TEFRA II, "tea . . . frah-two, and two frah tea-frah . . ." Hill humor.

But what TEFRA needed was Teflon, the impermeable artificial matter so often associated with Reagan; the bill planned a thunderous $98.4 billion tax hike over three years. To mollify expected critics Dole pushed TEFRA as a good-government measure, tax reform. That's what Democrats had harped on for years; here it was, he challenged. Whatever one called it, the bill's impact would be stark. It would take back roughly thirty percent of the special tax breaks offered in the 1981 tax cut bill, a direct repudiation of a third of the measure Dole had worked hard for the year before. But Dole stuck with the income-tax-cut portion of Reagan's agenda.

TEFRA's $98.4 billion hike broke down into large pieces—$30 billion would come from federal withholding of ten percent of interest and dividend income. The remainder would come from raising taxes on cigarettes, travel and telephone calls, cutting tax breaks for defense contractors and "safe harbor" leasing—enabling money-losing companies to sell tax losses to profitable companies—and imposing withholding of taxes for waiters' and waitresses' tips.

Despite his lengthy congressional career, Bob Dole had authored few major bills, but TEFRA indisputably was *his*. Although the Constitution prescribes that tax bills originate in the House, Ways and Means Chairman Dan Rostenkowski deferred to Dole on TEFRA; he was more than happy to let a Republican lead the way on raising taxes. Dole committed himself to TEFRA and kept the White House and Senate Majority Leader Howard Baker informed of its status throughout the spring.

The White House, to say the least, was recalcitrant. Dole lobbied the president himself and eventually persuaded Reagan that tax hikes were necessary to protect the economy. "My recollection of it was Bob was very supportive in the 1981 effort to cut spending and cut taxes and was instrumental in getting that done," said James Baker III, who was then chief of staff. "He also pushed the idea of TEFRA, which was not particularly popular, at times even with President Reagan. But we had campaigned on a platform of reducing taxes by $500 billion and we had, in effect, reduced 'em by $750 billion in the '81 competition with the Democrats, so we felt like it was important to make up the revenue from the standpoint of the deficit."

Working with Treasury Secretary Donald Regan and Assistant Secretary John Chapoton, Dole had to lobby his own colleagues on the Finance Committee. Outside the crowded committee room the hallways were lined with well-paid lobbyists representing dozens of businesses and industries affected by the closing of tax loopholes. They scuffed their feet so often against the wall it was repainted. Seeing the crowd of Gucci-shoed lobbyists one day, Dole joked, "They'll be barefoot in the morning."

The Finance Committee passed Dole's bill on a straight party-line vote with not a single Democrat joining them. Russell Long told Dole, "That's above my pay grade." Then the White House began courting members of the House and Senate, Reagan making nearly two dozen telephone calls to undecided members.

As TEFRA was taken up in the Senate on July 23 its future appeared shaky. Lobbyists crammed the hallways trying to buttonhole senators as they passed. A large group represented hotel and restaurant owners. They loathed the tip withholding provision because they believed it would add burdensome paperwork and make them into de facto agents of the Internal Revenue Service. Near midnight the withholding taxes on tips proposal was stripped out on a 70-25 vote. Down went a chunk of the bill representing more than $3 billion, an appalling setback for Dole.

The lobbyists cheered! They clapped each other on the back and streamed out of the Capitol, heading for a favorite watering hole nearby, the Monocle.

Scrambling now, Dole pulled his Republican colleagues into a private meeting in the Republican cloakroom. Around three in the morning the Senate approved a new amendment that would allow only half the cost of business meals in a person's home town to be deducted as business expenses, not the full cost. It was Dole's challenge to Democrats who had railed for years about the "three-martini lunch" business deduction. When the roll call began after 4 A.M. on the 24th, the package seemed dead. Suddenly, Senator Harry Byrd, the Virginia Independent, voted "aye," prompting others to hastily change votes to support the bill. Senator Jesse Helms voted to raise taxes on cigarettes, even though tobacco was the principal crop and a lifeblood in his state's economy. When it ended, TEFRA was passed 50-47 by the Senate with almost no Democratic support. Alarmed, the restaurant lobbyists rushed back in the next morning, pleading to replace the new business-lunch amendment with the tip withholding requirement. Dole agreed to do it in a later conference committee after upping the price.

Over in the House, supply-siders led by Representative Jack Kemp of New York condemned TEFRA as the undoing of Reaganomics, accusing Dole of going liberal on them. Dole answered in an August 8, 1982, op-ed piece in the Washington *Post,* saying Republicans had a "responsibility to lead." He professed that his tax hike plan was actually consistent with supply-side objectives because it neither gutted the income-tax cut nor discouraged savings. "We are not making a U-turn," Dole wrote. "We are merely adjusting the route to keep from going off the road. At a time of genuine distress we are holding fast to a program we're convinced will alleviate that distress, soon and in the long run."

On ABC News "Nightline" program August 16 Dole faced off against Terry Dolan, head of a conservative political action committee, and economist Dr. Arthur Laffer, the father of the conservative manifesto supply-side economics, who reportedly came up with the idea in the 1970s and wrote it on the back of a napkin. Moderator Ted Koppel noted that Reagan himself had spun Dole's bill as consistent with the policy. What did Laffer think of that?

"One thing you should never do is raise taxes in a deep recession or depression. And frankly, he's violating the first law of economics," Laffer said of Dole. "Closing loopholes, or whatever you want to call it, is literally a tax increase, and it's the wrong thing to do right now."

Laffer complained the tax hikes would nullify the job creation benefit of supply-side tax cuts, prompting Dole to defend his actions as aimed at cutting the deficit and helping working people, despite what woolly-headed academes thought.

"You ought to support your president," Dole told Laffer. "You don't have a more conservative friend than Ronald Reagan."

Laffer answered: "I've supported him when he ran against you, sir."

Dole shot back: "Now you're trying to do him in."

Laffer said, "No, no. He's switching policies on us. He's raising taxes and he ran against them."

Dole found himself backing his Republican president against conservatives, true to his own populist and moderate philosophy. As it played out, the full House approved the tax hike plan, 226-207, this time with a majority of support from Democrats. It was the largest tax hike in the nation's history, and it showed Dole's willingness to make tough choices to lower the deficit.

"You get a lot of fair criticism at times, I felt like I got a lot of unfair criticism," Dole said looking back to the TEFRA debate. "Even when you close the loopholes, the people who get closed say, 'Oh, you're for a tax increase.' My view is if somebody's getting an unfair advantage compared to everybody else in America, and we're all guilty of putting these little rifle shot amendments in, but when somebody gets a clear, egregious advantage, you'd better correct it. We were always looking for loopholes to close. Lot easier than raising taxes."

The Washington *Post* heralded Dole as the "New Lion" of the Senate, one whom pundits already were talking up as a presidential contender in 1984 if Reagan declined to seek reelection. "Dole has mellowed and matured," Time magazine said. Washingtonian magazine voted him the member of Congress with the best sense of humor, contrasting him with their worst, a tie between Kemp and Senate Minority Leader Robert Byrd of West Virginia. Dole never tired of the continual requests for a television, magazine or newspaper interview. Everyone wanted to know what the Finance Committee chairman thought. Dole was able to portray himself as a fiscal conservative and social moderate, which would play well in the nation's suburbs if Reagan forsook a second term in office.

DURING THE LATTER months of 1982 a monstrous time bomb threatened America's economic infrastructure. The multibillion-dollar Social Security system, the New Deal compact to provide income for the elderly, had been running out of money since the dawn of the decade. Because of the large post-World War II Baby Boom generation, the system could possibly go bankrupt by the end of the 1990s. Worse, its financial jeopardy was spreading worry throughout the single largest bloc of American voters, and the most punctual in their duty to vote: the elderly.

"Someone used to call the Social Security system a twenty-chicken alligator," Robert Lighthizer said. "You feed it twenty chickens a day, or it eats you."

The committee responsible for trying to keep America from being eaten, the Finance Committee, deadlocked on the issue. In early 1981 Reagan's budget director, David Stockman, had persuaded President Reagan to support a proposal to cut $82 billion over five years from Social Security, chiefly by cutting benefits to workers who retired at age 62 rather than 65. Struggling to make Reagan's budgets head toward his promised balance, Stockman and other White House advisers overlooked the considerable political consequences of riling older Americans. Democrats immediately pummeled Reagan for selling out his important constituency.

By late 1981 Reagan had found a way to minimize political damage to himself: he appointed a presidential commission to figure out what should be done. The seven-member National Commission on Social Security Reform was chaired by economist Alan Greenspan, who would later become chairman of the Federal Reserve Board overseeing the nation's money. Other members included Senator Bob Dole, House Speaker Tip O'Neill, AFL-CIO President Lane Kirkland, Florida Representative Claude Pepper, businessman Robert Brock and Robert Ball, former head of the Social Security system. The commission's efforts ground fruitlessly along throughout 1982 and appeared headed for oblivion by its early 1983 expiration date. In December 1982 Dole wrote an op-ed newspaper article published in the Washington *Post,* saying he had not given up trying to find a solution.

As Congress returned from its winter holiday recess in January, Senator Daniel Patrick Moynihan, the scholarly defender of moderate Democratic liberalism, approached Dole on the Senate floor, mentioning the article.

"Are we going to let this commission go down the tubes without giving it one more try?" Moynihan said, according to the Dole's 1988 campaign biography *Unlimited Partners.*

"Let's talk," Dole said. "Let's get ahold of Ball," who was Robert Ball, Tip O'Neill's representative.

The trio brought in the other commission members, notified the White House and for the next eleven days according to *Unlimited Partners* held private discussions with top White House officials at Chief of Staff James Baker's Washington home. They finally came up with a plan Reagan and leading members of Congress agreed upon: the Social Security Bailout. In March the House and Senate began debate, which stalled over an extraneous amendment sought by the banking industry. Earlier, bankers had bottled up a jobs bill with intense lobbying because they wanted a six-month delay of a new law requiring banks to withhold ten percent of interest and dividend income for taxes.

From the Senate floor Dole glowered and said, "They almost beat the homeless and the jobless and now they're after the senior citizens."

The bankers' amendment died after Senate Majority Leader Howard Baker called the banking lobby a "selfish special interest group." Dole's feud with them continued for months afterward. Instead of the fiery partisanship of yesterday, though, Dole's battles surfaced more because of his position of influence. Then, and in the years following, Dole grew testy when lobbyists tried to strong-arm him. He would dig his heels in and fight right back. He could be persuaded to support politically and ethically risky stands—that was the price of leadership, he often said—but he would not be forced.

Congress firmly approved the Social Security Bailout. As signed by President Reagan, it provided $165 billion over seven years, protecting retirement checks for thirty-six million Americans. The money came from raising the retirement age from 65 to 67 by the year 2027, delaying cost of living adjustments for six months and boosting payroll taxes paid by employers and employees.

★ ★ ★

BOB DOLE'S POWER rose in 1983. He was in the middle of every major legislative battle from taxes to overseas arms sales to farm policy. So did his wife's. That spring, Reagan nominated Elizabeth Dole for the position of Secretary of the U.S. Department of Transportation, overseeing the nation's highways, railways, airways, mass transit and Coast Guard, making her the highest ranking woman in government. At her confirmation hearing Bob Dole, sitting beside her at a conference table, introduced her with a deadpan observation: "I regret I have but one wife to give," he said, amid laughter, "to the nation's infrastructure."

Speaking to the Gridiron Dinner at the end of March, an annual gathering of the Washington powerhouses and journalistic elite, President Reagan cheerily observed he had not seen such a crowd since the government distributed surplus cheese. But it was Bob and Elizabeth who stole the show. Bob Dole rose to announce that in 1984 "Dole will not be a candidate." Elizabeth jumped up and brought loud applause when she smiled and said, "Speak for yourself, Bob."

The hard-boiled national press began writing about Bob and Elizabeth Dole, a powerful couple in a powerful city, painting each in favorable lights. Stories often observed *he* seemed mellower, probably because of *her,* while *she* earned praise for political savvy in her job as transportation secretary, perhaps with advice from *him.* In speeches Elizabeth joked that she warned her husband, "Just because you won in the Senate, don't expect to win in the house." People magazine ran a feature article showing the two of them making up the bed in their Watergate apartment. Bob began dozens of speeches, later noting that picture stirred one old-fashioned man to write to him complaining that the man's wife had begun insisting he help around the home. "Buster, you don't know the half of it," Dole said he wrote back. "The only reason she was helping was because they were taking pictures!"

Compared to many married couples, the Doles spent little private time together, though they seemed to thrive on their public careers and enjoy the brief time they shared. She left for work before he did, they did not share breakfasts or lunches and ate evening meals together only three or so times a week, usually at a restaurant. They worked all week and Saturdays, trying to break away Saturday nights and Sundays, though Bob frequently showed up on the Sunday talk-show circuit.

But they did fly together out to Russell for a July 22 celebration of his birthday and Elizabeth's upcoming July 29 birthday. They gathered at the

Dole home with Bina, Gloria, Kenny, Norma Jean and other family members. Gloria remembered Bob sitting in his mother's living room squeezing pennies into the penny loafers Elizabeth had given him to wear with his casual clothes. Bina, now eighty and frail, prepared a feast of fried chicken, macaroni and cheese, vegetables, fruit salad and homemade ice cream. "I think in some way she knew it would be her last time," Gloria Nelson said.

Back in Washington Dole strode onto the Senate floor July 27 to deliver a eulogy for Dr. Hampar Kelikian, the generous Armenian doctor and skilled surgeon who had tried to repair his shattered right shoulder after World War II and who had just died at age eighty-four. Richard Norton Smith, a speechwriter at the time for Dole, wrote the eulogy after a quick five-minute chat with the senator. In the speech, Dole praised Kelikian for waging war on many fronts: in scholarly medical journals, against childhood deformities, on the operating table for many men whose bodies had been damaged in war, all with an effort to "suffer with the patient."

"Today is our turn to suffer," Dole said. "For Dr. K has ended his career of service on this planet. His passing may count for little in the world's record, but for anyone whose path ever crossed his, this moment has its right to sorrow and the years ahead will be at least a little lonelier." As he began a section of the Robert Frost poem, "Nothing Gold Can Stay," Dole broke down. He put down his speech and walked directly off the Senate floor. His staff cowered to see him publicly express such inner grief. One bravely went up to him when he returned to his Senate office and said, in effect, "That was a nice speech."

"Oh, you know Richard writes so well," Dole said, pushing away the emotion.

At the end of August, sadness again summoned Bob Dole. Bina, who had a history of heart trouble, went into the hospital in Russell on August 30. She had a heart attack soon after—Bob flew back in from Washington —and was transferred to a hospital in Wichita, where she died on September 5. As he had when his father died, Dole sat for hours at the mortuary in Russell reflecting on his parents and their life. He loved his mother. He inherited his drive, assertive demeanor, even his appearance from her side of the family.

"Not that I'm knocking his father, who was nice-looking, but I think a lot of Bob's looks came from his mother's side," Gloria Nelson said. "He looks exactly like an uncle that's not with us anymore, one of the Talbott boys. Oh, my, he's just Uncle Joe the Second. There's an amazing resemblance between the two.

"Bob called his mother almost every week of his life," she added. "Whatever was going on or if something was worrying him or just to say hello. I think she was his strength. She and Dad both were behind him, giving him inner strength. He's told me that himself."

The Dole family
first home in
Russell, Kansas.
*(Courtesy of The
Russell Daily News)*

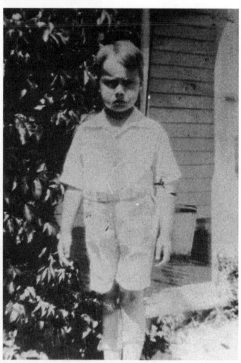

Bob Dole, roughly age eight.
(Courtesy of The Russell Daily News)

As a Junior High School student.
(Courtesy of The Russell Daily News)

Bob Dole in uniform.
(Courtesy of The Russell Daily News)

Camp Breckenridge,
Kentucky 1944.
(Courtesy of The Russell Daily News)

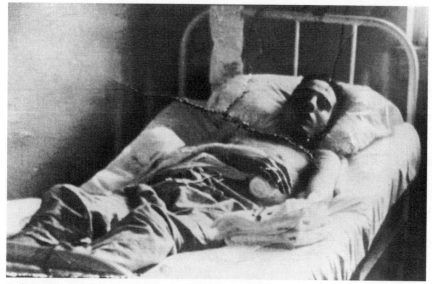

Bob Dole lying in a hospital bed after his World War II injury.
(Courtesy of The Russell Daily News)

Bob Dole exercising
behind his family home
after his war injury, 1947.
*(Courtesy of The Russell
Daily News)*

Bob Dole and his father,
Doran Dole, in front of
their Russell, Kansas
home about 1947.
(Courtesy of The Russell

Bob Dole and his
mother, Bina Dole, in
front of their Russell,
Kansas home about 1947.
(Courtesy of The Russell
Daily News)

Bob Dole in 1960 when he entered the U.S. Congress as a freshman House member. *(Courtesy of The Russell Daily News)*

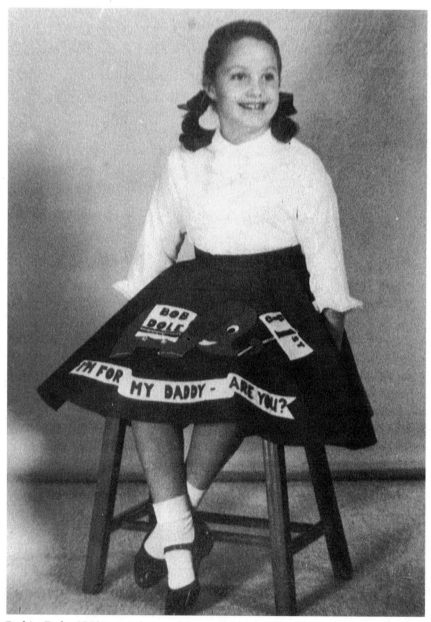

Robin Dole, 1960 campaign, wearing a skirt sewn by her mother, Phyllis, Bob Dole's first wife. *(Courtesy of The Russell Daily News)*

Bob Dole and President Gerald Ford in 1976. *(Courtesy of The Russell Daily News)*

Senator Bob Dole overcome with emotion in August 1976 as a vice presidential candidate, appearing with President Ford at a rally in his hometown of Russell, Kansas. *(Courtesy of The United Press International)*

Elizabeth Hanford Dole, left, Bob Dole, center, Vice President Al Gore, right, celebrating Bob Dole's 70th birthday in the Capitol, June 22, 1993. Bob Dole is holding up a pin, "Dole 96." Gore jokingly said to Bob Dole, "Is this a reference to your age or your ambitions?" *(Courtesy of Senator Robert Dole)*

Senator Bob Dole with President Clinton. *(Courtesy of Senator Robert Dole)*

Former President Richard M. Nixon and Senator Bob Dole in early 1994 at a commemoration of the 25th anniversary of Nixon's first presidential inauguration.
(Courtesy of Senator Robert Dole)

President Clinton, left, with Elizabeth Hanford Dole and Senator Bob Dole. The men behind from, left, are a Secret Service agent, Senate Majority Leader George Mitchell of Maine, and Tony Coehlo a former House member from California. Photo shot on April 14, 1994, the 25th anniversary of Bob Dole's maiden speech in the Senate, in which he discussed the status of disabled Americans, and the 49th anniversary of Dole's serious injuries in World War II. Clinton came to Capitol Hill to attend a luncheon Dole organized. *(Courtesy of Senator Robert Dole)*

REINS OF POWER

JAMES WATT, PRESIDENT Reagan's lightning-rod Interior Secretary, had built an impressive list of detractors by 1983, even before he offended the Senate Finance Committee chairman. The media had him under fire for attempting to open up federal lands to increased mining, timber cutting and oil and gas exploration. He angered the concert-going public by canceling the Beach Boys from a July 4 performance on the Washington Mall. He thought the California pop band too radical for an official government-run celebration. (Bob Dole invited them to Kansas, since they would have an opening in their schedule.) Then in late September Watt jokingly referred to an advisory panel in his department as having "a black, a woman, two Jews and a cripple." President Reagan quickly defended his cabinet secretary, saying Watt's remarks were improper but not an indication of bigotry. Democratic National Committee Chairman Charles Manatt called Reagan's support for Watt "pathetic."

A few days later a furious Bob Dole held a press conference joined by world-renowned violinist Itzhak Perlman, a polio survivor who used crutches. "If I'd been president he [Watt] would be gone," Dole bluntly said, according to the Washington *Post*. "There are other Republicans in this country who deserve to be protected. We want to retain the Senate majority and I think it's rather important we not keep erecting barriers

. . . We just can't stand, every two or three months, Mr. Watt making some comment to offend another twenty, thirty or forty million people." Denunciation of Watt raged on across the nation for several days afterward and he resigned.

Dole also skirmished that year with the White House over the federal budget. Through the year House and Senate members of tax-writing committees eyed gloomy forecasts that the federal deficit in 1984 would rise to around $200 billion and stay there "as far as the eye can see." The White House tried to soften the news by suggesting the economy was picking up. Unemployment had fallen from above 10 percent to about 9.5 percent. Republicans and Democrats aired proposals to impose spending cuts and tax hikes without reaching any consensus.

In July, Dole had urged the White House to convene a summit to grapple with the deficit. He was ignored. At the White House in October, Dole outlined a proposal to cut the deficit with a $150 billion package balancing tax hikes and spending cuts, including a politically sensitive $28 billion cut in Social Security. His White House allies of 1982—President Reagan, Chief of Staff James Baker and presidential assistant Richard Darman—were not with him in 1983. Raise taxes near the 1984 election season? They didn't think so.

Dole forged ahead and announced his proposal publicly. He and Pete Domenici, the New Mexico Republican who chaired the Senate Budget Committee, came on like the Brothers Grim. "We've got an emergency problem and it ought to be dealt with on an emergency basis," Dole said in a November 5 article in the New York *Times*. Domenici added, "My role is to remind the president and the Senate leadership of the facts."

Reagan, not one to let facts intrude on what he thought right, ignored the two Republican Capitol Hill leaders and soon told his 1980 campaign workers at a reunion: "I am unalterably opposed to Congress' efforts to raise taxes on individuals and businesses. I am prepared to veto those tax increases, no matter how they arrive, just as soon as they reach my desk." Among those praising Reagan and panning Dole was the conservative editorial page of the *Wall Street Journal*. The headline on a November 8, 1983, opinion piece was "Dole's Folly," and the editorial suggested Dole was captain of a ship sinking "to the bottom of Washington's treacherous political ocean."

"Pete Domenici and I were sort of the Deficit Twins in the eyes of some," Dole said, looking back. "In the eyes of the right-wingers we were public enemy number one. Maybe it's just old-fashioned Republican doctrine. You spend more than you take in, you don't do it very often, someday you're going to have to pay your bills. Maybe that's out of style."

Although Reagan's declaration seemed inviolable, Dole outlined details of another deficit cutting package in a Finance Committee meeting on November 16. His new $114 billion plan proposed $39 billion in spending cuts, coming from health programs and cost-of-living increases to Social Security, and $75 billion in tax hikes, including closing tax loopholes, a two percent tax hike on all forms of energy and a surcharge on the wealthy.

The Finance Committee members seemed open to Dole's approach but awaited the president's reaction. Treasury Secretary Donald Regan came to Capitol Hill for a closed-door meeting in the Finance Committee's conference room, firmly telling the members that the president would veto any tax-hike bill. Dole took the news soberly. Committee member David Boren, an Oklahoma Democrat, slammed a book down on the table and stalked out of the room.

Finance Committee members left the private meeting in a funk. "I think Donald Regan and the president live in a dream world with respect to the deficit," said Missouri Senator Jack Danforth, a Finance Committee member, in the Kansas City *Star*. "They are not being effective because they are not facing up to the world as it is with their eyes open." The president followed up, promising to veto any tax-hike bill. On November 18 the Finance Committee shelved the issue, quashing Dole's efforts for 1983. Congress adjourned for its winter holiday season, to spend time with family, hit the ski slopes, travel the world and visit with constituents back home.

With most everyone gone from Washington, Dole pulled together a final strategy to pressure the White House. When news slouched to a trickle in mid-December of 1983 Dole dominated the airwaves by presiding over three days of hearings on the deficit. He called forth a relentless army of expert witnesses to bemoan the "cloud on the horizon," the "long-range damage to the economy," who vouched for the need for spending cuts *and* tax increases in an election year, a folly only someone as unconventional as Dole would risk. "We're not prodding anyone. We're building a record," Dole said during the hearings, playing down his challenge to Reagan's advisers, according to the Wichita *Eagle-Beacon*. "It's a big issue and any politician who thinks he won't have to face it is wrong."

The White House declined to send anyone to speak at Dole's hearings; it was too busy cobbling together the budget proposal for 1985 due out in late January. The event made Dole a hero to independent watchdog groups distressed about the deficit. It made him the bane of President Reagan's inner circle.

"The White House had a meeting of the Bob Dole fan club," a Senate official joked in a *Wall Street Journal* article, "and nobody showed up."

Congressional Quarterly reported that the Kansas senator who greeted Reagan's presidency by supporting him more than 90 percent of the time in key votes in his first year and 85 percent of the time in 1982 had slipped to a tepid 78 percent support of Reagan on the key votes of 1983.

NOT ONLY HAD Dole's two-year chairmanship of the Finance Committee given him a soapbox from which to preach, it ushered him into a new realm of political fund-raising potential. In 1983 Dole's ambitions spread in two different directions, toward beefing up the numbers of Republicans in Congress and toward an eventual run for the presidency. He aggressively sought donations for Campaign America, the fund-raising committee he established to raise money for congressional Republican candidates. Tailored after a similar venture Richard Nixon had established in the 1960s, Campaign America was a "leadership political action committee," one of several dozen funds set up by prominent members of Congress. Indirectly, they imbued the leader with power-broker status and built up political IOUs. Like other members of Congress who headed similar ventures, Dole used Campaign America funds to fly around the country and appear on behalf of Republican candidates seeking office or re-election. According to Federal Election Commission records, he nourished the campaign coffers of fourteen of his Senate Republican colleagues by a total of $70,000. Senators each year were required to fill out financial-earnings statements showing summaries of their income outside of government service. The financial-disclosure reports showed income from investments, stocks, bonds, money-market funds, ownership of property, the value of gifts they chose to keep and from speaking engagements. At that time senators and representatives were allowed to give speeches to groups and collect speaking fees, honoraria. According to a December 13 article in the New York *Times,* Bob Dole in 1983 became a hot ticket on the lecture circuit. Dole was the leading recipient that year (and often in the years following) of honoraria, taking in $135,750. Dole donated $51,500 of the money to charity, keeping the rest to supplement his Senate salary of $60,600. In the *Times* article, Fred Werthheimer, president of the campaign finance watchdog group Common Cause, raised a theme he would hammer on over the next decade: "[Speaking honoraria] raise potential conflict-of-interest problems, and they're another way these interest groups can gain access and influence at the expense of average citizens."

Meeting with President Reagan in early January 1984, Dole proposed that the president convene and head a deficit summit with congressional leaders and Paul Volcker, chairman of the Federal Reserve Board. Asked on ABC's "This Week with David Brinkley" whether the president was popular, Dole responded: "I think he's very popular. I think he would be even more so if he were leading the charge to reduce the deficit."

On the same program Senator Daniel Patrick Moynihan, Dole's ally in the 1983 Social Security bailout, suggested setting up a presidential commission to find ways to cut the deficit. "We ought to probably face the facts that neither branch [of government] is going to seriously get involved in this issue in '84. If we set up a commission, it's not the worst idea to do in '85 what absolutely has to be done."

"President Reagan and the Congress will agree *this year* on deficit reduction measures," Bob Dole asserted in a speech to the National Press Club in late February. He portrayed himself as an advocate of Reagan and of those in Congress who wanted to deal with the deficit. "If it's not bipartisan, forget it," Dole said.

He directed his staff, chiefly tax expert Rod DeArment, to work up a new deficit-cutting bill, incorporating items that had drawn previous support and to seek ways to get the president on board. In 1982 Reagan had appointed a blue ribbon panel called the Grace Commission, named for its chairman, businessman Peter Grace, to propose ways to root out inefficiency and waste in government. Reagan applauded the Grace Commission's report and recommendations in 1983. Dole's tax staff culled through the report to pull out three specific recommendations that seemed politically feasible, among them one that would enable the Internal Revenue Service to cross-check those who received tax refunds with students who had unpaid student loans, and allow them to apply the return against the debt owed. The new bill was called the Deficit Reduction Act of 1984.

The Finance Committee approved the bill and sent it to the full Senate. Working through the night of April 10 to debate dozens of last-minute amendments, the Senate at five o'clock the next morning passed a bill designed to cut $71 billion from the deficit, then fled Washington for Easter recess. As approved, the bill included $3.1 billion in cuts recommended by the Grace Commission and increased liquor and telephone taxes. Beyond that, the forty hours of debate produced a bill characteristic of Dole's style—no huge tax hikes or spending cuts. Instead, in numbing complexity, it included more than two hundred relatively small provisions.

The House slightly scaled the bill back, and after conference committee meetings to work out differences, it approved a $63 billion deficit-reduction bill just before the July 4 recess.

"It was a very intense period of activity," said Missouri's Danforth. "Dole was a very good leader of the committee. Part of being a good leader, particularly in the Finance Committee, but probably for every committee, is creating the impression that the members of the committee have a stake in what the committee's doing. There was the sense that everybody belonged."

Seven months later, Common Cause magazine, the bi-monthly publication of Common Cause, revealed one specific amendment, known as the "commodity tax straddle," that Dole and House Ways and Means Chairman Dan Rostenkowski, the powerful Illinois Democrat, had tucked into the bill with no fanfare. According to the magazine, in a late night House and Senate conference committee meeting Rostenkowski proposed and Dole agreed to a tax provision in favor of three hundred thirty-three commodity traders, most of them working at the Chicago Mercantile Exchange. The Chicago Mercantile was a supercharged outpost for men, and a few women, willing to take enormous risks to win large profits in trading on commodities futures contracts from agricultural crops and treasury bonds. But in 1981, when Dole was chairman of the Finance Committee, he had led the fight to close the loophole, blocking wealthy traders and others with large incomes, such as rock stars, from juggling their profit-and-loss figures to reduce their tax liability.

The Internal Revenue Service investigated tax returns after 1981, looking for those who had shielded income with the tax straddles as a means to sidestep taxes, and built up a record of several thousand cases that were pending in U.S. Tax Court. The commodity traders returned to Dole and Rostenkowsi in 1984, according to Common Cause magazine, the senators essentially granting amnesty to the wealthiest traders, a tax break worth more than $300 million and freeing them from IRS scrutiny in Tax Court. Traders argued the straddle was absolutely essential in encouraging professional speculators to take long-term risks. The magazine said Federal Election Commission records showed that commodities traders and their political action committees had contributed more than $900,000 to House and Senate members. Dole and Campaign America had received $11,000 in 1981-1982, but donations rose sharply in 1983-1984 to $70,000.

"I think I was sympathetic to their argument," Dole said enigmatically. "And they did contribute to me."

After three years on the Finance Committee, Dole's aggressive style, combined with the hardworking efforts of his small press-office staff, brought him recognition as one of Washington's master power brokers. In early May, 1984, U.S. News & World Report named Dole the second most influential member of the Senate behind Majority Leader Howard Baker, and declared him the nineteenth most influential American after Reagan, House Speaker Tip O'Neill, a cast of top White House officials, television anchorman Dan Rather and Vice President George Bush.

Bob Dole enjoyed holding the reins of power.

As he had the year before, Dole in 1984 outdistanced his Senate colleagues by another yardstick. According to a May 18 article in the New York *Times,* the senator from Kansas earned $188,917 from speeches given to dozens of organizations in Washington and across the country. Of his total, Dole donated $82,500 to charities, many of them in Kansas. That year a new law went into effect limiting how much senators could keep, holding them to 30 percent of their salaries, roughly $26,000 in Dole's case because he earned somewhat more as chairman of a committee than the standard $72,600 Senate salary.

IN HIS SPARE time, recesses and weekends Dole flew around the country campaigning on behalf of Republican candidates for the fall 1984 elections. Although he jousted with President Reagan over tax policies, Dole stoutly defended him against criticism from the Democratic presidential front-runner Walter Mondale, Dole's old sparring partner from the 1976 vice-presidential debates.

Seeking to ignite excitement in his campaign, Mondale selected Geraldine Ferraro, a New York congresswoman, as his running mate, the first female vice-presidential nominee. Almost instantly Ferraro received tough questions from the media about her and her husband John Zacarro's personal finances. At first she said she would release both of their tax returns, then backed off, claiming it could hurt her husband's business.

Warming up before the official start of the Republican National Convention in Dallas in mid-August, Republicans decided to exploit the controversy. Their plans went awry. Bob Dole held a press conference on August 13 to demand that Ferraro release all of her financial information. "Full disclosure is not a partisan issue; it is a matter of ethics," Dole declared, according to the Des Moines *Register.* "Full disclosure includes income-tax returns."

Reporters immediately noted that Vice President George Bush had not released his tax returns in recent years. Should he?

Dole, distressed, said, "Sure, why not?"

Probing onward, a reporter asked Dole, "Why were you asked to come in here and do this?"

"Just luck, I guess," said Dole, smiling sheepishly.

Then real trouble hit. Had he released his own tax returns when he was Gerald Ford's running mate in 1976? Dole did not remember doing so. It turned out he had not, though his press staff the next day sent out statements that Dole in 1976 had released extensive summary information of his finances, following a disclosure format and statement Ford had used. The 1976 summary showed total adjusted and gross income, deductions, taxes paid and an estimated net worth of Bob and Elizabeth Dole, who had been married less than a year at that time. Two days after the press conference, Dole's office released a statement asserting that the summary revealed the "essentials of my 1040 returns." Bob Dole probably was not the best choice to take on Ferraro.

When the Republican National Convention officially got under way in Dallas, Reagan was polling far ahead of Mondale. Senate Finance Committee Chairman Bob Dole and Transportation Secretary Elizabeth Hanford Dole—known as "Washington's Power Couple" (behind Ronald and Nancy Reagan, of course)—addressed the convention and Americans tuned in for the prime-time television coverage. Dole spoke about the continuity of a two-term presidency under Reagan, something America had not experienced since the 1950's with Dwight Eisenhower, a Kansas Republican. He challenged the Republican party to diversify its appeal to all Americans, reminding listeners it was the party of Abraham Lincoln. As a counterstrike to Ferraro's candidacy, Elizabeth Dole addressed gender politics. "The idea that this election could be won on the basis of gender insults our electoral process," Elizabeth Dole said. "We are thinking women. No platitudes will buy us, no party will inherit us, no candidate will own us."

Talk buzzed around the convention that in four years Bob and Elizabeth Dole might run for the presidency, a Dole-Dole ticket. One reporter asked Bob Dole for his room number, and he joked: "1988. That's where Elizabeth is staying, I've been moved."

During this era moderates took note of Dole's abilities as a consensus builder. Pundits and party bigwigs murmured how his former conservative zealotry had transformed into readiness to work endless hours toward pragmatic solutions. Meanwhile, take-no-prisoners conservatives felt Dole had betrayed them; he had championed the 1981 income-tax cut, only to reverse course and push through bills that raised other taxes three years running. To younger stars of the New Right, the Baby Boomer generation of Republican House upstarts, Dole was a throwback. Dole had become "the tax collector for the welfare state," complained Representative Newt Gingrich, a Georgia Republican and leader in the New Right movement who was earning fame for his partisan speeches on the House floor on live cable television. Gingrich's critique would smudge their relationship for a decade.

That fall the party closed ranks behind President Reagan to help him toward an overwhelming re-election victory in November over Mondale, who won the electoral votes in his home state of Minnesota but not in any other of the remaining forty-nine.

THE PRESIDENCY SAFE, Dole turned his full attention to one of the stranger contests in America. For months now, Dole had been campaigning to succeed Tennessee's Howard Baker as Senate majority leader. Baker had announced at the start of the year he would not seek re-election to the post so he would be free to prepare for a campaign for the presidency in 1988. But Dole did not feel that way. Even if he eyed the presidential quest himself—and clearly he did—he thought he could do both. Unlike his low-profile job that tethered him to Washington and contributed to his defeat in 1980, Dole knew majority leaders got a lot of national press, generating name recognition.

Senate leadership races were and are the ultimate inside-baseball game of Washington insiders, senators pleading with colleagues for a vote. Dole and four other Republicans, Pete Domenici, Richard Lugar, James Mc-Clure and Ted Stevens—offering their colleagues a full spectrum of choices, conservative to moderate, low key to feisty, big picture to vote counter—made telephone calls, buttonholed Republicans in the Republican cloakroom and sent out notes touting their skills. As they campaigned, the five lived the life of lobbyists, that legion of favor-seekers who so often shadowed their every step, and they found it a bit rough on their egos.

"You walk into somebody's office and say, 'I want to see your senator,' " Dole told the Kansas City *Star* that fall. "They say, 'Well, he's on the phone or in a meeting.' Or they say, 'What's your name?' "

The night before the vote, Dole's top aides counted supporters, knowing that predicting the outcome was extremely difficult. In leadership races on both sides of the Capitol, members often played their cards close to the vest or intentionally hinted support to several friends. Because the votes were cast in secret, their actual vote was untraceable. Most believed conservative McClure would win on the first vote. On November 28 the Republican senators filed into the Old Senate chambers in the Capitol, a smallish dark room with heavy wood trim and historical atmospherics. Backers of each candidate delivered nominating speeches. Senator Barry Goldwater spoke up for McClure, giving what others later would recall as a quirky, not wholly effective testimony. Missouri Senator Jack Danforth, who had worked closely with Dole on the deficit wars, nominated Dole.

Dole's efforts had resulted in substantial budget savings. He had helped insure the solvency of the Social Security system, Danforth reportedly said. Dole husbanded Republican interests, built bridges to Democrats. Danforth reminded his colleagues that Dole had campaigned for most of them. He had a legislative record superior to the other contenders. Then Danforth, the tall, eagle-beaked, erudite, wealthy heir to the Ralston-Purina fortune, the sole clergyman-Senator, the reputed Conscience of the Senate, gave utterance to his heartfelt appraisal:

"Bob Dole has soul."

A decade later Danforth would say: "I think that inside Bob Dole is a very soft spot for the little guy. And that he is a latter day version of the old midwestern populist type of public person. It's very important for our party to have heart. To be something more than the business of America's business. In the early 1980's, with President Reagan in the White House, Republicans in the Senate, and an economic program that was trying to cut spending and cut taxes, it was important for us also to demonstrate that we, as a party, cared about ordinary people. That was very much a part of Bob Dole. This isn't something he creates artificially for the purpose of effect. In fact, because he comes across as something else, it was the reason it deserved a mention."

On the first vote, McClure was knocked out. On the second round, Domenici fell. On the third vote, Dole tied 20-20 with Ted Stevens, and Lugar was eliminated. In the fourth balloting, Dole won, 28-25, instantly becoming one of the most powerful leaders in American government. Moments after his election Dole appeared at a news conference. "Are you going to run in 1988?" a reporter demanded.

"I'm not worried about '88," Dole said, with that telltale pause. "I'm worried about lunch."

A reporter asked Dole how he would like having a chauffeured limousine, one of the perks that comes with the leadership job. "I think I promised two or three guys that I'd pick them up every day," Dole deadpanned. "That may be the margin of victory." That's right, same joke from 1964.

Elizabeth and Robin Dole, his daughter now living in Washington, had been more confident of the outcome than Bob. They presented him with a frisky schnauzer picked up at a Washington humane society kennel. The dog wore a cardboard nameplate around his neck—"Leader."

"It's an indication of where my leadership is going," Dole said, according to the New York *Times*. "House-broken, but not Senate-broken."

LEADER

"**I** THINK THERE were some senators who felt that, you know, I had a good support record for the president—according to Congressional Quarterly, the second highest in 1984. The highest conservative coalition record, and all that. Then, I also was willing to indicate some areas of disagreement from time to time—what I thought wasn't good policy. I know a couple of guys told me later, 'That's why I voted for you.' But nobody's looking for a confrontation. We like the president. We understand we're probably in the majority because of his 1980 victory."

Bob Dole was talking with Andrew C. Miller of the Kansas City *Star* about why he was elected majority leader of the Senate, a post that did not exist in American government until 1911, one that in the modern age would shove him into the role as the compromiser, the balancer between powerful egos of his Republican colleagues at one end of Pennsylvania Avenue and the objectives and goals of the telegenic president at the other end of Pennsylvania Avenue. Questions buzzed around Washington about what kind of leadership the ambitious Dole would bring to a chronically, even constitutionally, disorganized Senate. Was he chosen to coax the White House toward compromise, especially on tax and budget bills?

"We're going to retain the Republican majority in '86—that's our agenda—at the same time support the president's program where we can," Dole said. "We're members of the Senate, we have our own institution."

It was the kind of declaration his predecessor Howard Baker had never made. But that was the nature of the majority leader's job: the holder of the post could shape it to fit his personality. Because of Dole's drive, political observers and news commentators expected him to join two of this century's most dominant Senate leaders, Democrat Lyndon Johnson, the wily, arm-twisting persuader under President Eisenhower, and Republican Everett Dirksen, the theatrical compromiser who served as minority leader when Johnson succeeded to the presidency.

Howard Baker's style first emerged in the four years following 1976, when he was elected minority leader. "We're going to act like we're the majority," Baker said he told his colleagues. "Well, nobody in the Republican caucus had ever been in the majority, except Strom Thurmond, and he was a Democrat at the time. I tried to get them all talking to each other, the [liberal] Jacob Javitses and the [conservative] Jesse Helmses, to be friends and to work together."

As majority leader from 1980 to 1984, Baker tried to regularize the schedule so senators weren't working late at night. In his four years Baker worked as Reagan's liege. Baker's efforts to guide Republican senators to think of themselves as leaders paid off, too well. After the 1980 elections the Republican caucus was so large and diverse he had a difficult time controlling the Senate. The Republicans chose Dole because they wanted someone to move issues ahead.

"The first thing was to get everybody together and try to help President Reagan move his agenda," Dole said in an interview. "And also to get the confidence of Senator [Robert C.] Byrd, the minority leader, who initially was very wary that I might be too partisan, but later said he never had a problem with me. We didn't surprise each other. I was always a little intimidated by him because he knew the rules much better than anybody in the world. I never had been much of a stickler for all that stuff." In fact, however, Dole's colleagues had suggested he knew the rules perhaps second best of any senator; he was being intentionally modest.

During the holiday recess in 1984 Bob Dole moved into Howard Baker's offices in the Capitol, just a short walk down a hallway from the Senate floor. The offices offered a grand panorama of the Mall, displaying the power and beauty of Washington, which Dole often jokingly called the *second best* view in the nation's capital. Dole became the fifteenth man to hold the title of Majority leader, and the second Kansan, after Senator Charles Curtis, who served as majority leader from 1924 to 1929. No shake-up occurred when Dole took over; he made no immediate dramatic internal changes.

The Republican caucus also had chosen Wyoming Republican Senator Alan Simpson as the new Republican Whip, the number-two post. Simpson, a funny, gregarious conservative, tall and lean as a moose, complemented Dole because he naturally liked to make the rounds to gauge individual senator's views on issues, allowing Dole freedom to pull groups of senators into his office to debate, hammer out legislation, plan strategy.

Their relationship as leaders began with one of those defining moments in politics, punctuated by Dole's notoriously sharp tongue. Soon after the leadership vote, Dole made a comment about Simpson that Simpson first read in a newspaper article sent to him, a joke that lay lifeless on the printed page. A decade later he couldn't recall the exact comment, but recalled his reaction. Simpson confronted Dole:

"Bob, I was very hurt about that comment," Simpson said, leaning his six-foot-seven frame down to Dole, who stands six-two. "He looked incredulous and I said again, 'I didn't think that was fair and it hurt me.'"

"I didn't mean to do that," Dole said.

"You may not, but that's the way it felt to me," Simpson said. "Well, he was upset about that and he has never again said anything like that." A bond formed then.

As the new year began, President Reagan sought a substantial $235 billion cut in federal spending by targeting dozens of social programs over three years, and, while keeping a protective arm around his expanding defense program, pushed for a major reform to simplify the tax system.

The new Senate majority leader had his own ideas. Reform was a "great idea," deficit reduction was more important. Dole announced he favored an across-the-board freeze on federal spending, which would affect all programs relatively evenly. It was a striking turnabout for Dole. Only a year before he had rejected a similar freeze proposed by his Kansas Republican colleague, Senator Nancy Kassebaum. Dole said he had resisted Kassebaum's initiative because he felt inclined to support the president. After Reagan's initiatives passed and the deficit forecasts showed no improvement, he felt tougher measures were required. Dole sent a signal that everything should be on the table; his freeze would include defense spending and would cap Social Security cost-of-living increases, which he couched as a commonsense way of accomplishing meaningful deficit reduction.

The two high-risk proposals demonstrated the essence of Bob Dole the lawmaker, a man willing to change courses as the situation dictates, willing to tackle sacred cows. He also was reflecting the consensus of his Republican colleagues in the Senate, who wanted to get the deficit under control. If Dole's plan worked, the freeze plan would benefit the nation and enhance his reputation as the premier deficit-fighter among the possible 1988 presidential contenders.

Before he could pursue that agenda, however, Dole became embroiled in his first battle challenging him to decide between his new leadership role and his lifelong allegiance to agriculture. In February, Democratic Farm Belt lawmakers launched a filibuster against Edwin Meese III, Reagan's attorney general nominee, hoping to force Dole to demand that the White House compromise on a proposal to limit farm credit. That was and is how hardball is played in the Senate: one side freezes something the other wants for leverage to win its own goal. Farmers throughout the midwest were going bankrupt and facing foreclosure for overextending their farm debt during the late 1970s. Dole had told agricultural organizations they, too, would have to accept cutbacks in farm subsidies as their share of deficit reduction. In contrast to Howard Baker's collegial Senate floor demeanor, Dole notified all to be on guard, saying during the Meese filibuster, "I don't intend to be pushed around."

To break a rancorous four-day deadlock, Dole allowed a vote that expanded federal loan guarantees and commodity payments to farmers, a setback. President Reagan, however, vetoed the bill and it was not overridden, a qualified victory for Dole and his Republican backers.

At home in Kansas, a small group of peeved farmers started a Dump Dole campaign, aimed to unseat Dole when he was next up for reelection in 1986. In March, Dole delivered the 69th Landon Lecture, named for the Kansas governor Alf Landon, who had helped Dole get his start in politics, and whose daughter was Senator Nancy Landon Kassebaum. A dozen farmers protested the speech in which Dole asserted that the Reagan administration assisted farmers more than had predecessor Jimmy Carter. Farmers cornered Dole in a hallway afterward. "What are you personally doing to keep efficient farmers in business and bolstering small towns depending on agriculture as their lifeblood?" Dole said he was trying to form a coalition that could rally behind the upcoming farm bill and promised: "We'll be there for you."

That did not satisfy. "When the steak isn't on your table, you're going to finally listen," said Kansas farmer Dan Broxterman.

Dole reasoned that by not shielding his home folks he was demonstrating that his leadership responsibilities required him to think more nationally than parochially, "I think we're right on target," Dole told Miller of the Kansas City *Star* in March. "In my view we just keep on pushing deficit reduction and don't make any exceptions, even if it's fairly painful for the leader."

Dole now talked personally with Reagan about cutting defense and the growth of Social Security, noting deficit projections for 1986 and beyond showed a rising curve from $230 billion to $247 billion by 1988. Reagan was noncommittal. Dole and his deficit-fighting partner, Republican Pete Domenici of New Mexico, launched into weeks of closed-door meetings with Republicans and Democrats, adding items, subtracting items, putting the budget bill into a precarious seesaw that foreshadowed possible doom. Despite the pressures, one Dole aide who sat through those sessions said Dole did not berate or strong-arm his colleagues or Senate staff. A strait-laced midwesterner, he never cursed.

In early May, Reagan reluctantly agreed to Dole's proposal to make defense cuts of $17.7 billion and freeze cost-of-living increases for Social Security recipients. Senate Democrats, except Nebraskan Edward Zorinsky, who signed on for farm price support concessions, would have nothing to do with the package. Meanwhile, the twenty-two Republican senators up for reelection in 1986 trembled over the political consequences of voting against benefits for elderly voters.

Dole's package came to a vote on May 9. Despite more than one hundred meetings and parliamentary jousting between Dole and Senate Minority Leader Robert Byrd senators expected a cliffhanger. Dole had telephoned the White House to ask that Vice President George Bush be on hand to break a tie. Bush canceled political events in the southwest and flew back toward Washington. Dole relished the idea of making Bush, a potential rival for the 1988 Republican presidential nomination, vote with him on a politically risky measure. That way it couldn't be used by Bush against Dole.

With more real-life drama than Hollywood could muster, debate boomed on for hours, wearing down senators, aides and Senate clerk staff. Three senators were missing that night—Republican John P. East of North Carolina, who was hospitalized with a hyperthyroid condition, Democrat J.J. Exon of Nebraska, who had undergone gallbladder surgery recently and also was hospitalized, and Republican Pete Wilson of California, who the day before had had an emergency appendectomy.

After midnight on the warm spring evening a group of senators greeted a white ambulance pulling up to the Capitol. Out rolled Wilson on a blanket-covered stretcher. Dole's office had called Wilson earlier that day to see if he was well enough to vote, and against his doctors' wishes

Wilson came to deliver a possibly tie vote. East and Exon could not make it.

At 1:30 in the morning of May 10, with the vote on the budget deficit bill under way, a pale Wilson, wearing a bathrobe and hospital pajamas, seated in a wheelchair, was pushed into the Senate chamber. Vice President Bush had arrived and was sitting in the Senate president's chair in front of the Senate.

"What's the question?" Wilson said, deadpan, according to the New York *Times*. His Republican and Democratic colleagues hustled to their feet and applauded him. Wilson raised his hand to be recognized and said "aye." And his colleagues clapped again. The vote was tallied, 49–49, and Bush cast the tie-breaking vote, "aye," passing the budget 50–49. Several Democrats crossed the aisle to shake hands with Alan Simpson.

" 'You guys have more guts,' they said," Simpson recalled. "And it wasn't like, 'Ha, ha, ha, you're going off the cliff.' But that we had worked for a tough vote, a courageous vote they didn't think they could have made."

President Reagan in Lisbon, Portugal, telephoned Dole's office around 4 A.M., when Dole and several others were celebrating with a glass of wine.

"Mr. President, we had a very close evening," Dole told Reagan, according to the New York *Times*. "A $300 billion package is worth staying up all night for."

A Hollywood story would end there. But Washington isn't a storybook town, it's a deal-making town. The bill went to the House.

A month later, after receiving an ultimatum from House Speaker Tip O'Neill that the Democratic-controlled House would reject all Social Security cutbacks and complaints from House Republicans about raising taxes, Reagan compromised. And Dole's anger flowed hot.

"The president says no taxes, Tip says no COLAs," Dole said, according to a July article in the Washington *Post*. "They're saying they've got a deal. I don't know if it's a deal. I think it's surrendering to the deficit. Democrats and a few noisy Republicans want to play politics. They never made a hard choice in their lives."

James Baker III, then Treasury Secretary, said, "I think he felt, with some justification, that they had cut the ground out from underneath him because he got his Republican senators to take an extraordinarily courageous stand to try to control the growth of entitlements. And the White House ended up caving in to Republican House members who abandoned ship."

Apparently Reagan didn't see it that way once he really focused on the bill. Back in the 1984 presidential debates, Democratic challenger Walter Mondale had accused Reagan of having a secret plan to cut Social Security and raise taxes. Reagan testily promised he would not. "What kind of politics is it to raise gasoline ten cents a gallon and throw some people out in the cold in New England next winter?" one unnamed senior White House aide told the Los Angeles *Times*. "Or tamper with Social Security? I don't know what kind of politics the senators were thinking of when they thought that was good politics. The president is the only one who showed good politics. For the life of me, I can't understand it. The president is bewildered and a bit miffed."

Another lawmaker miffed at Dole was Jack Kemp, the New York champion of supply-side economics. In July the quiet feud that had simmered since 1981 erupted at a meeting of young Republicans, presaging later warfare between the two men. "Kemp wants a business deduction for hair spray," said Dole, a jab at Kemp's blow-dry coif of graying hair. Kemp later responded. "In a recent fire, Bob Dole's library burned down. Both books were lost. And he hadn't even finished coloring one of them."

Finally, in October, wearied of the fruitless wrangling on the deficit, Dole kept the Senate in a rare Saturday and Sunday session to wrap up eight days of debate and pass the "Balanced Budget and Emergency Deficit Control Act of 1985." Known as the Gramm-Rudman-Hollings bill for Senators Phil Gramm, a Texas Republican, Warren Rudman, a New Hampshire Republican, and Ernest Hollings, a South Carolina Democrat, the bill was intended to *force* Congress to cut the deficit. Gramm-Rudman, as it became known, would require Congress to set overall deficit reduction goals, cutting roughly $36 billion a year through 1991, theoretically to chop the deficit to zero. All spending bills approved by Congress would adhere to caps to reach that annual goal. New spending for favored programs would be offset by cuts in others. In corporate America this wasn't a revolutionary idea, but to the please-everybody Congress, it was. To avoid a political conflagration, Social Security spending was placed "off-budget," an accounting gimmick to keep the new limits from applying to benefits paid to the elderly. Even so, if Congress failed to meet its budget targets, Gramm-Rudman would kick in and automatically shut down the government, stopping the mail, the outflow of paychecks and the work of hundreds of government programs.

President Reagan backed Gramm-Rudman, as did senators as far apart philosophically as arch-conservative Republican Jesse Helms of North Carolina and liberal Democrat Edward M. Kennedy of Massachusetts. Dole heralded it as "a realization that the deficit problem was number one, front and center, in the minds of the American public. And a realization that the problem was not going to be wished away." When the House took it up in 1986 it also passed the bill, ostensibly holding all of Congress accountable for deficit reduction.

Dole faced more agriculture battles in 1985. Although Congress annually tinkers with farm policies, for several decades it has hashed out four- or five-year farm bills setting broad agricultural guidelines on everything ranging from farm-price subsidies to overseas export and production. Dozens of closed-door negotiations led by Dole and his staff resulted in a 263-page five year farm bill proposal containing sweeteners to satisfy lawmakers on both sides of the political aisle. Dole said it would cut overall costs by $11 billion while maintaining high subsidies for wheat, the main-stay of Kansas agriculture. Senators saw Dole the national leader addressing deficits, Dole the Senate captain producing a passable bill and Dole the Kansan protecting his home-state interests and those of others.

"It should pass. I hope I haven't overlooked anyone," Dole joked, while others groused it wouldn't provide enough help for farmers in financial crisis. Congress eventually passed the bill close to Dole's outline, a more expensive program than Reagan had originally favored but reluctantly signed.

Throughout 1985 Dole aimed his energies toward building support for a presidential bid in 1988. When asked directly, he demurred about 1988 but kept his intentions well-known with wry comments, such as in April when he spent a day in the White House Cabinet Room with other senators to discuss President Reagan's controversial proposal for $14 million in aid to the Nicaraguan contras, the rebels seeking to oust the socialist Sandinista government headed by Daniel Ortega.

"I went down to the White House Monday for a half-hour meeting on the contras," Dole said, according to the Washington *Post*. "It turned out to be an eight-hour session. It wasn't all bad, though—it was my first full day in the White House. I kinda liked it, but unfortunately it was the wrong room." He meant, of course, the Oval Office.

In 1985 Dole deliberately sought to make inroads with voters turned off by the Reagan administration, particularly women's groups and black organizations. An original sponsor of the legislation to designate civil rights leader Martin Luther King, Jr.'s birthday as a national holiday, Dole held a private luncheon with black leaders in his Senate office in July to discuss Reagan's civil rights record. The Rev. Joseph E. Lowery, president of the Southern Christian Leadership Conference, told Dole and other Senate Republican leaders that individual seantors would have to work hard to overcome the mistrust black leaders felt toward the president and his party. Hours after the meeting, Dole announced he was dropping his support for the nomination of William Bradford Reynolds as an associate attorney general. Reynolds had stirred the ire of blacks by refusing to enforce civil rights laws.

"If you don't like what you see in the Republican party, and not many groups are perfect, the best way to bring about change is join the internal debate," Dole told the Urban League, a national civil rights organization at its 75th annual meeting, according to the Associated Press. "I believe Republicans understand that there are those who must look to the federal government for help in opening the door of opportunity. I think most Republicans that I know are very sensitive."

If he ran for the presidency in 1988, Dole thought, this time he would get it right. He would raise big money, delegate, hire a sharp staff, create momentum and get attention. Bob had learned from the mistakes of 1980.

"You look back on it, we made a few friends in some of those states," Dole said in an interview. "Bad as the campaign was, it had no organization, not much money, poor Elizabeth was raising money on the telephone making calls at night, we had people calling all the Kappa Sigmas in the world, but, strange as it seems, that's how we put together the '88 [presidential organization], just people we met."

In mid-summer 1985 Dole took a large step toward establishing a viable presidential candidacy: he hired Donald J. Devine as the new director of Campaign America. Devine, a former University of Maryland professor who headed the nation's federal civil service system in President Reagan's first term, offered strong conservative credentials and fund-raising abilities. Capitalizing on Dole's rise in national prominence, Campaign America held several glitzy fund-raisers during the year, bringing in thousands of dollars, shedding its low-key image and providing Dole with a national organization for 1988. Devine urged Dole to play down his liberal credentials and play up his long-standing support of key items on the conservative agenda: passing a balanced-budget amendment and giving the president line-item veto power to knock so-called pork-barrel spending out of bills. Dole later followed his advice by allowing the Senate to vote on legalizing prayer in schools, which was defeated but helped him with conservatives. And he proposed a bill freeing President Reagan to fight terrorism throughout the world as he saw fit.

This step marked another shifting of emphasis by Dole. Just as he appointed himself Sheriff of the Senate to get attention in 1969; as he softened his hatchet-man image after 1976; as he became the Grand Compromiser as Finance Committee chairman; and as he became the consummate strategist as Senate Majority leader, Dole now tailored part of his agenda to win back conservatives. He wanted to "make a play for them," hoping at least they would not offer blind allegiance to Jack Kemp or be successfully courted by George Bush in 1988.

Dole's leadership altered one especially visible aspect of the Senate. Gone were bankers' hours. Instead, Dole instituted farmer-in-planting-season hours. He kept senators working to debate, vote on and pass dozens of bills. Under his stewardship the Senate passed 163 bills in 1985 compared to about half that in Howard Baker's last year, said his office in a six-page memo touting his achievements. Unimpressed, Democrats complained that for all the commotion, little of substance had been approved to cut the federal deficit below its $200 billion estimate.

AFTER YEARS OF hand-wringing, in 1986 a truly historic change arrived in the Senate in 1986: Television. The Senate approved a trial run for live broadcast. Dole had opposed opening the Senate up to the medium just the year before, but on March 12, 1986, he seemed to enjoy the prospect of televised Senate debate. "For the first time our proceedings will be heard by the people, unedited: all the debates, the filibusters, the roll call votes and, of course, all the bleeps, bloops and blunders." Beginning June 1, America tuned in, and the Senate suddenly became a useful soapbox for presidential aspirants. Free media! "Bob Dole stands to be the greatest beneficiary of TV," said Republican Senator Al D'Amato of New York in the New York *Times*.

FOR WEEKS DURING the spring of 1986 the Senate Finance Commitee negotiated the framework of President Reagan's tax overhaul proposal that would close dozens of special-interest loopholes for business. The sky was black with Lear jets. Lobbyists stampeded into the Capitol, taking up stations outside the committee room and later outside the conference committee, where a final tax overhaul bill was being negotiated between versions passed in the Senate and the House. Dole clearly enjoyed making lobbyists nervous, even though his political strategists aggressively courted them for contributions to his political ambitions.

One day, while staffers and senators sweated over conference committee negotiations on the 1986 tax bill, a dramatic reform of the tax code, one hundred bleary-eyed lobbyists and staff members lined a hallway outside an executive meeting room, chatting idly, a hum filling the air. The meeting room door opened and Dole strode out accompanied by an aide. The hallway fell silent, the only sound the two men's shoes clacking on the marble floor. Halfway across the hallway, Dole abruptly stopped, looking straight ahead.

"Could somebody find me a lobbyist around here?" he said, as though to his aide. Thirty lobbyists jerked forward. Acknowledging no one, Dole sped on, out of the hallway, heading to his office, smiling to himself.

During the spring and summer of 1986 Dole adjusted to a new White House chief of staff. Smooth James Baker switched jobs with more prickly Donald T. Regan at the Treasury Department. Asked by a reporter one day if Regan was abrasive, Dole responded, "not lately." Nancy Reagan was still unhappy with Dole because she did not think he should have run against Reagan in 1980. Still, a Congressional Quarterly study rated Dole as backing the president 92 percent of the time, 20 points higher than the Senate average of 72 percent.

If his relations with the White House were less than wholly heart-warming, Dole outright vexed Senate Democrats in April 1986. Some accused him of using his leadership authority to try to help the twenty-two Republican seats up for election in November 1986 and to further his ambitions for 1988. From the other end of the Capitol, House Speaker Tip O'Neill, the old-line Massachusetts liberal and good friend of Dole's, according to the New York *Times,* observed: "Bob plays a tough game of politics. the majority leader is running for President with both feet and both hands."

IN AUGUST, WHILE the Senate labored long, nerve-fraying hours to move dozens of bills forward working through the summer recess, a sensational breach of decorum erupted on the Senate floor. Senators customarily address one another as my "honorable good friend," or "my esteemed" colleague, even when they feel quite the opposite. A group of Democrats pushing for quick consideration of new economic sanctions against the white government of South Africa was frustrated that Dole seemed to be using his leadership powers to fill up the legislative calendar with Republican amendments, excluding Democratic initiatives. They clashed with Dole, who was fulfilling an obligation to President Reagan to vote on sending $100 million in aid to the Nicaraguan contra rebels. Dole insinuated that Byrd, the courtly West Virginian, was trying to "sneak" an amendment on the South Africa sanctions in for a quck vote.

"Does the senator think I sneaked when I offered this amendment?" Byrd said, affronted.

"No," Dole said. "But . . . someone can sneak in here and offer an amendment. I am not going to back away from that."

"I want the record to show that the distinguished majority leader is not saying that I sneaked and offered an amendment." Byrd said indignantly.

Later in the debate, Dole added, "I think it's time we ask ourselves, in all honesty, what kind of game we are playing here."

Byrd angrily shouted back, "I have had enough of this business of having the majority leader stand here and act as a traffic cop on this floor."

"I did not become majority leader to lose," Dole responded.

Stunned Democrats and Republicans worried that the outburst would damage the Senate's ability to function that fall, so close to an election when control of the Senate was at stake and could shift back to Democrats. But the tempest had blown its course rather quickly. The Senate that fall approved new economic sanctions on the government of South Africa with a "yes" vote from Bob Dole. President Reagan soon announced he could not support some portions of the bill, despite his opposition to apartheid, and therefore would veto it, turning to Dole to help him sustain an attempt to override. Stuck in another politically uncomfortable position, Dole made the decision to support his president.

"It has not been easy for me to decide on my own course," Dole told his colleagues on September 26. "To me, the absolute top priority has been to send a strong message to South Africa and to the world that the United States is fed up with apartheid and demands its immediate end. . . . [But] an even stronger message could be sent if the president and Congress could speak together on this issue." The Senate overrode Reagan, pressuring the white South African government. (Eight years later, free elections ushered in a new black president, Nelson Mandela, head of the African National Congress.)

Following the curious traditions of the Senate, Byrd and Dole returned to the Senate floor October 18, 1986, to offer end-of-session summaries. Dole called Byrd a "legend in the Senate" who had shared his knowledge of Senate rules often with Dole during Dole's two-year tenure as majority leader.

"I know Senator Byrd understands probably as well as any of us that today's foe could be tomorrow's ally," Dole added. "You do not burn your bridges in this place because the very person you may cut off at the knees is the person that you may want and you may not be able to find him if you have done that. You may want that person on your side in the next battle."

Standing at his desk, Byrd later noted that senators occasionally got carried away in their partisanship. Turning to Dole, Byrd said he wanted to break for a moment the Senate rule requiring senators to address each other in the third person on the Senate floor.

"I have learned a lot from you," Byrd spoke directly to Dole. "It is that tenacity and courage and stick-to-itiveness, and yet that good humor and joviality, that help to brighten our day. It is a pleasure to serve with you."

Dole returned the compliment, and the Senate adjourned.

IN THE NOVEMBER 4 elections, Republicans suffered dispiriting losses in the Senate as the balance shifted to 55 Democrats and 45 Republicans. Bob Dole lost the majority and he would switch places with Byrd in January. All four network anchors wanted Dole to comment, and he did by congratulating Byrd, the interviews finishing at 1:30 A.M. As he left, he saw balloons and streamers on Byrd's office door.

His disappointment was acute enough that he considered retiring from the Senate to conduct a full-time campaign for the presidency. Kansas had just elected a Republican governor, Mike Hayden, so if Dole retired, Hayden would appoint a Republican to the Senate seat, an important consideration for Dole.

MORE BAD NEWS was on the way for Republicans—this time from a newspaper in Lebanon: The American government had been secretly selling arms to Iran, under control of the Ayatollah Khomeini. A flurry of American news reports revealed that arms sales were made in the hope of securing release of several American hostages held in Beirut, and that millions of dollars from the sales had been illegally diverted to aid the Nicaraguan contras in 1985 and 1986 after passage of the Boland Amendment, which banned military aid to the Central American rebel group. Attorney General Edwin Meese held a news conference in late November to say the operation had been run by Oliver North, a Marine lieutenant colonel and national security adviser working with Admiral John Poindexter. At first blush it looked like Watergate all over again. Democrats demanded President Reagan explain all he knew about the arms-for-hostages deal, Republicans defended Reagan's statement that he was unaware of the deal until he was notified of it by Meese.

The crisis gave Dole the jolt he needed to jump back into the Senate fray. He spent Thanksgiving in North Carolina with Elizabeth's family. Thanksgiving morning he chatted with his friend Robert Strauss, the former Democratic party chairman, who was at his home in Texas. Dole told Strauss he was thinking of urging that a Senate select-committee be formed to investigate Iran-Contra and suggested Strauss bounce the idea off Byrd. Strauss called Byrd at his home in West Virginia, then called Dole back to say Byrd was thinking along the same lines. Byrd called Dole and sent up an agreement to propose the idea in separate appearances on two different Sunday morning interview programs that weekend. After they hung up Dole realized one straightforward way to shift focus away from the president was for Reagan to call a special session of Congress to set up a select-committee. He did not tell Byrd.

On November 30 Dole appeared on ABC's "This Week with David Brinkley." Brinkley told Dole he had heard apocalyptic predictions that Reagan's presidency might be mortally wounded in the scandal. Dole said he didn't believe that was the case. And then he unloaded his idea:

"He has three problems," Dole said of the president. "He has the American public. He has the Congress. And he has our allies overseas. And I think he must address all of those very quickly. He has to lay it all out. I would hope he would call a special session of Congress next week and form this select-committee. Otherwise, we're going to have fifteen or twenty committees investigating this problem."

In this one move, Dole managed to appear as if he were defending his president's integrity and trying to *help* Reagan clear the air quickly, while distancing himself from the president should the scandal prove his undoing. He also had one-upped Byrd.

ABC's Sam Donaldson said, "Well, the administration's story at the moment that's on the record is that Lieutenant Colonel Oliver North did all of this; that Admiral Poindexter, his boss, knew something was going on but didn't investigate it. Do you believe that?"

Dole responded, "I don't think Ripley would believe that."

In the following days Dole continued to maintain Reagan was popular and would survive. Reagan rejected the special-session suggestion, but Dole's comments catapulted Dole into the limelight during the next few weeks. He appeared almost nightly on the evening news and on television and radio programs, offering volumes of advice to the White House.

John Buckley, the press secretary for Jack Kemp, accused Dole of climbing "over the corpse of a popular president," criticism Dole responded to on a CNN "Evans and Novak" program December 13:

"I was chairman of the party during Watergate, and I remember going to the White House and being told by my good friend Bryce Harlow that this story wouldn't be around for two days," Dole told Roland Evans. "It was around two years and took ten years [for the Republican party] to recover, so I'm not going to sit back and watch everything go down the tube to satisfy somebody's press secretary."

Marlin Fitzwater, acting presidential press secretary from 1981 on, after James Brady was wounded in the assassination attempt on Reagan, became Reagan's official press secretary in 1987. He said Reagan was not offended by Dole's efforts concerning Iran-Contra. "Reagan didn't mind that," said Fitzwater, a Kansan. "President Reagan felt like he told the public everything he knew in the first twenty-four hours after he found out about it. His attitude was, 'Fine. Let 'em come.' "

Dole had been a fairly consistent supporter of the president, differing mainly on strategy to handle issues before Congress, and had worked effectively, if not always happily, with the White House during his tenure as majority leader. During 1987 the White House began to view him differently—as a presidential contender. And that created a new form of tension:

"By the 1987 period it was clear Dole was going to try to run for president, and that made him kind of an opponent of the White House, in the sense that everyone in the White House was a Bush person," said Fitzwater, who also would work for Bush. "And even Reagan made it clear he would be supporting Bush. That was the main source of the tension at the end, because everything Senator Dole would do was seen as trying to get some political advantage."

LIVE LONG AND PROSPER

IF PRESIDENTIAL CAMPAIGNS seem like wild circuses from the outside, the inside of one is like a churning Kansas tornado. In the 1988 presidential race, seven Republican candidates would battle that turbulence and each other for the mantle of President Ronald Reagan: Vice President George Bush, Representative Jack Kemp of New York, former Delaware Governor Pete du Pont, Christian tele-evangelist Pat Robertson, former Secretary of State Alexander Haig, former Senate Majority Leader Howard Baker and Bob Dole.

For three years Bob Dole had curried GOP support, sprinkled campaign donations from Campaign America, defended Reagan's agenda in the Senate and reached out to new audiences, blacks, women and minorities. The problem: Bob Dole was everybody's *second* choice behind George Bush, closest by job title to Reagan.

But in early 1987 Dole had reason for hope. As further details of the Iran-Contra arms-for-hostages transfer came to light, Bush's poll standings skidded downward, though he had not been directly tied to the scandal. The complexion of the presidential race suddenly changed in late February when Reagan cleaned house to shore up his public image and selected Howard Baker, the former Tennessee senator, as his new chief of staff. Baker then withdrew his name for 1988, a boon for Dole. Everyone knew

Dole had approached John Sears, who had run Reagan's 1980 campaign until he was fired before the New Hampshire primary, to join Dole's campaign. But their chemistry did not click. So, to ward off negative press, Robert Ellsworth, Dole's old House colleague from Kansas and Richard Nixon's administration official, announced on March 1 that he would serve as chairman of the newly-formed Dole presidential exploratory committee, leaving open-ended Sears' role, which never materialized. Dole's initial campaign group included Elizabeth Dole; Ellsworth; Bill Lacy, a former Reagan White House aide; Don Sloan, a Kansas City businessman; and two conservatives: Donald J. Devine, the former Reagan administration official hired in 1985 to run Campaign America, and David Keene, head of the American Conservative Union.

"The strategy was that the only way to beat Bush, because of the popularity of Reagan and Bush wrapping himself in the Reagan flag, so to speak, was to show him that he couldn't win," Ellsworth said, in a post-primary interview with Michael Gillette, who headed a 1988 presidential election study at the Lyndon B. Johnson School of Public Affairs at the University of Texas at Austin. During the August 1987 congressional recess Dole flew around the country, hitting seventy cities in twenty-nine states and always emphasizing he was electable and had on-the-job experience in running the government.

Then he and four other senators flew to Managua, Nicaragua, in September to challenge President Daniel Ortega, leader of the socialist Sandinista government, to agree to three-way talks between his government, the Nicaraguan contras and the Reagan administration. They sought a cease-fire in the civil war that had killed thousands of Nicaraguans. In a testy hour-long meeting, Ortega rejected Dole's idea, Dole accused Ortega of holding a "propaganda rally," and Ortega fired back that the United States was not sending aid but bullets against the people of Nicaragua, according to news stories. Days later, Dole added that he thought a "little three-day invasion" of Nicaragua would be welcomed by the Nicaraguan people. That tough stance and his strong defense that fall of Reagan's Supreme Court nominee, conservative Judge Robert Bork, whose confirmation the Senate later rejected in an acrimonious battle that contributed to an era of sharper partisanship, warmed conservative feeling toward Dole.

Dole also approached Bill Brock, Reagan's secretary of labor and a friend of Dole, for a key role in his campaign. The two eventually agreed that Brock would come in as chairman. Everyone in the Dole inner circle wanted Brock. He had earned a good reputation as a moderate Republican senator, he had turned around the Republican National Committee after Watergate as its chairman, he was Mr. Clean and unfailingly controlled. He was a well-connected millionaire from the upper crust of society. Brock, in Ellsworth's parlance, was a "Bigfoot," a big name, someone the cynical national media could latch onto and say, "Well, now Bob Dole is serious."

"Everybody thought it would be a ten-strike," Ellsworth said. "Everybody thought to have a sitting member of Reagan's cabinet—even if it was Bobo the Clown—resign from the Reagan cabinet for the purpose of becoming chairman of the Dole campaign would be a big blow to the Bush campaign."

On October 1 Elizabeth Dole had resigned as Reagan's Secretary of Transportation to devote herself full-time to her husband's campaign. Announcing his own decision on October 15 to leave Reagan's team, Brock said, "I wouldn't be doing this if I didn't think we could win." A few days later Dole announced that Richard Wirthlin, Reagan's pollster, would become the pollster for the Dole campaign. Political writers and academic pundits nationwide observed these developments and mostly blessed them.

One negative blip did hit the news in early November when Trans-Africa, an anti-apartheid organization, announced it would broadcast critical advertisements to coincide with Dole's formal entry into the presidential contest. The organization, as it had earlier in the year, criticized Dole for leading the fight for President Reagan to block Congress from imposing economic sanctions on the white-run South African government. "We don't want a president who will do business with racists in South Africa," the announcer said, according to the Associated Press. Dole called their charges a "phony" attempt to distort his civil rights record.

On a frigid November 9 in 1987 Bob Dole returned again to Russell to declare to the home folks he was off and running for the presidency. Bub Dawson, his old friend from Dawson's Drug Store, presented Dole with the same cigar box the town had collected money in for Dole following his World War II injuries. This time the box held more than $100,000. Dole promised to make the Republican party more inclusive, hinged his campaign on attacking the federal deficit and got in indirect digs at Bush. Both Doles felt Bush had served in many high government posts—ambassador, party chairman, head of the CIA and vice-president—but had made no special mark.

"I can make a difference," Dole told several thousand people gathered on Main Street. "I have made a difference. I will make a difference.

"I offer a record, not a résumé."

Behind the scenes, Brock was well aware of Dole's reputation for an inability or unwillingness to delegate. But Brock theorized that Dole behaved that way because he was dealing with people below him and that Brock, a peer, could "yell back, which in fact happened from time to time," said Fred Asbell, whom Brock brought in as his executive assistant. Brock first sent a swat team to Dole's headquarters. They wandered around asking staffers exactly what they did for Dole. Dole's hierarchy flabbergasted them.

"There were about ninety-seven informal lines of communication and behind-the-scenes deals," said Asbell in his interview with the Lyndon Johnson school. "Lots of things, more than I think he realized on the front end, were done deals . . . the media people, the polling contracts, a whole bunch of political field people, and a lot of stuff was in play." The staffs working in the Washington headquarters, in Iowa and in New Hampshire were off on their own like "Pluto, Mars and Venus."

"If he has a problem it's that he listens to too many people," acknowledged David Keene. "I joked once his organizational chart for his 1988 campaign was Dole at the top, then there's this long, long line below him with everyone from Bill Brock to his chauffeur. And Dole might have called anybody at any moment and acted on anything he heard."

The campaign developed three camps: the Brock people; Devine and Keene and other conservatives; and Dole's Kansas Mafia, like the Georgia Mafia of close friends who had surrounded President Jimmy Carter. Brock rented an entire floor above the existing campaign office in Washington. He furnished it elaborately and hired twenty-five new aides at vastly higher salaries than the Dole loyalists were earning, said Sloan, the Kansan. With Brock at the helm, the campaign budget jumped immediately by more than $125,000 a month. Some of the Kansas Mafia called Brock's quarters "Taj Mahal" or "The King's chambers." Dole's loyalists were irritated about the big guns stepping in to show them how a *real* campaign was run.

"Klingon alert! Klingons thirty paces," Kim Wells, a former Dole Senate staffer, and Bill Lacy would say as they passed each other in the headquarters hallways if a Brock person was nearby. They were referring to the television show "Star Trek," in which the bad guys, the Klingons, always threatened the good guys on the Starship Enterprise. Lacy and Wells started an underground movement, secretly making the Vulcan peace sign, and repeating Dr. Spock's famous phrase.—"Live long and prosper."

From the Brock group's perspective the Dole gang had indeed raised a comfortable $10 million but had no clear national strategy, a weak organization in New Hampshire and not much presence throughout the south for Super Tuesday's seventeen state contests. The Brock team reassigned Lacy and dispatched Devine and Keene to plan the campaign in lesser states, raising questions in the media about a staff shakeup. "In my mind, what we should have done was to execute [them] on November 1 and been done with it," Asbell said of unnamed members of the original Dole gang.

The first and most crucial test of the campaign would come in the Iowa caucuses on February 8, 1988. Early in 1985 Jo-Anne Coe, Dole's long-time aide, had contacted Tom Synhorst, who helped Iowa Republican Senator Charles Grassley get his reelection campaign firmly on track for 1986. Synhorst, son of an Iowa farm couple, thought Dole was the best candidate for 1988. In 1986 Synhorst had laid out a plan for Dole to win in Iowa, Synhorst said in his interview with the Johnson School. As he had done for Grassley, Synhorst convinced Dole to target the so-called little people, speak at dozens of town meetings he would set up, let people touch him, and avoid playing up initially to big newspapers, radio stations and business heavyweights in Iowa.

The week Bill Brock came aboard one of his top deputies, Skip Watts, called Tom Synhorst to tell him he was coming to Iowa. "When can we get together?" Watts said.

"How much time do you need?" said Synhorst, who kept Bob Dole hours, dawn to midnight. "We could meet at 5 or 5:30 A.M."

Watts said, "I'm not going to get up that early."

Watts flew out and they met in the early evening at the Marriott hotel in downtown Des Moines. He asked Synhorst specific questions about his operations and told Synhorst that when he returned to his home in Washington Brock wanted to meet him. Synhorst flew to Washington that Friday and told Brock he needed Dole in Iowa more. Regardless of what they planned in other states, Synhorst said, "If we don't win Iowa, it won't matter." The following Monday, Bernie Windon, another Brock aide, advised Synhorst he needed help. Synhorst got Windon to promise if he couldn't work with the person sent out to Iowa, Synhorst could reject him or her.

"He sent this guy out from Texas," Synhorst recalled. "He had a gold chain around his neck, and he had on this big fancy watch and pinkie ring."

During dinner the man from Texas told Synhorst he would look things over before deciding whether to stay, all the while stabbing the table with the prongs of his fork. "You can look at whatever you want," Synhorst said, "but it's my decision to make as to whether you stay or not." Early the following morning the man from Texas talked about all the things he needed in Iowa and said he'd be around four more days. "I thought, 'If I have to spend a week with this guy, it *will* derail me,' " Synhorst said. He quickly called Windon to complain. The Texan left on a 10:30 A.M. flight.

Another more senior Brock aide came to Iowa and told Synhorst he needed to produce a list of precinct leaders and prioritize it, then devise a plan to track the top ones week-by-week to develop lists of supporters, a large task. Synhorst put together the whole thing in a weekend. The Brock aide returned, stunned, and told Brock to leave Synhorst alone.

That week Dole flew into Iowa. Synhorst got on a plane with him and told him the Brock people seemed to want to take over. "If that's what you want, you will have no problem with me, period," Synhorst told Dole, according to the Johnson school interview.

"Dole got kind of this horrified look."

"Well," Dole told Synhorst, "that's not what I want, so it's not a problem."

Synhorst had planned for Bob and Elizabeth Dole to get on a plane with Senator Grassley and his wife Barbara to barnstorm Iowa between Christmas and New Year's Eve, building momentum when the other campaigns might be out of the state. Brock wanted them to take a vacation, to prepare for the battle ahead.

"Well, you know I've always believed that you can sleep *after* the election," Grassley told Synhorst when he mentioned it on another plane ride. "If you take a vacation now and you lose, you might end up the next morning and say, 'Maybe if I had just worked that week.' "

"I don't know," Dole mused. "I can't believe they think I'm going to want to sleep or be in the sun between Christmas and New Year's."

Back in Washington, Synhorst got into a heated argument with Brock's man Watts, who was concerned about the cost of the fly-around. After the meeting, Synhorst called Dole to tell him what had happened. Dole called Brock. He *was* going to fly around Iowa for the holiday. So Brock was the one who took time off, first for three days to Japan on business, then for a ski vacation with his family he had planned before he joined the campaign. Dole approved, but it rubbed the Dole loyalists the wrong way.

Synhorst set out to identify sixty to seventy thousand people supporting Bob Dole, and hoped to drive 60 percent of them to turn out on caucus night. Once on the list, "they were massaged with voter mail and telephone calls and so forth," Synhorst said. Every time Dole flew into the state, and he hit Iowa perhaps fifty times in 1987, Synhorst sent him to town meetings. No one had done them as extensively before and Dole often performed well. The meetings, in which townspeople freely peppered him with questions, gave Dole a chance to display his knowledge of issues and appear personable.

The Dole group believed federal campaign regulations contained a loophole allowing them to skirt state spending limits. In September 1987 Synhorst called a contributor in Blair, Nebraska, on the Iowa border and visited him in person to ask if he could set up a telephone bank with thirty phone lines in his office. The phone bank was used to call potential supporters and prepare nightly tracking polls to gauge Dole's standing on issues at the end of each day.

"It was just fast, efficient and very effective—little old ladies, retired housewives, sitting at the phone making these calls," Synhorst said. "That was unique; the town meetings were unique."

The Federal Election Commission frowned, however, on such activities in a post-campaign audit. In 1993 the FEC fined the Dole presidential campaign $100,000 for exceeding state spending limits by targeting activities into Iowa and New Hampshire from neighboring states, accepting illegal corporate contributions, accepting excessive contributions from individuals and not paying up front for use of jets owned by outside corporations. Separately, Campaign America was fined $12,000 for spending money to help Dole's presidential campaign, mainly in 1985 and 1986, a violation of federal rules that said it could only benefit other congressional candidates.

In 1988 in Iowa, George Bush toiled away too, as did tele-evangelist Pat Robertson—Bush through Republican party channels, Robertson through churches. Bush had won Iowa in 1980 but he was not as popular in 1988. When he flew into the state he came in the vice-president's Air Force Two, an albatross, as it turned out, in agrarian Iowa. The media described Bush swooping in aboard his sleek jet, riding in a long black motorcade with wailing police escort and a helicopter flying overhead, shuttling to planned events, hermetically sealed off from the real people. The Dole campaign played up the fact Bob and Elizabeth bounded around the state in a little twin-engine plane.

"He's one of us," was Dole's campaign theme.

And he was. From his quarter century of experience in agricultural and rural issues, Dole spoke Iowan. His home state was right next door. He had practically written the 1985 Farm Bill, which was helping reinvigorate the Iowa economy. In Synhorst's town meetings Dole often seemed to connect. Elizabeth campaigned with him and alone. "All the time people would say, '*You* should be running for president,' " Synhorst recalled people saying to Elizabeth. She would never answer questions from the press unless she knew what the questions were going to be, and she wouldn't take questions from the audience. "[She was] very, very careful, very methodical about her approach to everything. I think she was good."

It was Elizabeth who began telling people Bob's personal story, the first time he had let it be used in a national campaign. Elizabeth's standard stump speech included a segment covering Bob's modest life in Russell, his war injury and recovery, his years working to make something of himself. Before Bob spoke to an audience, his campaign often played an upbeat video biography of his life that ended with him delivering an impassioned speech to midwestern folks with a sun-drenched cornfield behind him. Then Bob Dole in person would walk in to address the audience. "He'd speak and there'd be a new context," said Mari Maseng (now married to columnist George Will), who was the campaign's communications director.

In December friction showed more between the candidates, particularly between Dole and Bush, sometimes on achievements, but also on their class differences. "I went to public schools," Dole would say, a dig at Bush's Philip's Andover prep-school upbringing. "Some of the candidates didn't have that advantage." And in Iowa Dole said on December 30, "When Ronald Reagan wants his program passed, he doesn't call George, he calls Bob." Bush countered by urging people to tell Dole to "get off my back."

"I'm not sure being in Congress all your life is part of the answer," Bush said in a speech at the National Press Club. "I think it may be part of the problem."

On January 8, 1988, Harris News Service in Kansas raised money questions in a copyrighted story about Dave Owen, who had saved Dole's 1974 Senate race. Owen worked now as Dole's national finance chairman and also manager of a blind trust for Elizabeth Dole. The paper said John Palmer, a former Dole aide, had signed a $279,000 promissory note to the blind trust in December 1986, ten months after Palmer's business, EDP Enterprises, Inc., received a no-bid contract worth $26 million. The contract was to supply food for army mess halls at Fort Leonard Wood, Missouri.

Under Owen's management the trust had also bought a million-dollar office building in 1986 in Overland Park, Kansas, a suburb of Kansas City, and had earned a commission from the sale and as a financial adviser to Palmer's business. The Small Business Administration investigated whether

Palmer was possibly serving as a front person for Owen to obtain a minority-business contract.

Controversy engulfed Dole in Iowa over whether he had been involved in the questioned transactions. Dole acknowledged later he had contacted the head of the SBA to help arrange a meeting with Palmer in 1983, but said that was a routine matter he would do for many constituents. No wrongdoing was found.

"I'm disappointed in David Owen, I can say that," Dole told reporters in Washington. "He's out of the campaign. He'll never be in the campaign again or anything else that Bob Dole has anything to do with." The Doles soon released twenty-one years of tax returns. The story died. The returns revealed that the Kansas populist and his wife had assets of more than $2 million, but small potatoes compared to Bush.

Investigators continued digging into Owen's finances and eventually found he had accepted $100,000 from Alabama businessman Paul Bryant, who was seeking to win a Kansas state contract to open a dog racing track. Owen had not reported it as income and was charged with tax evasion, according to the Kansas City *Star*. Owen also was charged with taking illegal business deductions for campaign contributions that went to Republican Mike Hayden, a Dole ally who won the state governorship in 1986. Owen was found guilty of tax evasion. He fought for an appeal but finally gave up and went to a federal prison in the spring of 1994 for a three-month sentence.

Ironically, Dave Owen would not have raised a penny for Hayden if Dole had not requested his help. When Owen had run for governor in 1982 he thought Hayden, then speaker of the Kansas House of Representatives, planned to support him. Owen then learned Hayden agreed to help Owen's Republican opponent, Wendell Lady. Wendell Lady lost the primary to Republican businessman Sam Hardage, and Owen never forgave Hayden. As for Dole, he never spoke to Owen again after the initial Harris News story appeared.

In January of 1988, a month before the Iowa caucuses, the Brock camp struggled to get control of the Dole presidential campaign. Brock wanted to get rid of Dole's "one of us" theme after Iowa.

"Why is that?" Keene said to Brock at an early meeting.

"It's fine for Iowa, because it's right next door, but that's not going to play in the country," Brock responded.

"Bill, that theme has nothing to with geography and everything to do with where you're coming from," Keene told him. "Of course, you wouldn't understand that, because you're one of *them*."

Beyond Iowa, the Brock group felt they had big problems. First, Bush's campaign team was better disciplined. Bush had a better organization in New Hampshire. They had deep strength for Super Tuesday, a sweepstakes of seventeen state primaries in March, most of which were in the South, home stomping ground for Bush's campaign chairman, the tenacious Lee Atwater.

Another problem was Bob Dole, according to Fred Asbell, Brock's lieutenant. Dole could not let go of the nitty-gritty details. He continued to read fund-raising letters, made and revoked decisions on an hourly basis. He would order sudden changes in scheduling and complain when the hastily-thrown-together events seemed disorganized. Instead of careful planning with field staff for Dole's trips, Asbell said, "It came to, 'Holy mackerel! He's going to be here tomorrow. What can we do?' It really got to be just a frantic deal."

And Dole tended to push himself too hard. "When I work long hours, I just get really tired and eventually fall asleep," said Asbell. "Bob Dole shifts onto ether or something. I don't know what he runs on. The tireder he gets, the harder he pushes. We all recognized fairly early that he was tired, and that the tireder he got, the grouchier he got. We would beg and Brock would beg, 'Please take the weekend off. Go to Florida, lay in the sun, rest and do something.' Dole would say, 'Plenty of time to rest after this is over.' Believe me, the problem was not lack of enthusiasm on the part of the candidate. If anything, it worked against us because we figured out that a number of the reporters were sitting around knowing that if this thing just pushed itself hard enough and long enough, this darker side of Dole would came back out again."

Five days before the Iowa caucuses Dole did erupt. Bush's Iowa director, George Wittgraf, sent out a press release accusing Dole of "cronyism" and a "history of mean-spiritedness." It raised questions about Elizabeth Dole and the federal investigation of her blind trust. Mari Maseng the campaign's communications director showed a copy of the press release to Dole after an event in a school. The only private space around was a broom closet. They jumped in to talk. She counseled him to speak more in sorrow than anger.

The following day in Washington, Bush sat in the Senate presiding officer's chair for a controversial vote on aid to the Nicaraguan contras. Bob Dole strode into the Senate and up to Bush. Dole pounded his fist on a desk and shook the press release in Bush's face, according to the Kansas City *Times*.

"Did you authorize this release?" Dole demanded.

"Yes," Bush said.

Dole said, "Did you read it?"

"No."

Dole said, "Do you know what it contains?"

"No."

Dole gave him a copy and demanded Bush apologize to Elizabeth. "His reaction was not as a politician but as a husband," said Maseng. The campaign's communications director. "He felt genuine rage that someone would do that to his wife."

Dole's ire died down, though the Bush camp refused to apologize. The presidential campaign had entered a bitter phase.

On February 8 Tom Synhorst's organizing paid off. Dole won the Iowa caucuses, yet the news focus of the day was evangelist Pat Robertson's second-place finish ahead of Bush. Dole won 37.4 percent of the vote to Robertson's 24.6 percent, while Bush received just 18.6 percent of the caucus vote. Dole, from neighboring Kansas, had been expected to win, but Robertson's second-place finish suggested the Bush campaign might soon be dead.

"The fact he finished second, that was sort of the story, so we really didn't get the benefit," Dole said in an interview. "I could tell almost the next day, and that took a little of the glitter off our victory."

The campaigns blasted off for other states, knowing the only real test ahead was the February 16 primary in New Hampshire. Dole's post-caucus polls showed a surge for Dole in New Hampshire.

The Dole brain trust now gathered in Nashua two days later to discuss strategy for the Granite State, while Dole was in another room doing satellite feeds into Super Tuesday states, the contests after New Hampshire, held on March 8. The Brock group wanted to project a moderate Bob Dole. Maseng and others wanted to project a conservative Bob Dole. The meeting foundered, no message emerged.

Dole did give one strong speech that week, Maseng recalled, the first day after the Iowa caucuses, to the New Hampshire legislature. He held up a personal check he had written for a fund to support the Nicaraguan contras, a symbolic conservative gesture that impressed the state lawmakers. "After that speech he became silent. Basically, because we began issuing a series of white papers on moderate, liberal issues, child care, the environment, the opposite message," Maseng said, the frustration still showing years later. "We rattled around the state in a mobile home and were never heard from again. And *then* the numbers washed back against us."

In the meantime the Bush campaign had regrouped, put Bush behind the wheel of a semi-trailer truck and pulled him out of his motorcade to chat with folks across New Hampshire, projecting a common-man image. Reagan remained immensely popular in New Hampshire, and Bush, in a Reaganesque gesture, promised he would not raise taxes, the right message in a tax-hating state.

The final weekend, in the midst of a fourteen-inch snowstorm, New Hampshire Governor John Sununu persuaded several television stations to run a Bush campaign ad called the "Senator Straddle" ad. It crushed Dole.

"George Bush is against an oil-import tax," the announcer on the ad said. "Bob Dole straddled, but now says he's for an oil-import tax. George Bush says he won't raise taxes, period. Bob Dole straddled, and he just won't promise not to raise taxes. And you know what that means."

Dole's ads, meanwhile, projected him as a moderate to liberal, rather than, as originally planned, a conservative. Mari Maseng called one of Dole's ads, "Gorbachev is a white wine drinker." It hinted Dole thought Gorbachev was all right because he and Dole had held glasses of wine aloft in a toast. "And we had an ad [of Dole] bragging about fixing Social Security, which conservatives immediately translated as, 'I raised your taxes,'" Maseng said. The Dole media team tried to prepare a rebuttal to the Straddle Ad, had trouble editing it and could not get it on the air in time.

But Dick Wirthlin's polls had shown Dole with a slight lead over Bush. The Brock group counseled Dole to project calm. Dole worried. The Sunday night before the primary, the Republican candidates met for a publicized debate in a college in Manchester. Before it began, Dole bumped into Charlie Black, the political consultant who had joined Dole on the 1976 vice-presidential race and now was working for Jack Kemp.

"What do you think of Wirthlin's polls?" Dole said.

"Obviously, I haven't seen them," Black responded. "But I saw him on TV last night declaring you the winner by ten points. You know, we're not polling, but I've been talking to [Bush's campaign manager] Atwater a bit and he's nervous as a damn cat. But I think you're losing ground. I don't think you've got this thing won by a long shot."

"That's what I think," said Dole, and they chatted about poll slippage and the impact of the Straddle ad. "My guys say I should take the high ground, all I gotta do is no errors and I've got the primary won."

"I'm standing here, Jack Kemp's campaign manager," Black said, "and he may rip into you in this debate. But I'm telling you, that's not the right strategy. You need to put some distance between yourself and Bush on your terms."

The debate didn't go well for Dole. At one point Pete du Pont brandished a piece of paper, saying it was a no-tax pledge and urged Dole to sign it; he refused. Later, Maseng speculated why: "Bob Dole is probably more ideologically opposed to raising taxes than Bush. But Dole is pragmatic. And there was no way he could physically take that piece of paper. There was no table and no one to hold it on the table. His right hand is not available to him. Plus there's just: 'I'm Bob Dole. You're not going to tell me what to do.' "

On primary day, Bush handily defeated Dole, winning 37.6 percent of the vote to Dole's 28.4 percent. Kemp came in third with 12.8 percent. "The Dole organization failed to campaign as long and hard as they could," said Robert Ellsworth in his explanation of the defeat. "It was a combination of incompetence and hubris."

In an interview, Dole said: "I think down deep most of the people around me knew if we didn't win Iowa and New Hampshire we were in trouble. We had bad polls. In the last week we sort of sat on our poll lead. And we had a big snowstorm. Bush was out there shoveling snow and driving trucks, things I couldn't do. So he had all the news coverage. We were wandering around grocery stores shaking hands. I think Bush and Sununu did a superior job. We got up that morning to visit the polling places and there were George Bush signs solid, everywhere we went. And if you need any last-minute reminders who really has it in the campaign, that was it. I must say, I probably thought about it every night for a year afterwards to figure out what happened myself. One thing that happened, nobody could or would make a decision. We had lots of different ideas, but somehow it didn't happen."

Primary day, demoralized by the Sunday night debate, deflated by Bush's unfolding victory in New Hampshire, the Dole powder keg that was lit in Iowa blew. NBC captured a moment during the day when a du Pont supporter walked up to Dole at an event and challenged him, "You voted for tax increases six hundred times in your career. Well, can you defend that?"

Dole's voice rumbled like low thunder, he scuffed his toe around in the snow and muttered, "Go back in your cave."

Just in case viewers didn't hear, NBC reporter Lisa Myers helped out: "Dole said, 'GO BACK IN YOUR CAVE.' "

That night in an NBC primary election special, anchor Tom Brokaw bantered with George Bush about his win. "I've got Senator Bob Dole who's standing by in his headquarters," Brokaw said.

Sitting in a darkened room staring at the black hole of the television camera pointed at him, Dole felt lousy. He had the flu. He managed a small smile. He had no television monitor in front of him to see what viewers at home would see. Brokaw turned to Bush: "Anything you'd like to say to him at this point?

"Nope," Bush said with an uncomfortable smile, "just wish him well, and we'll meet him in the south."

"And, Senator Dole, is there anything you'd like to say to the vice-president?" Brokaw said. On his earphone Dole heard the conversation, but did not realize they were on live with Brokaw. He thought it was the usual chitchat that went on between producers, anchors and those being interviewed before the real thing.

"Yeah, stop lying about my record," Dole said, glaring into the camera.

Maseng, who also had the flu, sat bolt upright. Dole walked over after the interview. "How bad was it?"

Bad. The national media seized the story: "Bob Dole's mean streak returns." "The dark side of Bob Dole attacks George Bush." News shows replayed the videotape of Dole's outburst. The day after New Hampshire, Dole flew to Oklahoma. The Bush camp already had lined up Governor Henry Bellmon ahead of time for a 10 A.M. press conference to attack Dole. Bellmon used Dole's "stop lying about my record" statement to complain about how mean and vicious Bob Dole was.

"We were prepared to attack him on other things," James Shearer, Bush's regional political director, said in an interview with the Johnson School. "I can't remember what they were, because when I saw this on live television it was like a gift from God. We truly did as much as we could do to help set the mood of the press, and in effect, get them to write the stories we wanted. We wanted Dole on the defensive . . ."

Dole's campaign briefly righted itself with wins in the South Dakota primary and Minnesota caucus, two midwest states Bush had made a play for but pulled out of before the voting. Then Strom Thurmond, the ancient South Carolina Republican, whose state primary was a crucial three days before Super Tuesday, endorsed Dole. While he had pursued Thurmond for weeks, the endorsement forced the Dole campaign to spend money and the Doles' time in South Carolina. It drained money from Super Tuesday states they hoped to win—Missouri, Oklahoma, Tennessee, North Carolina and Kentucky. "It's the old story of the dog chasing the car: if he catches it, what's he going to do with it," said Fred Asbell, Brock's lieutenant.

But Bob Dole wanted to do everything in his power for this, his best chance at the presidency. "It was just intense, he was going all out," said Charlie Black, who talked to Dole every couple of days after Kemp dropped out in New Hampshire. "And the fact that he had it for a few days there, between Iowa and New Hampshire, and saw it slipping away was driving him crazy. I got the impression no matter how late he worked he wanted to work another hour that night, in case he might find a few votes."

A long-smoldering power struggle caused more bad news on February 25 in Florida. Dole had asked conservatives David Keene and Don Devine to join him on the campaign plane to help him work out a new message. Keene wrote a memo on one of the campaign's computers, perhaps hoping it would be discovered, essentially outlining a takeover. Brock found out about it and hopped aboard the campaign plane headed into Florida. Even from in the back of the plane, the press corps felt bad vibes.

While Dole spoke before a business group in Ronnie's Restaurant in Orlando, Brock met with Keene and, as reported in the Washington *Post,* said, "I'm pulling the string. You're finished." Donald Devine joined them and Brock told him: "I might as well deal with both of you. This is not going to work. You are off the payroll as of today. You're off the plane in Jacksonville."

The plane next landed in Jacksonville. Within earshot of the press, Brock told Fred Asbell, "Get their bags off the plane." While Brock held a news conference to explain their departure, Keene and Devine held their own news conference at the airport, revealing all the gory details. Brock had ordered their bags thrown off the plane onto the runway tarmac, they complained. Keene called Brock "petty," but said he did not want to hurt Dole's chances for the presidency.

"They made a big deal about leaving the bags on the tarmac, but in fact there never were any bags on the tarmac because we never got them off the plane," said Asbell. Dole, stunned, "just stepped back and let Brock clean it up," said Asbell. Of Devine and Keene, he added: "In my judgment, very little of what they did was working for Dole's interest. They got tons of bad press for him. They groused about it for weeks." Keene, Devine and other critics later noted that perhaps Brock's bags should have been dumped onto the tarmac. Brock, who had worked for Richard Nixon's campaign in 1972, seemed not to understand how presidential politics had changed by 1988. Brock put many people on retainer, hired limousines, chartered airplanes and helicopters, ran up hotel bills and spent money in states Dole probably could never win. "The rap on Bob Dole was he'd never give up control, he'd be his own manager, he'd do everything himself," Keene said. "He *did*. He gave it all up to Brock. And then he got fucked."

Dole lost South Carolina. The initial $4 million budget for Super Tuesday had dwindled to $1.3 million, too little to sell a candidate wholesale on television. The Brock team seemed to spread money everywhere, pulling it from the southern border states the campaign originally targeted, signaling the Bush campaign to put money for television ads into those states—Missouri, Oklahoma, North Carolina—"to stomp out the last few sparks," said Maseng.

Dole had to win a few Super Tuesday states to recharge in the midwest and pray to stay alive until the California primary. Yet on Super Tuesday eve, although Dole came close in Missouri, North Carolina and Oklahoma, he lost all seventeen states. Dole and the campaign staff had flown to Illinois that night for the next primary. At dinner one evening in the Oak Park Hyatt Hotel, Bob, Elizabeth, Bill Brock and others tried to construct a strategy to still win the nomination. Kim Wells said things looked pretty grim.

"You're taking negative pills again, Kim," Brock told him.

"No, he's just being realistic," Dole said.

In Washington soon after, Don Sloan, the Kansas City businessman and Dole campaign co-chairman, got into Dole's car for a ride back to the Watergate to advise him to quit. Out of pride and Brock's urging, Dole resisted. "'We could win California, we could turn this thing around,'" Dole told Sloan.

Dole lost the Illinois and the Wisconsin primaries to Bush, then called a news conference on March 29 in Washington to withdraw. "My friends know that I am a fighter," Dole said, according to the New York *Times*. "I make no apology for that. It is simply the way I am. They also know that I am an optimist. If I weren't, I wouldn't be here today. I have been beaten before, and no doubt will be again. But I have never been defeated, and never will be."

Was Bill Brock the fatal flaw of the campaign? In an interview, Dole said no. Although Brock joined the campaign late in the election cycle, he was Dole's friend and the big name Dole had been convinced he needed. A combination of factors—the Dole campaign staff tensions, chaos fostered by Dole himself Bush's organization, Reagan's annointment of Bush and media coverage—all contributed to the defeat. And Brock, it seemed, was not up to date on national politics . . . "When you're out of it, eight or ten years, you're out of it," Dole said.

Once the primary season ended for him, Dole sent some of his staff to meet with Bush's staff to coordinate what the Doles could do to support the vice-president's campaign against Democrat Michael Dukakis. Dole himself actively campaigned for Bush. "He didn't miss a step," Dole's daughter, Robin, said. "It took me longer to accept that the best candidate wasn't going to win. He's got some ability to keep all these details and relationships straight. He's always been a Republican and a believer in what the Republican party stands for and he's always been out campaigning for as long as I can remember for Republicans."

The GOP faithful gathered in August in New Orleans for the Republican National Convention and Bush's coronation. Rumors circulated that Bush might be considering either Bob *or* Elizabeth Dole as his vice-presidential running mate and they let it be known they were interested. Richard Nixon weighed in, suggesting publicly that Bob and George Bush would make an invincible team, a congressional expert and a foreign policy expert. But some Bush advisers feared the acrimony of the primary season would resurface between them if Bush became president.

The call came to their hotel room. Bush's choice was neither Dole. That was fine with them, said Kansan Kim Wells, the senior Dole presidential campaign adviser and former staff aide from Kansas. But Dan Quayle?

13

SHOTGUN WEDDING

"**A** NEW BREEZE IS BLOWING, and the old bipartisanship must be made new again. To my friends, and yes, I do mean friends, in the loyal opposition, and yes, I mean loyal, I put out my hand," George Bush intoned in his presidential inaugural address of January 20, 1989. "The American people await action. They didn't send us here to bicker."

The new breeze blew awhile, long enough for quick confirmation by the Senate in late January of three Bush appointments: Elizabeth Hanford Dole as secretary of labor; James A. Baker III as secretary of state; and Richard Darman as director of the office of management and budget. Then it fell slack over Bush's nomination of former senator John G. Tower as defense secretary.

Material gathered in a Federal Bureau of Investigation background check of Tower was leaked to the media in February about his post-Senate work as a consultant to the defense industry. More damaging, apparently, were allegations that Tower was a drinker and a womanizer. Republicans and Democrats manned battle stations. Senate Democrats demanded Bush withdraw Tower's nomination. Republicans tried to discredit the allegations. The Senate Armed Services Committee, chaired by Democrat Sam Nunn of Georgia, delivered a party-line vote against Tower's confirmation.

Bush stood by fellow Texan Tower, and the president laid the responsibility for getting him confirmed into the hands of Senate minority leader Bob Dole. The big question was how Dole would work with his once-bitter opponent in this new phase of his political career. Dole's personal head count of votes showed Tower losing, but Dole thought Tower was not receiving a fair hearing and decided to fight. For him, it was a high-stakes mission for his Republican party against the Democrats, who had seemingly loaded up to hit the new president on one of his first nominees.

"It became a Dole crusade," said Walt Riker, Dole's press secretary at the time.

Like most presidential nominees, Tower had refused to talk to the media during the confirmation process, which had stretched to three months of silence amid charges from his opponents. In late February Dole was irked to discover that Nunn had assigned special investigators to probe Tower's background. Riker, to put the Democrats on the defensive, early Sunday, February 19, leaked the story about Nunn's action. A few days later Tower called Riker offering to swear off drinking if he was confirmed. The offer set off discussions between Dole and the White House on how, when and where to make the announcement. On February 26 Dole brought along Tower to break his silence on ABC's "This Week with David Brinkley." Dole first assured those listening that Tower had overcome his problems.

"There are millions of Americans out there who have been able to do that," Dole said. "John Tower has never been an alcoholic. He never suffered from alcoholism. They say he drinks too much. That's in his past. Are you going to condemn somebody for something that happened ten years ago?"

When his turn came on the same television program, Tower asserted he had never been an alcoholic nor dependent on alcohol. "However," he added, "to allay fears or doubts on this matter, I hereby swear and undertake that if confirmed, during the course of my tenure as secretary of defense, I will not consume beverage alcohol of any kind or form, including wine, beer or spirits of any kind."

ABC's Sam Donaldson turned to Tower: "Now, when allegations are raised that you're a womanizer, should you take a pledge not to go out with women?"

He had been single for more than three years, Tower said. "But womanizing is a broad term," he told Donaldson. "What is your definition of the term?"

"I don't know," Donaldson said. "I would just simply say to you, that if you take—"

"Well, I think most women know it when they see it, Senator," reporter Cokie Roberts interjected.

Tower's pledge on the program did little to placate senators' expressed worries about Tower, but Bush remained steadfast in his support. Dole tried another tack. On the Senate floor, March 3, he made a bold appeal to let Tower face his accusers, his former colleagues of that exclusive club. "It is the spirit of decency and fair play," he said, "that compels me to ask you, Republicans and Democrats, to give John Tower his day in court—right here in the United States Senate." The Democrats didn't bite, but Dole did not quit.

"I heard him [Dole] on the phone with the White House saying, 'Try this, try this, what about this? Hey, why don't you do this?' " said Riker.

"I think we're going to fight this to the end," Dole said on Brinkley's show March 5. "I'm proud of President Bush for standing by John Tower. And it's sort of a cop-out, all these senators coming on these programs, saying, 'Well, I've known John Tower for twenty years, but I'm going to rely on some bartender somewhere or some story that's not corroborated in the FBI report.' " On the show, Dole accused South Carolina Democrat Senator Ernest Hollings of "vicious personal attacks" in releasing information damaging to Tower.

On the Senate floor the next week Hollings faced off against Dole, complaining about his Sunday comments. Dole responded, "You called him an alcohol abuser."

"I did!" Hollings shot back. "That's the record."

Senator Robert Byrd, president pro tem of the Senate, with whom Dole had clashed on the Senate floor and later made up with in 1986, admonished Dole for violating a Senate rule requiring senators to address each other in the third person, and the angry debate over the nomination continued among other Republicans and Democrats, each often glaring across the aisle at each other.

Back in his outer office, Dole called the White House to talk with Chief of Staff John Sununu, the former New Hampshire governor rewarded with that post for his campaign work on behalf of Bush. They should propose that Tower be confirmed on a six-month trial basis, Dole told Sununu. At his confirmation Tower would sign a letter of resignation to be accepted if his performance on the job was deemed a failure by the Senate. That would throw the question back to the Democrats.

"It was to say, What are you really interested in? Destroying this guy or do you want to give him a chance?" Dole said, according to Riker. Working with Tower, Dole proposed it to the Senate. No deal. Finally, on

March 9, capping several days of rough debate, the Senate voted and rejected Tower 53-47.

"The president of the United States didn't lose here," Dole grimly told his colleagues after the vote. "The United States did. And John Tower didn't lose either. We have witnessed a confirmation process gone reckless." The Senate, Dole lamented, had "become a hotbed of character assassination." Bush soon nominated former Wyoming Representative Dick Cheney, and the Senate confirmed him as Secretary of Defense without controversy.

Perhaps the major result of the whole imbroglio was that it showed White House skeptics that Bob Dole would give his all to support President Bush amid a new reality. Bob Dole, now sixty-five, admitted in April that his chance at the presidency appeared over, so he had turned to working with his one-time political rival, tensions with the White House notwithstanding.

"I think it's probably finished for me, but you never know," Dole said in an interview at his Capitol office, with neither sadness nor real finality. "Things could happen. I'm not planning on that or doing anything. My role now is to make George Bush a good president. I'm certainly not trying to keep anything alive." While wariness continued among their staffs, Dole said he felt none concerning Bush. "These things run their course," Dole said. "I think there's some in the Bush administration who still view Dole people as somehow aliens. And we don't appreciate that when we hear about it, but that's not the president. It's his staff. I understand we're going to get along."

Both men apparently realized they needed each other to succeed: For Dole, Bush could provide an agenda to bolster the party and perhaps help Republicans retake the majority in 1990, promoting Dole back into the majority leader's post. For Bush, Dole could fight Democrats to win approval of Bush's agenda, thereby burnishing his image as a successful president. Dole and Bush were professionals. They put the acrimony of the presidential campaign behind them.

"It happened like a snap of a finger," said Dole's friend Robert Ellsworth. "It took longer to feel good about it, to feel how it was and have confidence it could work and that it would work."

Alan Simpson, the Republican Whip who worked closely with Dole during the Bush years, said Dole quickly developed a style. "When George Bush would do something and ask Dole to help, Bob Dole would do everything in his power to do it," Simpson said. "There were times

Bob would say, 'I think this is a terrible idea,' and told the president that it was bad, but then marched ahead to try to win."

Looking back in 1994, Bush wrote: "The reaching out was made very easy by Senator Dole. After I got the nomination, the scar tissue was still there, but Bob is a thorough going pro, and he went right to work to support the ticket. Once I became president, Senator Dole lined up his troops and supported me in every way possible. The personal relationship, which had never been strained except during that primary period, was stronger than it had ever been. My respect for his leadership knows no bounds."

One day in late May Dole led syndicated newspaper columnist Jack Anderson and a television camera crew into his office for an interview about terrorism. With the tape rolling, Anderson pulled from his pocket a handgun and a bullet, which "an accomplice" had smuggled past security guards and metal detectors. Anderson said he performed the stunt to dramatize the need for better security to protect members of Congress from terrorist attacks. It angered Dole and drew a rebuke from members of the press corps who covered Congress. The U.S. Attorney's office briefly contemplated charging Anderson with a felony; it is illegal to carry a gun inside the Capitol.

"I'm trying to save lives," Anderson said, according to the Associated Press. "People on Capitol Hill responded as they so often do—by attacking the one who's trying to expose the scandal."

The incident echoed the first time Dole really had been threatened. In 1986, when he was Senate majority leader, a former Kansas prison inmate mailed a letter bomb to Dole. Federal officials tipped off Dole and alerted the Federal Bureau of Investigation, the U.S. Postal Service and the Senate Sergeant-at-Arms to intercept the package. It was inoperative. Capitol Hill postal workers had routinely X-rayed all packages sent to congressional offices after a bomb exploded outside the Senate chamber in 1983.

"I guess that's one thing about slow mail," Dole joked in disclosing the letter bomb incident to a chamber of commerce meeting in Davenport, Iowa, in 1986, according to the Associated Press. "The batteries had died."

BOB DOLE HAD TRAVELED on diplomatic missions in the 1980s to the Soviet Union, Central America and other strategically important areas. But in August 1989, Bob and Elizabeth Dole left for a ten-day trip that would linger with them for years. Their destinations: Armenia, Poland and the

Netherlands. First, they flew to Armenia, the native country of Dr. Hampar Kelikian, the surgeon in Chicago who had knit together Dole's right arm after his World War II injuries. Seven months earlier in Armenia a massive earthquake had rippled through the country, killing 30,000 people and leaving 600,000 homeless. The Doles delivered medical supplies and saw tragedy everywhere, dozens of amputees, hundreds of destitute Armenians, flattened cities. "There's no way you can measure the devastation until you see it," Dole said when he and his wife arrived in Poland soon after. "It's always hard when you see people's faces. It's tough. It's not a junket to go to Armenia."

On the plane ride into Poland, Elizabeth pored over State Department briefing books. Did Bob read them? "Naahh," said Riker. Bob Dole verbally quizzed a state department official on the trip about what he should know. That was their pattern—she would pile on research, he would absorb information in on-the-run briefings.

They arrived in Poland on the eve of the first democratic elections in the communist-controlled country in forty-five years. The historic transformation occurred after a decade of prodding by the labor movement Solidarity, born in Gdansk's shipyards and led by the charismatic, working-class Lech Walesa. The Communist vise on Eastern Europe was weakening through the policies of *glasnost* emerging in the Soviet Union.

That afternoon the lawmakers of Poland's parliament, the Sejm, gathered to vote. A hush fell over the large hall as 378 members raised their hands to elect Tadeusz Mazowiecki, a lean, reserved scholar, the first noncommunist prime minister in a generation. Four voted against him, forty-one abstained. Bowing his head, Mazowiecki accepted a standing ovation.

That evening the Doles attended a caucus of Solidarity leaders in the Parliament's Column Hall, known for its twin rows of cream-colored columns. Bob Dole, not one to make rhetorically soaring foreign policy speeches, spoke of what he knew.

"If I can give any advice as a legislator for twenty-seven years, whatever you do, do it now, do it early, do it while you have the support of the people and the world community," he told the group, which applauded him.

The following day the Doles delivered letters of encouragement from President Bush to Mazowiecki and to Communist President Wojciech Jaruzelski. Their small entourage then flew to Gdansk to meet Walesa, a former shipyard worker whose bold bid for democracy earned him the Nobel Peace Prize. During an hour-long meeting at his Solidarity headquarters in Gdansk, Walesa leaned toward the Doles and made a motion with his hands as though he were raising a heavy garage door.

"We have lifted the Iron Curtain," Walesa said. "But it is getting heavy. We need help."

The Doles had next planned a leisurely visit in The Netherlands with C. Howard Wilkins, a wealthy Wichita, Kansas, businessman and fund-raiser for Dole. Wilkins had given $100,000 to the Republican party in 1988 in a so-called soft money contribution for party-building activities and was awarded the ambassadorship by President Bush. But at Bush's request the Doles cut short their meeting with Wilkins and flew directly to Kennebunkport, Maine, Bush's family retreat, to report on their trip. They carried the message that Walesa sought $10 billion in foreign aid from the United States. He wouldn't get that much, even though he would appeal in person that fall in a speech to a joint session of Congress.

Throughout the first two years of the Bush presidency, Bob Dole practiced a different form of leadership under President Bush than under President Reagan. Rarely did Dole line up his Republican troops in an adversarial position to Bush's. Instead, he acted as the chief advocate of the Bush agenda, fighting for Bush's capital-gains tax cut, then abruptly bailing out when Bush agreed to drop the tax cut for modest increases in the minimum wage in 1989. Dole faced off frequently against contentious Democrats led by Senate Majority Leader George Mitchell, the Maine Democrat and former judge who tended to smother sharp critiques in a voice of modulated reason.

A NEW DECADE BROKE, the 1990s, and with Congress away on recess, that snoozy time of year when little news trickles out of Washington, the New York *Times* on January 16, 1990, ran an op-ed piece in which Dole advocated a shift in foreign-policy priorities. Walt Riker said: "It came out of meetings in South America the year before, where Senator Dole found out there were people down there fighting for democracy, but at that time all the attention was on Eastern Europe, Hungary and Poland. One of the presidents [in South America] he met with said, "We're fighting for freedom, too. We want to have democracy just like Eastern Europe and nobody cares about us.""

"What I am suggesting," Dole wrote in his op-ed article, "is to reexamine some of the huge aid programs in a few countries—the so-called earmarked countries—that take most of our current aid budget. Right now the big five—Israel, Egypt, the Philippines, Turkey and Pakistan—

receive more than two-thirds of our foreign aid. Does it make sense at this historic moment to provide these countries practically all of our aid at the cost of foreclosing dramatically promising new aid initiatives in Eastern Europe or other important countries? Consider this simple fact: A 5 percent cut in current aid would provide about $330 million—enough to respond to the needs of new democracies such as Poland, Hungary, Panama, and countless needy countries that under current allocations will receive not one penny of foreign aid . . . Can't those pressure groups that have turned some of our foreign-aid programs virtually into entitlement programs realize that making some minor adjustments in aid allocations can simultaneously serve the countries of their special interest, and serve America?"

His piece triggered something of an explosion. The proposal was an unusual foray by Dole into politically charged foreign-aid issues involving Israel and Egypt. Together they received $5.7 billion of a $14.8 billion foreign-aid pie, the two largest recipients of American foreign aid as a result of Camp David accords signed with President Jimmy Carter in the late 1970s. Dole's proposal had been out only a few hours when the American-Israel Public Affairs Committee issued a statement acknowledging Dole's concerns but suggesting that "we should not hurt our existing vulnerable democratic allies in the process of helping potential democracies. Instead, we should look toward strengthening the tools of diplomacy by increasing the foreign assistance account."

Elsewhere, the reaction was mixed. Syndicated columnist Charles Krauthammer called Dole's proposal "nonsense" and a "pernicious" attempt to undermine five allies that teetered on the "knife edge" of economic and social turmoil. Yet the State Department endorsed the idea of giving greater flexibility to the allocation of foreign aid, as did Robert C. Byrd. The controversy intensified when Dole next raised questions about granting $400 million in housing-loan guarantees to Israel while the United States had its own unmet housing needs. And Dole spoke up about a Senate resolution he initially supported—but later perhaps came to regret—recognizing Jerusalem as the capital of Israel, choosing sides in a dispute over a city historically important to Jews, Christians and Muslims.

"His recent actions and words I find tragic," said Hyman Bookbinder, a veteran of the Washington scene as a representative for the American Jewish Committee. "It reflects a lack of patience with a difficult process that's going on in the Middle East. I do not consider him anti-Israel. By his comments, though, he has become the darling of the anti-Israel forces."

Four Republican House members held a press conference in the House radio television gallery, led by Dole adversary Newt Gingrich. The sour group took Dole to task proposing to cut Israel's foreign aid, and for tarnishing the Republican party's image through comments attributed to Dole that appeared in the Jerusalem *Post*.

Dole fired back a letter: "Normally, if I disagree with a fellow Republican, I speak to him privately about any problems instead of holding a press conference." He pointed out that he had a 26-year record of support for Israel and was directing his comments toward the pro-Israel lobby, not Jewish organizations or the Israelis. The context of the interview, he wrote, "was my assertion that the leaders of the pro-Israel lobby are shortsighted and selfish in their zealous efforts to protect Israel's aid levels at any cost." He added a cutting postscript meant for Gingrich: "Apparently, you've forgotten your private words of praise for my proposal to cut foreign aid earmarks—which would have resulted in a 5 percent cut for Israel. Or weren't those words for public consumption?"

IN THE FALL of 1989 Bob Dole had ventured into foreign policy on a far more personal matter. The issue arose out of a sense of the Senate resolution introduced by Dole, one of those commonplace forms of legislation that flow from the Senate by the dozens, often with perfunctory approval, little fanfare. At the time, it caused a minor stir in U.S.–Turkey relations. By February 1990, it had grown into an international incident.

On February 20 Dole stood at his leadership post in front of the Senate to defend his one-paragraph resolution designating April 24 as "National Day of Remembrance of the Seventy-fifth Anniversary of the Armenian Genocide of 1915-1923." "For too long we have ignored history," Dole said. "For too long we have bowed to the pressures of an important ally and powerful interest groups. For too long we have failed to speak the truth about genocide." He maintained it was time to recognize the 1.5 million Armenians who were killed during those years by the Ottoman Empire, now Turkey, because of ethnic heritage. In response, Turkish Prime Minister Turgut Ozal denounced the use of the word genocide and the Turkish lobby came out in force against Dole's resolution, writing letters and making telephone calls to dozens of senators. The White House was in a quandary, having tried to head off the vote on the resolution out of fear of antagonizing a close American ally, even though as a candidate Bush also suggested U.S. recognition of the fact of genocide in Armenia.

Byrd began a filibuster to block a vote on the resolution, bottling up most Senate action for three days. Dole called it a "David and Goliath issue," pitting broken-down Armenia against well-heeled Turkey. He got in a few digs at Israel and Democrats who had been condemning the Chinese government's treatment of its dissidents. Dole hung photographs of Armenian children in his office. He showed an astonishing drive, "perhaps the highest intensity I've ever seen from him," marveled a prominent Senate staffer whose boss opposed Dole's resolution. "He wouldn't give up, he was absolutely determined to win, mainly out of personal obligation to the doctor who had helped him. It wasn't related to Kansas in any way. This was personal."

After eight days of Senate floor outbursts and behind-closed-doors quarreling, Dole pulled his resolution off the Senate calendar, warning he would try to find other avenues to recognize the Armenian deaths.

SEVERAL TIMES A week during his presidency, Bush invited congressional Republicans to the White House to talk about strategy on issues. Once Bush and Dole had established a working relationship, in spite of awkwardness over Armenia, Bush would take a few extra minutes to talk privately with Dole, Bush's press secretary Marlin Fitzwater recalled. Their relationship grew from Dole's defenses of Bush's agenda against Democratic attacks, and through personal gestures. When Bush heard Dole's sister Gloria had cancer, he called to offer Dole the services of his personal physician, a gesture Dole appreciated.

In early 1990 Bush vetoed a bill that would have allowed Chinese students whose student visas expired to remain in the United States for at least two additional years to protect them from prison or torture if they were deported back to China. The measure came nine months after the massacre by Chinese soldiers of hundreds of protesters in Beijing's Tiananmen Square. Bush, ambassador to China in the early 1970s, issued instead a temporary administrative order not to deport Chinese students who wished to remain in America. This amounted to the same thing, but softened the message to China. The House, unconvinced, overwhelmingly voted to override the president.

Mounting a blitz of telephone calls by Bush and other top officials, Dole persuaded thirty-seven Republicans to stand by their president, and they blocked an override in the Senate. Afterward Bush sent a photograph showing Dole holding the vote tally standing beside a surprised Bush. He wrote a note underneath: "Impossible—But you did it. Thanks for everything, George Bush."

★ ★ ★

ONE AREA OF Bob Dole's career that continuously aroused controversy as he became nationally prominent was his fund-raising activities. Watchdog organizations questioned whether Dole had offered any *quid pro quo* favors or campaign contributions. Over the years Dole repeatedly denied trying to help his contributors with favoring legislation.

His practice was to turn letters over to his staffers for review to see if the pleader had a case. If they involved tax matters, the staff person would check with the Treasury Department. "Whether they're Republicans or Democrats, people at Treasury are pretty hard-nosed," Dole said in an interview. "Generally, if they're saying 'No way,' I understand it. Sometimes because it's Bob Dole or [Senator] Pat Moynihan or whoever might be the chairman, they might be a little more flexible. I don't think in any of those cases we've overridden Treasury. If I did that to the system, that'd be bad. I don't know if we can have any friends anymore, we are beating ourselves up about no gifts, no this or that," Dole continued, heading into a related area. "If you have a close friend, then you're suspect. But if he wasn't your close friend he wouldn't invite you to dinner."

Dole's involvement with ethanol, the nation's largest ethanol producer, Archer-Daniels-Midland Co. of Decatur, Illinois, known as ADM, and its president, Dwayne Andreas, indicates how close Dole did go to the line with one friend. Andreas, born of modest means in Minnesota, assiduously cultivated friendships for decades among the country's powerful Democrats and Republicans. Andreas gave $120,000 to Nixon's campaign fund in 1972. Throughout the 1970s and 1980s Andreas, his family and the ADM political-action committee gave individual donations to Republicans *and* Democrats, and $2.7 million in contributions to Republican candidates and "soft money" donations to the Republican party, allowable for use in party-building activities, according to "Common Cause," a watchdog group in Washington. The group, known as Common Curse by its detractors for its analyses of campaign donations, later found that the Andreas' and ADM's political action committee had donated thousands of dollars toward Bill Clinton's presidential bid and for congressional Democrats as well.

Prodded by Jimmy Carter's Energy Secretary, James Schlessinger, Andreas' company in the late 1970s began large-scale production of ethanol, a corn-distilled fuel used in a blend of 10 percent alcohol with 90 percent gasoline to make gasohol. Andreas first met Bob Dole as a young congressman from the wheat fields of Kansas in the 1960s through either George

McGovern or Hubert Humphrey, two Democrats well known to Andreas. Dole supported legislation in 1978 providing a tax break amounting to a subsidy of 60 cents a gallon for blended gasohol to make it competitive with gasoline production. In the 1980s he was a consistent supporter of the ethanol industry. By the late 1980s Andreas' business held 60 percent of the ethanol market. Over the decade to 1990, ADM, its foundation and the Andreas family, had contributed more than $160,000 to the Dole Foundation for the disabled, Dole's press office said in an interview with the author; and more than $80,000 to Bob Dole's political campaigns, according to Federal Election Commission records in Washington.

John E. Ford, a former U.S. Agriculture Department official who was president of the American Corn Grower's Association, a group of southern and western corn growers, said in an interview with the author that in negotiations over the 1990 Clean Air Act, Dole protected ADM, to the detriment of small ethanol producers. "The piggishness of ADM has caused a real problem for the corn industry," Ford said in a 1990 interview with the author. "The whole corn industry, the politics of it, is controlled by one man."

Kansas produced a lot of corn, four other small companies in Kansas manufactured ethanol, Dole countered. Besides, ADM owned sixty grain elevators in Kansas and had a flour milling division. "People think this is a Decatur, Illinois, big ethanol thing," Dole said in an interview. "So they're (Kansas) constituents, too. Big time."

In 1982, according to a 1987 article in the New York *Times*, Elizabeth Dole and her brother purchased a three-room condominium for $150,000 in Bal Harbor, Florida, at the Sea View Hotel, whose board chairman was Andreas. Other condo owners at the hotel at the time were House Speaker Tip O'Neill; President Reagan's then-chief of staff, Howard Baker, the former Senate majority leader; Robert Strauss, the former Democratic National Committee chairman; and television journalist David Brinkley. Andreas often gathered politically powerful people at the Sea View for social occasions, and the few days Bob Dole actually vacationed during any given year tended to be at the Florida condo. In the winter of 1994, Dole appeared on Brinkley's show one Sunday from Bal Harbor. As it ended, Dole urged Brinkley to come on down to escape icy Washington. "I shall shortly," Brinkley responded. Then the show cut to an advertisement for ADM. The moment was an harmonic convergence.

From the early 1980s Dole also borrowed ADM's corporate jet on occasion to fly around the country for political events. Legal under Federal Election Commission rules, Dole reimbursed ADM for first-class airfare.

Since the cost was below the cost of flying the chartered jets, questions were raised about indirect campaign contributions. Besides ADM, Dole flew into the 1990s on corporate jets owned by other companies, among them the Torchmark Corp., Cargill Co., the Coastal Corp. and NTC Inc., according to Dole campaign spending reports filed at the Federal Election Commission.

In a 1990 interview, Andreas agreed Dole had been helpful to the ethanol industry, *not* because of their friendship or contributions. "We in ADM don't lobby and I don't myself talk to politicians about ethanol," the seventy-two-year-old Andreas said. "I'm sure I haven't talked to Dole about ethanol three times in my life. I only see him two or three times a year, and it's never on business. Dole is agriculturally oriented and naturally wheat growers, corn growers and all farm organizations are very, very staunch supporters of ethanol and that's the main point of Dole's constituency, being from Kansas.

"Hubert Humphrey once told me, 'Don't talk to a politician about your business because they can't afford to be caught doing something for a company,'" Andreas continued. "That's what Hubert Humphrey taught me and I've always subscribed to it."

ANDREWS AIR FORCE BASE, ten miles east of Washington, houses the 89th Airlift Wing, including two Boeing 747 Air Force I jets for the president's official duties. The base provides airplanes for official travel for the vice-president, cabinet members and members of Congress. Andrews is as crisp, spare and unglamorous as most military installations. To that austere setting in the steamy summer of 1990 retreated several dozen of the country's top congressional leaders, Bush administration officials and a clutch of senior staff, fleeing the distractions of media and lobbyists. If the deadlocked Congress failed to pass a 1991 fiscal year budget by October 1, the Gramm-Rudman-Hollings law would force sequestration of federal money, instantly furloughing thousands of government workers and closing government agencies nationwide. The mail would stop. A shutdown could ground air passenger service, derail trains, sideline freight trucks. The potential costs to the economy were in the billions.

Under pressure from a rising federal deficit and Democrats, President Bush had agreed in June to break his No New Taxes campaign pledge to pass a budget. Ironically, Bush had backtracked on the very issue he had used to kill Bob Dole's presidential ambitions in the 1988 New Hampshire primary—calling Dole "Senator Straddle." Now he needed Dole. Dole was the lead negotiator required to bring in his forty-five Republican Senate colleagues, work out a plan with Senate Finance Committee Chairman Lloyd Bentsen, a Texas Democrat, and fence with House Republicans still wedded to the no-taxes pledge. He also had to work with White House Budget Director Richard Darman and Chief of Staff John Sununu, who got the straddle advertisement on the air the final weekend in 1988 before the New Hampshire primary.

The negotiators haggled for weeks around conference tables at Andrews Officer's Club. By mid-September leaks about the negotiations flowed from Andrews. "Dole was furious about it," Riker said, and Dole on the Senate floor complained about "all the garbage." The group abandoned Andrews, returning to Capitol Hill. Shortly thereafter Dole offered two ideas to break an impasse. He first suggested raising income taxes on the wealthy, and the White House hastily shot that down. Next, he offered a double-play strategy in which two bills would be voted on one after another, the strategy he used in 1986 to link sanctions against South Africa with continuing military aid for Nicaraguan contra rebels. This time he proposed voting first on a bill with spending cuts and tax hikes—sort of a Democratic package—then on one containing the administration's cherished capital-gains tax cut and extension of tax breaks—a Bush package. If the first passed and the second failed, the first would be nullified. That plan fell apart. Dole was fighting in the trenches, balancing between his colleagues and his president.

"Some of my colleagues say: Why are you up there doing this? You ought to be out there with us—no new taxes," Dole told the New York Times in late October after Bush signed emergency orders temporarily extending government spending. "But I'm the leader, I'm the Republican leader. I'm not Newt Dole, you know," he said, a poke at Newt Gingrich the House Republican and anti-tax hard-liner.

"The frustrating thing for Dole was to try to get the administration to sort out where they were," said Sheila Burke, Dole's chief of staff, who had been at Andrews with him. "He tried as best he could to represent them as well as his colleagues in the Senate. The Democrats were insistent that they wanted to speak with the president and didn't want to have to deal with substitutes. It was difficult to try and get a clear message." She said the negotiations offered a view of Dole's fundamental legislative style. "It is to keep trying to reach some consensus by looking at different alternatives rather than locking themselves into one position. In that sense he's a classic legislator. He views his responsibility as getting to the end of the process, developing a consensus, so he's always got the view: Well, let's try one more idea before we give it up. A never-say-die attitude."

Finally, after Bush had signed emergency measures to keep the government running, in late October the negotiators pounded out a $495 billion deficit-reduction bill that was steaming toward passage by Congress. On October 27 Dole stood on the Senate floor, praising members of the president's team with whom he had worked, beginning with Nicholas Brady, secretary of the treasury, then John Sununu.

"And the president's Chief of Chaff—Staff—John," Dole said, according to the Kansas City *Star* in an apparent slip, but then continued with a chuckle while Sununu looked down from the visitor's gallery. "Chaff might have been right, John. Chief of Staff, John Sununu." And he continued on, heaping praise on Bush and others. Afterward, Dole corrected the Congressional Record record to say only chief of staff.

14

HEAVY BUCKETS

Hɪsᴛᴏʀʏ, ᴏғ ᴄᴏᴜʀsᴇ, is never neat. President Bush might have poured his full energies into resolving the budget turmoil in the fall of 1990 were not his thoughts pulled away to a small country in the Middle East. On August 2, Iraqi dictator Saddam Hussein invaded his neighbor Kuwait with 100,000 Iraqi troops, providing Bush a convenient diversion into his area of expertise—foreign policy. Yet at first the takeover of the oil-rich sheikdom looked like a messy international incident perhaps exacerbated by mixed-up American foreign policy messages.

Throughout 1990 Saddam, believed to control the world's fourth largest army, threatened to burn Israel to the ground and had intimidated his neighbors—Iran, Kuwait and Saudi Arabia. Earlier, in the 1980s, Saddam had fought a brutal war against Iran, using chemical weapons against Iranians and on rebel Kurds in his own country. Rather than drive him into isolation, the Bush administration followed former President Nixon's strategy with China in the early 1970s and attempted to draw Saddam into discussions through conciliatory gestures. Among the messengers was Senate Republican Leader Bob Dole.

In early April 1990 he led a group of senators to meet officials in various Middle East nations. On April 12 Dole and Senators James McClure, an Idaho Republican; Howard Metzenbaum, an Ohio Democrat; Alan Simpson, Wyoming Republican and Senate Republican whip; and Frank Murkowski, an Alaska Republican, flew into Baghdad. Iraqi military officials escorted them to a Boeing 727 for a flight to the northern city of Mosul, where eventually they came face-to-face with the Iraqi leader.

Dole presented Saddam with a letter signed by the five senators, which Saddam proceeded to read. "Just as President Bush said yesterday in his telephone conversation with us, we want to improve our relations with your country and your government," Dole said in his opening remarks, according to a transcript released in September by the Iraqi embassy, which the senators said was accurate but incomplete. Saddam responded in a long monologue that ended: "We know that an all-out campaign is being waged against us in America and in the countries of Europe." Dole told Saddam that a person at the Voice of America who had editorialized against Saddam had been fired because his views did not represent those of the American government. That turned out to be untrue, though Dole was unaware of it at the time.

Dole observed that he had read Saddam was developing a virus for warfare to wipe out entire cities. "Are you developing this virus, these biological weapons?" he asked.

"Do the Americans possess biological weapons or not? Does Israel possess biological weapons or not?" Saddam answered.

"Not in the U.S." said Dole. "Biological weapons have been banned in the U.S. since the Nixon administration."

The group talked about weaponry in the Middle East. Soon Simpson spoke up. "I believe your problems lie with the western media and not with the U.S. government," the Wyoming senator said. "As long as you are isolated from the media, the press—and it is a haughty and pampered press—they all consider themselves political geniuses. That is, the journalists do. They are very cynical. What I advise is that you invite them to come here and see for themselves."

Saddam admitted, even for him, the media could at times be "a headache."

"In the U.S. they view me as a stubborn man," Dole soon said. "President Bush has been trying to build a kinder, gentler America. I want a stronger, tougher America."

Saddam said, "In this regard we lean towards President Bush."

"I am not speaking about myself, Mr. President," Dole said a moment later. "I hesitate to do that because I lost the use of my right arm forty years ago because of the war. That reminds me daily that we must all work for peace."

Simpson said Saddam sat riveted as Dole gestured to his right arm. The group broke up on a businesslike note without any concrete pledges. When the transcript was released in September, newspaper columnists and television commentators jeered Simpson for offering public-relations advice to Saddam. Simpson said in an interview: "I did use those words, that's true. I wanted to tell him, 'Well, if you have nothing to hide, let them in.'"

In late July, as Iraqi forces were mobilizing to move into Kuwait, April Glaspie, the U.S. ambassador to Kuwait, met with Saddam and warned him against invading Kuwait, while also suggesting that the Bush administration hoped to keep diplomatic channels open and had no opinion of regional disputes. Saddam annexed Kuwait three days later.

Beginning in late August, President Bush dispatched thousands of American troops and tons of tanks, anti-aircraft guns, helicopters, fighter jets and bombers to military fortifications established in the desert of Saudi Arabia, the beginning of Operation Desert Shield. Saddam ignored the sabre rattling. Meanwhile, Bush and Secretary of State James Baker III were building international support to kick out Saddam if he wouldn't voluntarily abandon Kuwait. On recommendations from his military advisers, Bush in November doubled the size of U.S. forces in the gulf region to nearly 500,000 American soldiers despite divided public opinion on U.S. participation in a war.

General Colin Powell, chairman of the Joint Chiefs of Staff, was one who often briefed Dole during the Reagan and Bush administrations on military and national security matters, including the invasion of Panama, funding for the Nicaraguan contras and the buildup of Desert Shield. "He and I consider ourselves good friends," Powell said. "He has a great sense of humor and sometimes it has a certain bite to it. Even in the most serious of discussions, he never became overly intense or so wrapped up that the tension level rose. He'd always break the tension with a bon mot or a cute expression or a joke. I was never reluctant to go see Dole or worried he would not be in a mode to work on a problem, solve a problem."

BOTH BOB AND Elizabeth Dole flew to Saudi Arabia to visit with soldiers from the First Infantry Division, the "Big Red One," deployed from Fort Riley, Kansas. Sensing abiding public ambivalence after his return, Dole was among the first to propose that Bush seek congressional approval if he decided to go to war. Dole had lived through the bickering in Congress over Vietnam, the demonstrations, the daily body counts; he wanted Congress to be on board, so if a war did not go well Bush could point to Congress' endorsement. Working through the United Nations, Bush and Baker persuaded the U.N. Security Council to vote to deliver an ultimatum to Saddam: leave Kuwait by January 15, or risk war.

In the days leading up to the deadline in January, Congress debated and voted on two resolutions. One, proposed by House Majority Leader Richard A. Gephardt of Missouri, demanded that Bush allow economic sanctions longer time to constrict Iraq. "The only debate here in the Congress is over whether we slowly strangle Saddam with sanctions or immediately pursue a military solution. We say we can win without a war," said Gephardt during the House debate.

The other, proposed by Senate Republican Leader Bob Dole, supported Bush if he chose to lead America into war. "Sanctions without a credible military threat would never have a severe impact on Iraq or Saddam Hussein," Dole said on the floor just before the final votes. "What we are attempting to do is to strengthen [Bush's] hand for peace, not to give him a license to see how fast we can become engaged in armed conflict."

Senate Majority Leader George Mitchell, who advocated Gephardt's theme in the Senate, has said, "For myself, there really wasn't any disagreement over the objective. It was just how to get there. I felt that tight economic sanctions had not been given a chance to work and they should be before military action was undertaken. I was not opposed to military action, just at that time."

Debating into the weekend, the Senate defeated the sanctions 46-35, then on Saturday, January 12, the Senate threw its support to Bush by a narrow margin, 52-47. The House followed, 250-183. After the vote, Dole summoned the Iraqi ambassador to the United States into his office with Simpson and other Republicans. This time the tone was unmistakably hostile. "We told him, 'You're doing this to yourself, fella,'" said Simpson. "'This is about naked aggression and you're going to get it in your ear.' He was furious."

In drawing senators together to support the president, James Baker said of Dole: "We had something like thirty-plus countries supporting the president. It was important that we have the United States Senate supporting him if he was going to take the country into war, so it was a critical vote. We had the resolution from the United Nations, we had authority constitutionally to go. We thought we had the authority, but we wanted the political support. And it was extraordinarily helpful to get it."

Dole himself said in an interview, "I felt we had to roll the dice. I've often wondered what Bush would have done if he'd lost. We had eleven Democrats help us out. And Saddam Hussein helped us out, too."

The afternoon of January 16, the flow of official telephone calls into Dole's Capitol office increased. Late afternoon, reporters began calling Dole's press secretary, Walt Riker, saying they had heard rumors war would start that night. The networks began calling more frequently. Suddenly, a batch of officials trooped through Riker's press office into Dole's inner office: Robert Michael, the House Minority Leader; George Mitchell, the Senate leader; some National Security Council staff and Central Intelligence Agency Chief Robert Gates. Riker's phone rang. It was ABC.

"They knew it. They said, 'Planes are in the air,' " Riker said. "I hadn't heard anything official so I couldn't tell them anything. It was really chilling: I heard the locks on Dole's office click shut. I'd never heard that before. They were locked from the inside."

The group in Dole's office stayed half an hour, then Dole emerged. "His face was red and somber, almost watery-eyed," Riker said. "I told him, 'We're getting all these rumors something's going on.' "

"Nothin' yet," Dole declared.

Dole returned to his office, shut the door. Moments later, Riker's phone rang.

"Hey," it was Dole speaking quietly, "you'd better hang around tonight."

Riker thought, "We're going to go to war."

"Obviously, it affected him having been in a war," he said of Dole. "He understood the gravity of it, because young men were going to die."

Before President Bush went on the air at 9 P.M., Simpson wandered into Dole's office. He, Dole and staffers watched Bush's news conference, the affirmation that the United States was at war to liberate Kuwait. Riker dispatched a statement from Dole: America was united to repel Saddam Hussein. "The cause of this war is Iraqi aggression, not American determination."

During the night, Dole took and made telephone calls and he kept asking about CNN's anchor Bernard Shaw, crouched in a Baghdad hotel with CNN reporters Peter Arnett and John Holiman, providing unnerving eyewitness accounts of the unfolding air bombardment. Dole liked and respected Shaw, he worried about him.

Forty-five days later, having crushed the once-vaunted Iraqi military threat and chased it out of Kuwait, President Bush ceased the American assault and stopped the war, triggering an outpouring of goodwill from Americans upon the nation's military forces. The victory seemed to lay to rest two decades of psychic turmoil from Vietnam. The cottage industry of armchair generals and military experts that had sprung up during the war questioned whether Bush had halted the war too soon, whether he should have ordered American troops into Baghdad to capture and eliminate the Iraqi dictator. But overall, despite the deaths of 244 Allied troops, among them 146 Americans, of which as many as 30 percent may have died in friendly fire, the war was considered a success. Bush's popularity-poll numbers soared off the charts.

"In Desert Storm, Bob was particularly effective," Bush wrote in a letter to the author. "His own combat experience helped him understand the stakes. He read his colleagues like a book, informing me where work needed to be done to get certain key senators on board. Desert Storm went so well that many now forget the run-up, with the claims of 50,000 body bags, the dire warnings from certain senators that we would have the blood of innocents on our hands, etc. Senator Dole was strong, knowing that we could not compromise with the evil of Saddam. He was not eager to go to war, but who was?"

Mitchell called the military engagement a qualified success. "The result was successful, in that Iraq was expelled from Kuwait," he said. "It was unsuccessful in that Saddam Hussein is still there, still oppressing the people of Iraq and still threatening the region."

Dole could not help firing a partisan shot of his own in a March 13, 1991, op-ed article for the *Wall Street Journal*. "As a proud America welcomes home its Desert Storm heroes, it is sobering to realize that a shift of only three votes nine weeks ago could have turned this smashing victory into a catastrophe," Dole wrote. "We now know—categorically—that sanctions were a losing game, despite the passionate claims of the opposition . . . Let's face it., Desert Storm's defeat in the U.S. Senate would have been one of history's most serious blows against a president in a crisis."

The article included sixteen statements from opposing Democrats culled from the Senate floor debate before the war-authorization vote: "We are going to make a tremendous blunder." . . . "The rush to combat is now tragically shortsighted." . . . "The administration is making a great mistake." And so on. Dole declined to attach names to the statements, assuming the American people would make the connection.

"Many pundits are predicting that 1992 will be the next test of accountability, that essence of Democracy," Dole continued. "Our votes on the domestic agenda will no doubt be part of that test. Like it or not, so will our votes for, or against, Desert Storm."

The *Journal* the following day identified the names of those whose statements Dole had cited. Dole was partially right. Bush's success in Desert Storm frightened away the Democratic party's top tier of possible presidential contenders—House Majority Leader Richard Gephardt and Senator Al Gore of Tennessee—but unfortunately for Bush and Dole, by the time Arkansas Governor Bill Clinton achieved the Democratic nomination in July of 1992, Desert Storm, politically, was little more than a hazy memory.

THAT SPRING DOLE'S attention swung toward the Soviet Union. He had visited Moscow the year before, meeting with President Mikhail Gorbachev and Boris Yeltsin, who soon became the democratically elected leader of the Russian Republic, the first of the Soviet republics to splinter. After his trip Dole had urged the Bush administration to initiate more U.S. contacts directly with the Soviet republics and democratic reformers such as Yeltsin.

Dole and Senate Majority Leader George Mitchell invited Yeltsin to come to the United States, drawing an initial cool response from the president, who later agreed his administration would receive Yeltsin. In mid-June, a Soviet airliner touched down at Andrews Air Force Base. As Yeltsin stepped from the plane he was greeted by Bob Dole, the only member of Congress on hand; the White House had sent a low-ranking State Department official. The political implications of welcoming a possible challenger to Gorbachev were seen as a problem to Democrats on the Hill and to the Bush administration. So was Yeltsin's reputation. The year before, he had visited Washington and apparently had such a good time the Washington *Post* Style section portrayed him as a well-lubricated, carousing buffoon. Dole looked beyond caricature.

The following day Dole held a photo-op in his Senate office for Yeltsin, presenting him with a white straw cowboy hat, bandolero-style, from Shepler's, a western outfitter in Wichita, Kansas. "It's for big people," Dole said, "and for great leaders." Obliging, Yeltsin smiled widely and stuck it on his head. Dole handed him a "top grain, saddle leather, hand-laced" Western belt, waist forty-four inches, with an oval belt buckle bearing the Kansas state seal. The name stenciled into the back of the belt: "BORIS." Yeltsin wrapped it around his waist and beamed.

Reporters asked Yeltsin with whom the United States should deal, him or Gorbachev. "With both," Yeltsin replied through a translator. Two months later, in August, a defiant Yeltsin stood on a tank near Russia's

White House to help unite Russians in blocking a coup attempt against Gorbachev, an event carried live worldwide on Cable News Network.

ANOTHER SORT OF war erupted in the fall of 1991, in the heart of the United States Senate. The battle began over confirmation hearings of Clarence Thomas, a black former head of the federal Equal Employment Opportunity Commission and President Bush's nominee to replace retired Supreme Court Justice Thurgood Marshall. In September the Senate Judiciary Committee asked aggressive questions about Thomas' views. Then the hearings became an international news event in October as Anita Hill, a black Oklahoma University law professor who had worked with Thomas at the Department of Education in the early 1980s, alleged Thomas had sexually harassed her by making suggestive comments about pubic hair on his Coke can and requests for dates, which she had turned aside. Hill's cool testimony inflamed many women across America. The issue of sexual harassment became a cause celebre. Thomas held his ground, angrily denying he had made any unwanted advances toward Hill, ridiculing the Judiciary Committee's hearings as a "high-tech lynching."

When America got a hard look at the Judiciary Committee, it saw a row of awkward white men, Republicans on one side bitterly complaining about unknown committee staffers leaking FBI files and repugnant allegations, Democrats on the other drawing out details of the alleged harassment and probing for psychological motivations.

Behind the scenes, Dole coordinated the Republican senators' strategy with Missouri Republican Senator Jack Danforth, Thomas' former employer, who was indignant over the slanders aimed at his onetime protégé. "Jack Danforth was obviously somebody who was committed to Thomas and had been engaged in talking to members individually," Dole's chief of staff Sheila Burke said. "I think Dole wanted to be as supportive and as positive as he could. He met with members and helped them talk through strategy. So it really was as a leader, in the sense of gathering his people together, helping to design a strategy with the kind of tack they might take in terms of questions."

The hearings ran through a Saturday and Sunday, broadcast live on CNN and in long time blocks on the other television networks. Just before the vote the following week, Dole said on the Senate floor, "I think we ought to give the benefit of the doubt to the nominee, Clarence Thomas, who for 107 days has been hanging out there, twisting in the wind while every effort conceivable, every effort ever known to man was used to discredit him and defeat his nomination. He has withstood the test. He is a stronger person because of it." Thomas was confirmed on a narrow vote of 52 to 48 in the full Senate.

A WEEK LATER the Bush administration signaled that it wanted to move forward a civil rights bill that had been bottled up all year, a move interpreted by congressional Republicans as a commitment to improve civil rights protections without mandating quotas of minorities in the workplace. Democrats perceived Bush as trying to take advantage of some goodwill from black Americans outraged over the Thomas hearings. White House counsel Boyden Gray and Senate Republican leaders gathered around a conference table in Dole's office, arguing over language, thumbing through dictionaries and thesauruses to find acceptable terminology. In a kind of tag team exercise, Dole offered compromises to Danforth, the bill's chief sponsor, who would leave the room to confer with Democratic Senator Edward M. Kennedy, and then return. The tactic eventually resulted in passage of the civil rights bill in late October. Democrats gloated that the White House compromised; Republicans countered that Democrats had given the most ground. Either way, Dole served as the conduit through which a deal was struck advancing civil rights protections in the workplace.

DURING 1991, DOLE settled into what was as close to a routine as he ever got. On weekends and recesses, he flew out of town on borrowed corporate jets to fund-raisers for Republican candidates or to promote Campaign America. During the week he worked his Republican colleagues to counter or cooperate with Democrats, depending on the issue. He sent out almost daily statements from his press office on education, jobs, unemployment benefits, arms control, foreign policy and impending Kansas issues such as rural hospitals, agriculture, improvements at military bases.

All the while, debate on the Senate floor thrummed on. When Democrats criticized too sharply, Dole dropped what he was doing to respond. "It was a time when he believed he had to go out and match whatever the Democrats were saying," said Riker. "It was putting the gloves on and getting into the arena. Where every day the Democrats would be teeing off on Thomas or Bush or whatever, Dole would have to go out there and somehow mute it or balance it. Dole would go out and defend the president, or get other senators to defend the president."

Every Tuesday, Republicans and Democrats retired to closed-door policy luncheons to discuss upcoming legislation and plan strategy. Leading Republicans, Dole usually opened with a general statement, then called up various senators who were leaders on different issues to give status reports. The discussions could be spirited. They certainly were one day.

Dole found out that a band of conservative senators were meeting at the White House with Chief of Staff John Sununu, seemingly behind the Senate Republican leader's back. "He brought it up at a meeting, to get it out in the open," Riker said. "Some of the more conservative senators stood up and denied there was anything sinister behind it. And then Dole said, 'If you want to elect a new leader, we'll have that vote right now.' Dole was serious. It froze everybody in their tracks. It was dramatic because it came out of nowhere. It made it clear who was the real leader and what his mission was: Bob Dole was the one to work with the White House and help shape its agenda. These were big stakes, and we couldn't have a fractured party."

The meeting eventually cooled down and broke up. As people left the room, Dole walked up to Senator Malcolm Wallop, a conservative Wyoming Republican suspected of heading off the reservation. Dole spoke face-to-face with him, making an amiable comment to defuse tensions.

Dole's determined style prompted comparisons with Lyndon Johnson, perhaps the most aggressive Senate leader of this century, and Howard Baker, Dole's predecessor as Republican leader. But when Johnson was the Senate Majority leader from 1959 to 1961 he had a balance of 65 Democrats to 35 Republicans, wide latitude to lose members and still win passage of his agenda against Republican President Dwight Eisenhower. In 1980, Howard Baker arrived as Senate majority leader, heading 53 Republicans to 47 Democrats, and steered them with President Reagan's mandate to impose limited government. As minority leader in the 1990s, Dole had only 43 Republicans to support Bush and a generally less unified Republican party. Dole needed every single Republican body, and resorted to firm persuasion to hold them together. He did not endear himself to his cross-generational opponent, Republican Newt Gingrich.

In a December 1, 1991 appearance on NBC's "Meet the Press," the House Republican whip said, "I love Ronald Reagan . . . he was a great man that changed America," then complained that Dole was among a group of "pre-Reagan Republicans," implying Dole was an old-fashioned throwback.

Dole soldiered on for Bush. He actually managed to say a few nice things when Sununu was forced to resign in December of 1991 after months of revelations about his frequent use of government airplanes and chauffeur-driven cars for personal business, to go the dentist, for skiing, to attend a stamp collection meeting. Perhaps his personal view of the man showed through a joke Dole often told in 1991 about meeting Sununu at the White House: "I knew he was in trouble when we met and he asked if I had the seat in the upright position and the tray table locked."

But Dole's professional relationship with Bush was sound and generally closer than the one he had with Reagan. "I could sit and talk with Bush and it wasn't any strain on either of us. I think he respected my views sometimes," Dole said. "With Reagan, I had a good relationship with him, but it was different. He wasn't tuned in to all these little details. That was fine. He said he was only going to be here eight years. Why should he learn all that stuff or learn everybody's names? 'They knew their name, why should I learn their name?' That was his attitude."

Dole was not one to call presidents, he did not want to bother them. During Reagan's eight years he spoke privately with Reagan on the telephone fewer than ten times. Bush, in contrast, telephoned often. Once in the fall of 1991, when Dole was at the White House, Dole mumbled something about possibly not running for reelection in 1992.

"Come on back in the back room a minute," Bush said, leading Dole into a private room and turning to face him.

"You've got to run again," Bush said. "I really need your help."

"Well, I like what I'm doing," Dole said, "but, like everybody else, you think, maybe this is the time to leave."

Dole quietly bounced his future off friends and family. His daughter, Robin, told him not to make up his mind based on what others thought he should do; he should do what was right for him. David Keene, the political consultant who linked up with Dole in 1978, offered his frank opinion: "You don't have anything to prove to anyone," Keene said. "You can quit. But you'll die."

In the summer of 1991 Dole noticed he was getting up more frequently at night. He had an annual medical exam in July and had a PSA blood test done to check for prostate cancer, for prostate specific antigen. Bad news, the results showed an elevated level, strongly suggestive of the disease. He had a follow-up blood test a month later, with similar results, and a biopsy that confirmed it: Bob Dole had cancer. He dove into research about the disease and options for treatment, radiation or surgery. He found that prostate cancer, a disease of men over age forty, strikes 110,000 men each year and kills 34,000 a year; it is the second leading cause of death in men behind lung cancer.

That fall he flew out to Kansas for political visits and stopped in his home town of Russell. Sisters Gloria and Norma Jean, his brother Kenny and Kenny's wife Anita gathered at one end of the dining room table in his parents' house, which he and his daughter Robin had bought after his mother's death. Bob sat at the other end.

"Well, I'm going to have surgery," Dole told them, and choked up. The family worried about the news and tried to comfort Dole.

"It was a scary time," Robin recalled.

With no previous hint to the public, Walt Riker sent out a press release on December 17 announcing Dole would undergo surgery the next morning to remove his prostate. Bob and Elizabeth drove that morning to Walter Reed Army Medical Center in Washington and Bob underwent a three-hour radical prostatectomy, a common but far from simple procedure. Typically, patients receive a spinal or epidural anesthetic, a catheter is installed, then the surgeon makes a twelve-inch incision from the belly button downward. Working inward, the surgeon maneuvers around to remove the prostate gland, checks for spreading cancer, and sews the patient back up. In Dole's case, the surgery apparently got all of his cancer.

The operation usually zaps even younger men's strength for weeks. On January 3, the first day the Senate came into session in 1992, 16 days after his surgery, with a catheter still attached underneath his clothes, Bob Dole returned to the Senate floor. His responsibility that day: to welcome a new senator, Pennsylvania Democrat Harris Wofford, who had defeated Dole's choice, Republican Richard Thornburgh, President Bush's attorney general.

"I must confess I was surprised to see him elected," Dole observed of Wofford. "But I also remember what he said to me after the election. He said now we will have time to become acquainted and work together. I certainly accept that in the spirit in which it was conveyed to me by the junior senator from Pennsylvania."

Encountered two weeks later in his office, Dole was suited up for battle. Just back from Florida, he had the tan, the quip, about 85 percent of the attitude. He was happy no further treatment was recommended by his physicians. "I feel pretty good, except that it's going to take a couple of months to recover," Dole said. "I'm not going to push myself. No early meetings, no late nights, sort of a daylight warrior for a while." Dole's doctors had told him that one in ten men develops prostate cancer.

"So"—his eyebrows lifted with a grin—"I figure I saved nine other guys."

On January 24, Dole flew out to Kansas to hold a press conference in

Topeka, coinciding with an annual GOP state convention. He was up for reelection in 1992 and had caused worry among Kansas Republicans and Democrats by putting off a decision. Republicans needed time to rally behind a successor, if there was to be one; Democrats hoped Representative Dan Glickman, a popular Wichita Democrat and the only politician thought to have a chance against Dole, would run.

Dole walked into a conference room at the Ramada Inn, a weathered hotel not far from the state capital. One hundred people crammed into the room, more than a dozen reporters, Dole backers and GOP faithful. Dole stepped up to a podium and stood there, a ready look on his face. John Petterson, a veteran Kansas reporter, finally spoke up: "Well, are you going to run?"

"Yes," Dole said.

Applause! The Dole backers clapped in relief. That was it. Shortest announcement speech in Kansas political history. Sure, he answered questions for a while, but he offered no platitudes. His cancer was beaten, that's what had held up the announcement. Of course he would run again. Elizabeth was the only one who knew in advance; he had told her at 9:30 that morning on the way to the airport in Washington. When he strolled back into his Capitol office in Washington a few days later he was greeted by a four-foot-square placard with one word in big letters: YES.

That spring and summer Dole became, in his own words, the "prostate poster boy." In public appearances he urged men to get tested for prostate cancer, granted television, newspaper and magazine interviews to talk about the disease, and sent personal letters to those who wrote to him about it.

"He felt almost a *compulsion* to let people know that this cancer can be cured," Elizabeth Dole said. "The thing that surprised me about that is, he is a private person, and he just spoke out immediately and forthrightly about a very private matter. I remember reading a People magazine article [focusing on his crusade about the disease] and I thought, This is great! He spoke out about his own situation. I think he takes his opportunity to influence public policy very seriously." That August, Dole set up a blood test booth at the Republican National Convention in Houston, one of the event's few bright spots.

Dole's bout with cancer may have delayed the formal announcement, but he had not neglected the real heavy lifting needed to get elected in the 1990s. His Senate campaign fund, fattened by high-dollar Washington fund-raisers and hundreds of small donations, had more than $2 million in cash on hand. Over the previous two years, he had used his influence with the Bush administration to fly a squadron of dignitaries into Kansas. Elizabeth Dole, in her capacity as president of the American Red Cross, the commander of the Strategic Air Command, the Air Force secretary and chief of staff, the Army chief of staff, the head of the Federal Emergency Management Agency, the Agriculture secretary, the NASA administrator, Kuwait's ambassador to the United States, Boris Yeltsin and even former President Richard Nixon dropped into Kansas through mid-1992 to bolster Dole's image as a politician who could get things done.

In another high-profile way Bob Dole had exercised his influence to reach the hearts of some Kansans with help from his colleague, Senator Robert C. Byrd. One day in 1990 the West Virginia Democrat walked up to Dole and said, "Bob, you don't do enough for your state." It was not an idle bit of chitchat. Byrd had given up his Senate leadership post to head the Senate Appropriations Committee, the money-dispensing committee in 1989, with the promise to West Virginians he would steer $1 billion of federal money home. Byrd's diligent work in the vineyards would earn him a rising crescendo of dubious accolades—the prince of pork, the king of pork, finally the "Pope of Pork," for carving four-lane highways where rugged country lanes existed before, for sprinkling research grants upon unglamorous colleges, for in effect hijacking hundreds of federal employees and ancillary government agencies with them. Byrd ruled who among the Appropriations Committee's twenty-nine Senate members—and special others—would receive goodies earmarked in spending bills specifically for their states.

Acting on Byrd's advice, Dole redoubled his decade-long efforts to bring federal projects and dollars to Kansas. In 1991, he steered $107 million in appropriations to various projects, and secured another $800 million-plus in defense spending at the state's military bases. The following year he won hundreds of millions more in earmarked spending. Over a period of years he secured money for four buildings on state college campuses, two of them named for him. Millions of dollars of highway money, some of which the state had not requested, flowed into Kansas. Dole tried to get Wilson Lake, a large man-made Army Corps of Engineers reservoir near Russell, declared a national recreation area by the National Park Service. When the park service opposed the idea, Dole got an appropriation of $900,000 to spruce up the lake with a new boat ramp, picnic and camping facilities.

Wasn't it Dole who so assiduously fought the federal deficit in the 1980s? Democrat Gloria O'Dell, a woman of little political experience persuaded to challenge Dole in the 1992 race, made that point, without inflaming most Kansans.

"I hope we're not greedy or hogs, but I don't think we get more than our fair share," Dole said in early 1992. "My view is, I'll be willing to vote to freeze all programs, all projects, everything, as long as it applies to every state."

"He is not one of the big pork-barrel spenders," admitted Margaret Hill, a spokeswoman for Citizens Against Government Waste, a watchdog group in Washington, a feeling echoed by an appropriations committee staffer who said, "Bob Dole does it with humor, thoroughness and circumspection. It's not gimme, gimme, gimme. It's I want this and see what you can do."

The committee found a way the following year to send several hundred million more dollars to Kansas. Slipped into one bill was a special appropriation of $1.4 million to develop an industrial park in Russell, Dole's home town.

In early 1992 Dole gained a measure of notoriety in a book, *The Best Congress Money Can Buy,* by Phil Stern, who laid out a case study of Dole's work on behalf of the E. & J. Gallo Winery. Gallo family members over the previous three years had given $97,000 to Dole's Senate reelection committee and to Campaign America, his political action committee. Dole worked to protect Gallo's business with a tax break. At least that was the book's interpretation.

ARKANSAS GOVERNOR BILL CLINTON, survivor of months of inquiry into his personal affairs and stiff battles with other Democrats, won the presidential nomination at the Democratic National Convention in July, 1992. Clinton and Tennessee Senator Al Gore rolled out of the convention on a cross-country bus tour that attracted favorable news coverage and a noticeable surge in Clinton's polls. And the nation waited as the Bush camp crouched, planning who-knew-what strategy for the mid-August Republican National Convention in Houston. Nervous about the Clinton-Gore media phenomena, Dole dove in, just as he had done as a vice-presidential nominee in 1976. In late July he called Clinton "disingenuous" about his Vietnam military draft record, accused Gore of shopping his Gulf war vote around for a prime-time spot on television in January 1991, and sardonically noted Gore at least had been to Vietnam—as a journalist. He didn't have to remind anyone he, Bob Dole, had been gravely wounded in real battle and that George Bush had been shot down over the Pacific in a real dogfight. Clinton and Gore projected themselves as moderates, products of the Democratic centrist movement that arose in the 1980s. Dole countered on the Senate floor that they "have already proved their first-class liberal credentials."

The Clinton-Gore war room fought back. Politics in the 1990s had become a lightning-fast exchange of vitriol. "Bob Dole is a very straight-forward, snarling attack dog when he wants to be," Clinton's press secretary Dee Dee Myers said in late July. "That was the role he played when campaigning in 1988 *against* George Bush and now it's a role he's playing *for* George Bush in 1992."

Gore's Press Secretary Marla Romash echoed: "Bob Dole has descended into personal insults and blatant falsehoods because he doesn't want to face the truth of George Bush's record or his own record of coddling Saddam Hussein and leading America to a war it would not have had to fight if it wasn't for their mistakes."

It was a sour autumn. The Republican National Convention projected an image of intolerance. Engaged too late, the Bush campaign foundered with the ailing American economy. Ross Perot, a Texas billionaire who had challenged both Bush and Clinton earlier in the year, then dropped out, rejoined the presidential campaign in the fall as a third party candidate. Even when Bush's people had given up on Perot, Bob Dole served as an intermediary, trying to draw Perot in. But Perot's candidacy would help cripple Bush. Far-right conservatives considered abandoning Bush. Bob Dole campaigned for and defended Bush to the end.

"You have to carry some pretty heavy buckets," Dole joked in the fall. "Sometimes you don't want to even pick up the buckets."

Marlin Fitzwater, who returned to work for Bush as his press secretary on the day Bush was inaugurated in 1989, said the relationships between Bush and Dole changed over the four years. "The staffs for the men, our staff and Dole's, were pretty much estranged at that point," Fitzwater said of the first days. "But by the end of the administration that had reversed entirely. In fact, I suspect if President Bush were forced to identify the single most loyal person in his mind it would have been Bob Dole. He told me many times how much he appreciated Dole's support and how surprised he was that Dole never deserted him, when others had, particularly people like Kemp and Gingrich, Buchanan, Bill Bennett, who were running for cover on one issue or another. The president always felt Dole played straight with him, in the sense of saying the same things privately that he said publicly. That was one of the most frustrating things President Bush always felt . . . that many political allies would voice public support and tell the press privately, 'Well, I really thought that was a dumb idea.' There were few instances of that with Dole, or at least he was clever enough so that there never were any fingerprints.

"At the end, it was just so ironic," Fitzwater added with surprise, "in the last six to eight months of the presidency, and even during the campaign, President Bush often felt Bob Dole was really one of the few people he could turn to, who would not waver and who had stuck with him."

THE CHAPERONE

Election night, november 3, 1992, Governor Bill Clinton had won the presidency on a theme of "Don't Stop Thinking About Tomorrow," a popular song that spoke to Clinton's campaign of youth and change. The Arkansas Democrat shoved aside Republican George Bush with no small help from cantankerous Ross Perot, who attracted 19 percent of the vote as an independent candidate. Ending a twelve-year reign, Republicans were banished from the White House, from the leadership of all government agencies, from dominating the nation's domestic and foreign agenda. Democrats owned all—the House, the Senate, the White House. Even a couple of older liberal Supreme Court justices were known to be teetering on retirement. It was a bleak night in the land of the Big Elephants. Republicans gritted their teeth and the hot lights of national network television clicked on. There, blinking into the camera, with a somber gaze, was Senate Republican Leader Bob Dole.

"We've seen the last two years the Democrats beat up on George Bush almost daily," Dole declared to CBS anchorman Dan Rather, "and I think my responsibility as the Republican leader will be to unite the Republicans, the independents, the Perot supporters, because Bill Clinton's not going to have a mandate. We won't probably win, because we won't have the numbers, but maybe we can frustrate some of his spending and taxing programs."

That night to NBC's Bryant Gumbel, Dole said: "They've got a big advantage now. They've got the whole enchilada. They can't say there is gridlock." And to ABC's David Brinkley Dole declared, "We'll make the best fight we can."

As the election approached, and Bush's defeat seemed likely, Bob Dole had viewed it as an opportunity that would not come again: the eyes of America would be on Bill Clinton, but also on him, the most prominent Republican left standing after the wipeout at the White House. Dole prepared to position himself to rally Republicans. He did not travel to Kansas the night he easily won a fifth six-year Senate term over Democrat Gloria O'Dell, a former state official. He remained in Washington; bigger fish to fry.

The day after the election Dole strolled into the Senate television press gallery for a news conference. In the 1980s he had been Senate majority and minority leader for Ronald Reagan and minority leader for George Bush. How would he play this new incarnation as minority leader of 43 Republicans facing a phalanx of Democrats that stretched from one end of Pennsylvania Avenue to the other?

"For all those folks who are handling the Bill Clinton mandate, 57 percent of the Americans who voted in the presidential election voted against Bill Clinton, and I intend to represent that majority on the floor of the U.S. Senate," Dole declared. "Obviously, we'll cooperate with the new administration if it advances the best interests of our nation. But we'll stand up against bad policy, we'll offer common-sense alternatives on the most important issues confronting America, whether it's health care, the deficit or jobs.

"So, I think he got some good news and some bad news last night— Governor Clinton," Dole continued. "The good news is that he's getting a honeymoon in Washington; the bad news is that Bob Dole is going to be his chaperone."

While other Republican leaders made customary conciliatory noises, Bob Dole's instantaneous call to arms had stirred his supporters and startled those who had voted for Clinton.

Over the next few days Dole joined House Minority Leader Robert Michel, an Illinois Republican less confrontational by temperament, to assert they would lead the "Loyal Opposition," meaning, in the best light, that they would help their party formulate alternative ideas to Clinton's agenda. Some Democrats and critics interpreted Dole's warnings as evidence Republicans would block the agenda of the first Democratic president, out of spite. The New York *Times* reprimanded Dole in an editorial titled, "The Politics of Rancor."

"There I was," Dole said in an interview, explaining his initial out front obstreperousness. "Well, I guess I thought the best man lost. And we didn't do very well in the Senate either. I still had the same hope that Bush had [to win]. And we'd been pretty much out there on the campaign too, with all of the Vietnam stuff. I'd been in Arkansas. They were pretty tough, too. They played hardball down there. I think a lot of it is disappointment, you know, you really get clobbered. I thought it was also time to establish myself as the leader. I think it was about 50-50. There weren't any heroes in the first few days."

On November 10 Dole convened Senate Republicans and members of Bush's cabinet at Washington's refurbished and gleaming Union Station for a tribute to the departing president.

"The good news is, Mr. President, your place in history is secure," Dole said as Bush sat nearby. "The liberals on Capitol Hill and their allies in the media will not admit it, but the American people know better, and so do we: George Bush helped change the world, and that's very important to all of us."

When Bush rose, defeat still etched in his face, he spoke with his singular style about his loss and the appreciation he felt toward Dole. "He never, ever put his own personal agenda ahead of the president's, and that's kinda the way it ought to work when you have the White House," Bush said, looking around the room. "And the propensity, the tendency when there's a defeat of this magnitude, of this hurtfulness and of this enormity, is to criticize. To find somebody to blame. Regrettably, some Republicans and many Democrats have fallen into this marvelous second-guessing trap, figuring it all out and analyzing to the detriment of somebody else, and tearing down somebody in order to ooooch yourself up a little with your wisdom. Not Senator Dole.

"From the minute the election results were in," Bush said, headed for the home stretch, "he has been courageous in standing up against the common wisdom, saying nice things about the president and Dan and Barbara and all of this. In addition, he's shown where the leadership really is now in this country in terms of party . . . I think people understand it, I think they respect the way he has assumed, without arrogance, without any kind of bitterness, a significant leadership role to hold our party together. The idea that this party has seen its demise, and I love these little analysts, these media that I tried to annoy and failed. To hear them analyze, you'd think history had been indelibly writ that the party is out of here. I don't believe it for one single minute. The thing I've admired about Bob is he's taken on this mantle of leadership that he has *earned* through his years as leader and said, Look, we're here to do battle. We're here to do what's right for the country, we're going to stand on principle when we think you're wrong. And that's exactly the way it should be."

Republicans did not launch immediate warfare against Clinton. Most of his first cabinet nominees sailed through in January, except the nomination for attorney general, Zoe Baird, who became ensnared in legal problems because she and her husband had failed to make social security payments for their nanny. Dole only grumbled that the family and medical leave bill, formerly vetoed by Bush, which Congress passed and Clinton signed in January 1993, was a costly mandate on small business.

Dole threw his first roadblock in late January when Clinton announced plans to lift immediately the ban on gays in the military, an issue that ignited a fierce controversy among veterans, gay Americans, the fervently religious and civil libertarians. On NBC's "Meet the Press" January 31 Dole professed wonder at Clinton's diversion from his campaign theme— "It's the economy, stupid," observing in quintessential Dolian fashion, perhaps it was because "We'd now have the Bush recovery in full steam."

Dole said that Clinton, a man who never served in the military, did not understand the close-quarters realities of military life, an unsubtle dig at Clinton's avoidance of the Vietnam war draft. Reporter Lisa Myers asked, "You have consistently voted against discrimination based on race, on age, and on disability. Why is it that you feel comfortable discriminating against gay people?"

"Well, I don't," Dole answered, adding he still opposed discrimination. "Serving is not a right, it's a privilege in the United States. And there are certain restrictions. It just seems to me we are spending too much time on an issue that could be delayed."

Faced with mixed-polls results, resistance from Senate Armed Services Chairman Sam Nunn, a Georgia Democrat, and other Democrats, Clinton backed off, pledging to lift the ban in six months, allowing for Congressional hearings and advice from military leaders on how to accomplish that goal.

In mid-February Clinton delivered a virtuoso performance unveiling his first budget proposal in a speech before Congress, carried live on national television. It was praised in the national media for style more than substance and criticized by Republicans as a return to Democratic tax-and-spend policies of the past.

Waiting in the wings, all wired up, was Bob Dole. To NBC's Tom Brokaw, Dole declared Clinton's plan was a "big, big, big tax increase. I want the president to do a good job. I want him to be successful, but I want him to do more on the spending side, more spending cuts."

Clinton's detailed budget released days later urged quick passage of a $16.3 billion emergency economic stimulus package. "Emergency" meant that it would be financed by deficit spending, by increasing the federal deficit. Dole reacted quickly.

"What do you want to do that for?" Dole demanded of Clinton in a telephone conversation soon after. "It's just adding to the deficit, we don't need it."

Clinton replied, "I've concluded we need this."

Dole was irked. "I think someone else convinced him he needed it," Dole said.

Republican senators sniffed around items in the bill, disputed ways of attacking it, debated alternatives, found no common ground. Then at a Republican caucus meeting in early April, Missouri Senator Jack Danforth stood up and told the group:

"This is just straight spending that will worsen the deficit. We can all agree that mindless spending is not the key to anything."

That was the hook that brought them together. Eyeing an emerging consensus, Dole persuaded all forty-two Republican colleagues to send Dole a spontaneous letter pledging to oppose any stimulus bill that also lacked deep spending cuts. For the next three weeks Dole pounded that theme nationally, filling up the airwaves, the fax machines and talk shows. His colleagues dug into Clinton's proposal and found that the emergency spending plan called for community development block grants that might go to build a warming hut at a skating rink, several pools and a ski lift, not exactly dire needs. Worthless pork barrel spending for mayors, many of whom were Democrats, they charged.

The White House counterattacked with a list of seemingly worthy projects in Republican senators' states that would be killed if the bill failed. On April 11 Bob Schieffer, the CBS "Face the Nation" host, asked Dole how he could vote against a bill that would provide $34 million for highways, $300,000 for Head Start for low-income children and $51 million for small business loans and grants. Dole responded with the basic Republican theme of opposition:

"Well, it's very easy," Dole said, "because you say, sure, if this comes up in a normal process where it's paid for, where it's offset with cuts somewhere else, then I would probably vote for most of it, maybe not all of it.

[But] I think most Kansans say cut spending first, and if you can't cut it, at least pay for it. That's the message from Americans across the country."

Republicans began a filibuster in early April. To end the filibuster, sixty votes were needed to pass cloture. Cloture would put the bill on the Senate floor for a vote, where passage seemed possible because Democrats held a fifty-seven seat majority to the Republicans forty-three. The Republican resolve held firm through four separate votes for cloture; the stimulus bill was going nowhere. On April 21 the Clinton administration abandoned the stimulus plan.

Republicans now saw they could legislate, when they chose, with a policy of opposition, or as opponents would say, obstruction. The victory came only days before Clinton marked his first one hundred days in office, a symbolic measure of presidents taken since Franklin Delano Roosevelt pushed through much of the New Deal architecture in his first one hundred days. Clinton learned Republicans in Washington weren't the "wandering beggars" he had steamrolled in Arkansas, said Wyoming's Alan Simpson, Dole's deputy on the Senate floor. So invigorated were Republicans that even Dole's old adversary offered praise.

"It's the best spring of Bob Dole's political career," House Minority whip Newt Gingrich told the Washington *Post*. "He has done an absolutely astonishing job."

Dole's win immediately prompted a surfeit of questions whether he might make a third presidential bid in 1996, and he did nothing to quash that line of inquiry. Asked if Clinton misjudged his pitch of the stimulus bill, White House political director Rahm Emmanuel told the Los Angeles *Times* in a story headlined "Bob Dole is Back on Top of the Hill": "Yeah, we made a miscalculation. Nobody knew Bob Dole was going to start running for President within the first hundred days."

Then something happened that made waves in Washington, a town of egos as inflated as its architecture and elaborate unwritten rules of deference. Clinton tried to get even. It became BOATGATE. In early May Clinton spoke at the White House Correspondents' Association dinner, where by custom speakers are supposed to make fun of their political foes. Clinton accused Dole of killing the stimulus bill even as he was seeking a little pork barrel spending for a special Kansas project. About the stimulus bill's community development grants, Clinton joked, "Senator Dole and all those Republicans said, 'You just don't understand this thing is full of pork. It's a dadgum scandal.' I was appalled, and then I read yesterday in The *Wall Street Journal* about a senator from Kansas who asked for $23 million of that money to convert a senior citizens center to a boathouse in Kansas . . . He was right, after all."

Dole was not laughing. His staff spent Sunday "researching the issue to within an inch of its life," as the Washington *Post* put it. Dole's office on Monday issued a press release with a large black headline: "WHITE HOUSE'S $23 MILLION LIE." In step-by-step detail, accompanied by letters from Dole and Representative Dan Glickman, a Wichita Democrat, the release noted he asked the federal government to waive interest in the building—it had spent $500,000 to refurbish the structure in 1980—because it was vacant and scheduled to be torn down. The boathouse renovation was to be paid by private funds.

Dole said, "There's no $23 million boathouse, no deficit spending, no new money, no connection with the president's deadbeat stimulus bill, and no truth coming from a White House staff that is ill-serving the president with these sophomoric attacks." He demanded an apology from Clinton.

Soon White House Communications Director George Stephanopoulos stepped forward to say the president regretted using "hyperbole" in his speech. That did not quite appease Dole. On May 7 a letter signed jointly by Dole and Clinton was sent to the group hoping to renovate the boathouse, conveniently faxed to newsrooms across Washington and Kansas: "We hope the $23 million worth of free publicity we have generated for this project will make for smooth sailing in Wichita."

With the battle over the stimulus bill won, Dole rallied his troops for war. Their enemy was Clinton's entire budget proposal, a $500 billion deficit-reduction bill they slammed as leading to enormous tax increases, paltry spending cuts and a new BTU energy tax that would penalize middle-income Americans, the very people promised a tax cut by candidate Clinton. The president challenged Republicans to offer a better alternative, and they responded with a proposal for broad freezes on spending, vague on specific cuts. The White House played hardball, issuing a statement reminding Americans that Dole, suddenly an opponent of income-tax hikes and increased gas taxes, had suggested raising both in the 1990 budget deliberations at Andrews Air Force Base.

Suddenly, President Clinton changed tactics. He decided to try to break bread with his nemesis, have a *social* encounter. He got in touch with Robert Strauss, Dole's old friend and former Democratic party chairman. Strauss orchestrated a supper summit. On July 1 Bill and Hillary Clinton walked into Duke Zeibert's, the ultimate Washington insider restaurant. Harry Truman ate there, as did presidents Nixon, Ford and Carter. The Clintons sat down at a table with Bob Dole (Elizabeth was out of town) and pal Strauss as a gentle mediator. Nearby, a table full of reporters strained to hear them talk over a fish dinner about health care, exercise and stress reduction. The two-hour get-together was cordial. But Strauss' hoped-for detente did not happen.

"They seemed to enjoy themselves," Strauss said of Dole and the Clintons. "I think it's a shame they didn't follow through more, that either one didn't get more out of it than they could have, which is what I hoped would happen, a little more dialogue. But it's hard for a president to have dialogue."

As the budget vote neared in the Senate, Clinton made a nationally televised appeal on August 3, immediately followed by a Republican response from Dole. Clinton portrayed his now $496 billion five-year deficit-reduction plan as one that would put America's economic house in order, a Reaganesque echo. "This plan is fair," Clinton said. "It's balanced. And it will work."

Dole moments later countered, "We oppose this plan because it takes America in the wrong direction, because we believe by working together we can do much better." Dole said the plan failed on four points: it was a large tax hike, it cut little spending, it created few private-sector jobs and it wouldn't solve the deficit. At best, Dole said, the deficit would still hover around $200 billion in the fifth year.

In the Senate fiscally conservative Democrats grumbled. Senator Bob Kerrey, a Nebraska Democrat who fought Clinton for the Democratic presidential nomination in 1992, warned on the Senate floor that he would oppose Clinton's bill if it did not include distinct cuts in entitlement spending—Social Security, Medicare, veterans' benefits—all of which could drive the deficit upward. Kerrey's aria jeopardized Clinton's fragile package. Dole pulled Kerrey aside to suggest that Kerrey vote with Republicans to kill Clinton's bill and spend the month of August working out a new bill with cuts incorporated. Kerrey demurred, winning only a final-hour nebulous promise from Clinton to look at a spending cut bill in the fall. The mood in the Senate was so poisoned, Kerrey felt all Republicans could not be trusted. To him, he told reporters, Dole's offer was the same as being sold a watch in a back alley.

In the final hours of August 5 the House passed the budget bill by 218-216, and on August 6 the Senate passed the plan 51-50, with Vice President Al Gore casting the deciding vote. Kerrey voted with the president. On "Meet the Press" August 8, NBC reporter Lisa Myers asked Dole about Kerrey's comment. Dole seemed hurt: "I mean, I made it in good faith. I said, If you really want to get deficit reduction, let's do it now. He's given up all his leverage."

Dole seemed to relish his growing prominence, even the notoriety. Actor Dan Akroyd performed a humorous skit on "Saturday Night Live" that spring portraying Dole attacking Hillary Clinton. If Bill Clinton could blow his saxophone on Arsenio Hall's show, Dole would accept Jay Leno's invitation to the "Tonight Show" for some good-natured bantering. Dole appeared that fall on the popular television show "Murphy Brown," with actress Candace Bergen, and on Conan O'Brien's late night NBC talk show. Newspaper cartoonist Pat Oliphant showed Dole leading the "Branch Bobbians," a reference to the Branch Davidians who had died in an inferno in Texas. The balloon at the bottom read: "We have a right to go to Hell our own way." Another cartoon depicted Clinton as a kid asking his father, Dole, for "a few billion to buy stuff" and getting turned down. A new T-shirt proclaiming "Dole, Sit Down and Shut Up" sold briskly in several Washington, D.C., stores. They were created by a disgruntled small-business owner who said Dole seemed hell-bent on blocking Clinton. Newspaper columnists and television commentators began calling Dole Dr. Gridlock and Dr. No.

"We were able to not derail other things but at least delay," Dole said in an interview about the budget battle, in which he then offered a distilled philosophy of his approach to government service. "That's what it's all about, the two-party system is competition. I'm not defensive about it. It turned out the economy's doing quite well without that added incentive. Sometimes you have to oppose. Some of these social programs and all these mandates, I've been opposed to those long before he ever got here. It was not opposition to Clinton. I don't think gridlock ever sold. I think maybe early on with a brand-new president you have to pick your targets, you can't just say I'm against everything."

For once, that August, Bob Dole joined other members of Congress in the annual summer recess. He took a vacation. Unlike most, he traveled to New Hampshire, his third visit that year to the important presidential primary state. In a week-long tour, Dole gave speeches, spoke to newspaper editorial boards, appeared on morning television news shows, acting every bit the candidate, and finally admitted it.

"We're not going to kid anybody, we're up here looking around," Dole told the Associated Press in Wolfboro on August 19. "It's fair to say that like a lot of people, I know what the calendar is and I know what's coming up in a couple of years. I haven't made any judgments yet, but it's not illegal to come to New Hampshire to take a look at politics."

★   ★   ★

WHEN CONGRESS RETURNED after Labor Day, Bob Dole was sporting a new attitude, pledging to work more with Clinton on important issues. In a speech before Congress and the nation on September 22, 1993, Clinton laid out his health care reform proposal in broad terms. Dole immediately raised questions but his tone was modulated, not strident.

In November Congress turned to passage of the North American Free Trade Agreement, a pact negotiated by President Bush that President Clinton had slightly modified and then embraced. Dole worked for passage of NAFTA because he felt it would boost American jobs by promoting freer trade between the United States, Canada and Mexico. American labor organizations representing auto, steel, textile and other manufacturing industries strongly opposed NAFTA and found a champion to try to defeat it —House Majority Leader Richard A. Gephardt, a longtime labor supporter.

The two teams squared off. On the side for NAFTA stood Clinton, Dole, leading House and Senate Republicans and all the living former presidents, Nixon, Ford, Carter, Reagan and Bush. On the side against stood Democrats Gephardt and Michigan Representative David Bonoir, the number three House leader, many House and Senate Democrats and Ross Perot, complaining that NAFTA would export American jobs to Mexico.

"There will be three votes on this agreement," Perot warned. "This is the first one. The second vote will be in '94, and the third one will be in '96."

Dole, who had courted Perot and his supporters after the 1992 election, said that on NAFTA, "Ross Perot is wrong." After weeks of debate and protests outside the Capitol by anti-NAFTA forces, the trade agreement was approved in both houses of Congress with substantial Republican support.

In early 1993 President Clinton had pledged to sign the Brady bill, named for President Reagan's first press secretary, James Brady, who was seriously wounded in the attempt on Reagan's life in 1981. In the years following Jim Brady's partial recovery, Sarah and Jim Brady founded the organization Handgun Control to challenge the powerful National Rifle Association lobby. The rising violence on America's streets in the 1990s mobilized public opinion in favor of the Brady bill, requiring gun buyers to wait a week before purchase, thereby allowing time for background checks of those seeking guns.

In the mid-1970s Bob Dole had won a Defender of Individual Rights award from the NRA for forestalling attempts by the federal Bureau of Alcohol, Tobacco and Firearms to impose national firearms registration. In 1991, however, Dole helped write a compromise Brady bill that passed the Senate but eventually died. The plan included a five day waiting period, which would expire after two years, when a national computer background check would be up and running! In 1993, reflecting his more conservative Republican Senate colleagues, Dole came out fighting against the Brady bill. The bill's supporters accused him of obstruction, but the bill was passed and Clinton promised to sign it. Sarah and Jim Brady held a news conference in the Capitol, ebullient and vowing to fight for further curbs on gun availability. As the news conference broke up, Dole slipped in the rear door to congratulate the Bradys. Sarah Brady pressed him to look at the next proposal she would offer.

"I hope we can talk it over," Sarah Brady said to Dole. "Certainly, we've been trying to talk to you about the Brady bill." For two years she had requested a personal meeting with Dole with no success, though she met with "everyone else on the Hill."

"I ran into him once in a hotel and he mentioned the bill briefly and said, 'When I'm back in Kansas it doesn't seem to be that big a deal,' " Sarah Brady said Dole told her. "I always had the feeling it wasn't an issue he wanted to have that much to do with. But he took sides and that was surprising. I was disappointed."

In late December 1993 Dole took sides on another potentially explosive issue: Whitewater, an Arkansas land deal involving the Clintons and former business associate James McDougal, and Madison Guaranty Savings and Loan, a thrift McDougal owned that failed. New York Senator Al D'Amato, who had survived a Senate ethics committee inquiry into his own business transactions, demanded that the Senate Banking Committee look into the Clintons' dealings with McDougal, only to be rebuffed by the committee chairman, Donald Riegle, a Michigan Democrat.

But at the same time Iowa Republican Representative Jim Leach, who usually muffled his partisanship under rumpled sweaters, spoke out for similar hearings for the House Banking Committee.

Dole joined in, displaying his political skills at keeping the Democratic party off balance without overtly criticizing the Clintons. Through letters his office released to the media and appearances on news shows in early January 1994, Dole pressured Attorney General Janet Reno to name a special counsel.

Special counsels named by attorneys generally work under the Justice

Department. Reno had a choice: seek either a special counsel or a special prosecutor. Dole pointedly avoided asking for a special prosecutor. A separate three-judge panel selects special prosecutors, ostensibly lending them more autonomy.

Under President Reagan Dole had engaged in a three-year public feud with Special Prosecutor Lawrence Walsh, assigned to investigate the Iran-Contra affair, the arms-for-hostages deal that implicated a dozen officials in the Republican administration. In late December 1992 George Bush had issued pardons for several convicted of felonies in the scandal. Dole regularly complained that Walsh was on an endless witch-hunt, wasting millions of taxpayer dollars. Walsh's investigation did cost nearly $40 million, the most expensive since the special-prosecutor law was passed in the late 1970s, but it also revealed willful lawbreaking.

To Dole's pressuring on Whitewater, Attorney General Reno replied that if she decided to appoint a special prosecutor "it's still my prosecutor and there will be questions about that person's independence." Dole disagreed. A few days later, Senator Daniel Patrick Moynihan, a New York Democrat, also suggested that if Clinton had nothing to hide, why not seek a special counsel, a shift that shook loose other Democrats and turned the tide against Clinton. On January 11 the president himself asked Reno to choose an independent counsel to investigate Whitewater and Madison Guaranty.

Dole immediately held a press conference in the shopworn Senate Radio TV gallery on the third floor of the Capitol. Reporters clambered in. Now that Dole had his special counsel, he upped the pressure by calling for a special Senate investigating committee to look at Madison Guaranty and the Clintons, similar to the Watergate committee that bored into Richard Nixon two decades earlier. Adam Clymer, a veteran reporter for the New York *Times,* spoke up:

"Senator Dole, you asked for a special counsel and said [Reno] had the authority [to appoint one]. Now if you get that and if you get a select committee, do you promise not to ask for something more?"

"Why?" Dole said, with a conspiratorial smile at Clymer. "Have you got some ideas?"

The room broke up in laughter.

Few, if any, realized that years before, in 1979, Dole had argued the exact opposite line on special counsels and prosecutors concerning a case involving Democratic President Jimmy Carter. On March 20, 1979, Bob Dole and six Republican colleagues wrote to then-Attorney General Griffin Bell, seeking appointment of a special prosecutor to investigate loans, transactions and other issues between the National Bank of Georgia and the Carter family. Bell had appointed a special counsel. Dole and the other senators said the special counsel was "inadequate in this case."

"It is extremely difficult, if not impossible, to expect the executive branch to conduct an investigation of its own chief executive to an impartial and just conclusion," the Republican senators wrote.

Looking back, Dole admitted they were playing politics then. But he said he was turned off on special prosecutors when a special prosecutor investigated whether Jimmy Carter's chief of staff, Hamilton Jordan, had used cocaine. Jordan was cleared in 1980 but his reputation had been tarnished unfairly. Then Lawrence Walsh's work cemented Dole's antipathy.

"I don't feel this way today," Dole said of his 1979 letter. "Plus, I thought Walsh, even though he was a nominal Republican, lost touch. It got to be a propel-Lawrence-Walsh effort."

Dole moved on in the winter of 1994 from Whitewater back to health care, an issue of vital importance to the Clinton presidency. In his State of the Union message delivered to a joint session of Congress the evening of January 25, Clinton demanded passage of comprehensive reforms, because "we have a health care crisis in this country." Holding up a pen, the president declared: "If you send me legislation that does not guarantee every American private insurance that can never be taken away, you will force me to take this pen, veto the legislation and we'll come right back here and start all over again."

Seated in his office on the other side of the Capitol, Dole immediately followed Clinton with the official Republican response, also broadcast live on national television. Dole countered: "Our country has health care problems, but no health care crisis." Alongside the sober-faced Dole was a large chart that resembled an electric power grid for a small city. Dole said it represented all the new bureaucracies that would be created under Clinton's health care plan.

"Now you and I are way down here, way at the bottom," Dole said, pointing to the very bottom of the grid. "We can fix our most pressing problems without performing a triple bypass operation on our health care system."

The following day the Democratic National Committee fired off a fax containing several comments made by Dole both in 1991 and as far back as 1971 using the words "health care crisis."

The poll numbers on Clinton's health care plan slid south in the ensuing weeks, prompting Dole to pronounce key elements of Clinton's plan "dead." This was a bit of hyperbole on his part. Yet Dole had had an experience as a leader in a 1986 catastrophic health care bill that Congress passed, then rushed back to rescind the following year after outcry from older Americans, who faced some higher costs. In late spring of 1994, Dole said he told Clinton: "I see the same thing happening with health care now. We're not preparing the public. We might pass it, but then there could be a big, big backlash."

After his first year Clinton often found himself locked in a power struggle with congressional Democrats. Dole had been struggling for longer to stay ahead of the shifting Republican makeup in the Senate.

"I think that what's happened is that the Republican party in the Senate has moved pretty far to the right, and that the leader who tries to corral all Republicans goes where the center of gravity is," said Missouri's Jack Danforth, who was retiring at the end of 1994. "I think it's pulled Bob. He tries mightily to please the right wing of our party, which I think is implacable usually anyhow. But I think he is a centrist at heart."

His centrism got him in trouble. On March 30, 1994, Dole worked with Senate Majority Leader George Mitchell to round up Republicans— including arranging for a couple to ride on Vice President Al Gore's plane returning to Washington—to vote to break a filibuster by Jesse Helms, the conservative North Carolina Republican. Helms was trying to force inclusion of a school-prayer amendment into an education bill, according to a memo written by an unnamed Republican staffer. The memo raised questions about Dole's effectiveness in the future as a leader of the loyal opposition.

"Senator Dole and I regularly exchange information two or three times daily," Mitchell said, perhaps predictably playing down the event. "I regularly accommodate Republican senators in terms of travel."

CLINTON, LIKE MOST presidents, also was bedeviled with foreign-policy problems, not considered his strongest suit. And Dole was always ready with advice and criticism.

In the fall of 1993 Dole sought to rein in Clinton by proposing Clinton obtain congressional approval for further action in Somalia. The idea failed. Dole subsequently turned around to help Clinton by opposing efforts to set a firm deadline for withdrawal from Somalia. Dole later complained that the Clinton administration's policies regarding the ethnic warfare in Bosnia and the former Yugoslavian region were muddled. Concerning suffering in Haiti, Dole opposed the idea of U.S.-supported invasion to try to restore order and imposition of economic sanctions against the military-run country, believing sanctions would only hurt the poorest people in the Western Hemisphere. Dole backed renewing Most Favored Nation trading status for China without imposing sanctions requiring the Chinese government to improve human rights for dissident Chinese or Tibetans living under Chinese rule in Tibet, despite strong protest from human rights groups. Exports to China were important, Dole thought, and the United States might need China's leverage in dealing with potentially hostile North Korea.

Dole's and Clinton's conflicts, while at times intense and likely to continue beyond 1994, were as much a function of the American form of government as honest differences in their views, said George Mitchell, the Senate majority leader. "Most democratic systems are based upon the parliamentary method, in which the chief executive, the prime minister, is the head of the legislative majority," Mitchell said. "So you can't have, in Canada, Great Britain or Germany, France or Australia, a chief executive who is of a different party than the legislative majority. In our system you can and do have that. As a result, the legislative leader has both a role in governance and a role as a leader of the opposition. And there's a tension that's reflected on a daily basis."

Knowing that inherent tension, Washington politicians occasionally go through rituals designed to bridge gaps. On April 14, 1994, the forty-ninth anniversary of his war injury, as he had every year for a quarter century on that date, Bob Dole spoke on the Senate floor about the status of Americans with disabilities. Afterward he held a luncheon in his office for forty people, civil rights advocates and disabled individuals. Not wholly unexpected, President Clinton dropped in.

Offering a tribute to his adversary, Clinton told the gathering he had reread Dole's first Senate speech. "It was one of those magic moments in the history of Congress and maybe of our country, which reminds us all, for all of our differences, there's a common chord that unites us when we are all at our best," Clinton said. "I just wanted to come by here and pay my respects. Not only for that [speech], but for all the work he's done since for Americans with disabilities. And I'm very grateful."

Clinton had come as a lamb to Capitol Hill, lying down peaceably with the lion, Bob Dole, if only for a moment.

THE REPUBLICANS' MAN FOR
ALL SEASONS

TWO DAYS BEFORE former President Richard Nixon's funeral in the spring of 1994, Kansan Robert Ellsworth, Nixon's ambassador to NATO, dispatched a memo to his old friend Bob Dole concerning the eulogy Nixon's family asked Dole to deliver. "No amenities," Ellsworth wrote. "Only one theme. Simple language. Leave a picture with the audience. End dramatically, emotionally." Perhaps end the speech: "God Bless Richard Nixon. God bless the United States of America."

Flying aboard a government-chartered jet packed with Republican lawmakers and former Nixon aides and confidants to the funeral on April 27, Dole stopped by Ellsworth's seat with a draft of his eulogy. It began, "I believe historians will say . . ." That was like Dole, Ellsworth had thought. Look to trained scholars, important thinkers, to render an opinion of Nixon.

"No," Ellsworth told Dole. "People want to know what *you* think, Bob."

Dole walked back to his seat. Sheila Burke, Dole's chief of staff, came back to Ellsworth with a new draft: "I believe the second half of the twentieth century will be known as The Age of Nixon." Ellsworth smiled.

That afternoon, beneath heavy gray clouds in Yorba Linda, California,

Bob Dole forcefully defended the polarizing thirty-seventh president to his family and friends and the nation watching on television. Dole only indirectly mentioned the Watergate scandal. Instead, he soberly asserted that Nixon's singular gift to the world was his fighter's spirit, his will to rise every day and "confound my enemies."

Although speaking for Nixon, every line in Dole's speech seemed to parallel his own life. Nixon, Dole declared in his bass prairie voice, was "one of us," a dreaming young man, a student who scraped by, a proud husband and father—"how American."

To millions, Nixon was a hero who honored their belief in "working hard, worshipping God, loving their families and saluting the flag," Dole said. "He called them the Silent Majority." Dole, too, had spoken out for the Silent Majority. Like Nixon, Dole had "lived to the hilt," brave, strong and "unyielding in his convictions," a man "who never gave up and who never gave in."

In front of Dole at the funeral sat a tableau of living presidents and their wives—Gerald Ford, Jimmy Carter, Ronald Reagan, George Bush and Bill Clinton, all men whose presidencies Nixon had affected. But Dole perhaps bore the strongest bond with Nixon.

Nixon and Dole heard the same night trains whistling through their home towns as boys. They grew up poor, educated themselves with single-minded devotion. Each man persevered through noisy triumph and hollow defeat. All those similarities seemed to ring down into Bob Dole's soul through his eulogy and welled up at the last two lines.

"May God bless Richard Nixon," Dole concluded. Then tears filled his eyes. "May God bless the United States."

Dole slammed his notebook closed, spun away from the podium, marched to his seat and sat down next to his wife Elizabeth, who looked stricken. Henry Kissinger, Nixon's secretary of state, reached forward to touch Dole's back.

Ellsworth was seated nearby. Bob Dole, he thought, a man raised in an era and culture that demanded men be reticent, Bob Dole the so-called hatchet man, had shown *emotion*. People wiped away tears, eyeglasses came off.

The four eulogists finished, the funeral concluded with a sermon from the Reverend Billy Graham and people rose to leave. Kansas Representative Pat Roberts, a Republican who held Dole's old First District House seat, walked up to Ellsworth. "Dole blew it!" said Roberts. "No one will ever forget it."

Others offered mixed reviews. As Ellsworth boarded the jet to return to Washington that afternoon, he passed by Dole and reached out to grip his friend's left hand in both of his.

"*Great* speech," said Ellsworth.

Dole seemed mortified.

"*You* made me put those last two phrases in, and *that's* what did me in," Dole said. That evening dozens of telephone calls rolled into Dole's Capitol office, most praising Dole's speech. Talk show hosts, morning news anchors and the big newspapers mentioned the surfacing of compassion in Dole's eulogy. Ellsworth telephoned Dole the next morning to see how Dole felt now.

Elated.

"You remember, Nixon always said you had a great voice," Ellsworth told Dole.

Not only were their lives similar, but Bob Dole was Richard Nixon's friend. More than any other politician in recent years, Dole looked up to Nixon as a mentor. They had come a long way since the tensions created in 1973 when Nixon forced Dole out as chairman of the Republican National Committee. Ten years later, the debacle had prompted Dole at a Washington Gridiron dinner jokingly to call presidents Ford, Carter and Nixon "Hear no evil, see no evil, and Evil."

As the Kansan rose in stature from conservative to compromiser in Congress, a relationship between the men developed through notes and telephone calls. In 1987 Nixon and Dole were brought together by their mutual friend Ellsworth. "I went up to see Nixon I don't know how many times in '87," Dole recalls, "to get some foreign policy ideas because he was always good. I still feel he had more at the tip of his fingers than all the rest of them put together, myself included. I don't think he was always right, but he had the knowledge and the information."

After Dole lost the New Hampshire primary to Bush in February of 1988 and was wiped out by him in the Super Tuesday states in March, Nixon called Ellsworth.

"Nixon was always saying things you must do," Ellsworth recalled. "He told me to tell Dole he must never quit. Tell him he must keep fighting." Dole, emboldened, fought on two more weeks before conceding the race to Bush.

In Dole's Capitol office, in his jumbled press office, hung a photograph of Dole and Nixon sitting in Nixon's library in 1993. As when they first met, Nixon was shaking Dole's left hand. Dole always appreciated that gesture. Below the picture, Nixon wrote: "To Senator Bob Dole—a past, present and future leader of the Republican Party. With best wishes from Dick Nixon." Inside his own desk in his Capitol office, Dole kept personal letters from Nixon dating back to the 1960s, more than a dozen typed and handwritten notes.

November 28, 1984, the day Dole won election as Senate majority leader, Nixon wrote: "As Disraeli would have put it, you have now reached the top of [the] greasy pole in the Senate. The vote you received is a recognition of your superior brain power and your years of loyalty to the Party in many tough battles."

Nixon to Dole on January 13, 1991, after the Senate voted to authorize the Persian Gulf war: "To hold all but two Republicans on the Gulf vote was a brilliant achievement."

On Dole's 1992 announcement to seek reelection, Nixon wrote: "The Redskins big win was good news. Even better was the news that you will run again. The party needs you. The Senate needs you. Most important, the nation needs your continued intelligent, responsible and courageous leadership."

Reflecting upon the Republican National Convention in 1992, Nixon wrote: "Dear Bob, no one on the political scene today can handle humor more effectively than you can. My regret is you were not in a better prime time slot. Regards, RN."

In 1992 Dole brought Nixon to Kansas for an honorary dinner despite protests from Kansans still fuming about Watergate. In January of 1994, Nixon attended a luncheon ceremony Dole organized in the Capitol in Washington to commemorate the twenty-fifth anniversary of Nixon's first inauguration. The old bulls of Congress stopped by, a stream of young congressional staffers shuffled in for an autograph, Nixon rested on a sofa in Dole's office. On January 27 Nixon wrote in his thank-you to Dole: "I thought the most astute comment I made during the luncheon was that Clinton and you are in the same class when it comes to mixing with people. I give you an edge, because I believe you would be good with people even if you weren't in office or seeking office. I am not sure that would be the case with him."

"One thing that impressed me about Nixon was he always had something positive to say," Dole recalled. "A lot of confidence in me, I guess. There may have been another side to Nixon I didn't see. I must say I was disappointed when I heard some of the tapes [secret recordings Nixon made in the Oval Office]. The four-letter words. Very surprising."

★ ★ ★

A WARM SPRING Saturday in 1994, Bob Dole, wearing an open collar white shirt, khakis and running shoes, sat on the patio outside the Hart Office Building across the street from the Capitol. The Hart housed his second office, reserved for Kansas issues. He pored over a travel schedule for June that looked "crazy." He would leave in a few days for the fiftieth anniversary of the Allies' D-Day invasion, where he would be cheered by veterans followed by a foray into northern Italy to tread again below Hill 913, where German soldiers cut him down April 14, 1945, a rendezvous with his own mortality. He also contemplated his future.

On that Saturday, the office was quiet, a brief reprieve in the usual whirlwind around Dole. Leader, Dole's schnauzer who spent workdays in the Hart office, either was not around or resting his loud bark. When Bob Dole was not traveling out of town he came in on Saturdays to study issues and telephone Kansans, political people and those whose letters had struck him. He signed piles of photographs, just as he had when he first came to Washington.

"I don't know how much time I spend just autographing pictures," Dole said, bright sun on tan, rugged face. "I don't know how the president must handle it. He must have a machine. But people don't want machines. 'If he doesn't sign it himself, don't send one!' they write. Oh, these people, they can tell a machine. On Saturdays, it's kind of nice to do all those things, make a few phone calls."

Bob Dole seemed relaxed, reflective, witty. One could glimpse how close friends and family said they saw him, a warm, engaging, loyal and intense man. It was a far cry from the Bob Dole with whom adversaries worked, the man on the evening news, the Washington establishment figure—the one who acted as a blunt, combative general in daily warfare with Democrats.

Over the last thirty-four years in Congress Bob Dole had taken political stands on his terms, based on his evaluation of political realities and facts assembled, categorized and sifted in his mind poured in from dozens of sources. "You cannot make Bob Dole do something he doesn't want to do," said Mari Maseng Will, who was communications director of Dole's ill-fated 1988 presidential bid. She implied the converse as well; he would do only what he wanted.

"I think he takes himself very seriously and he's very disciplined," Elizabeth Dole explained. "He feels that this is tough business, serious business and he's serious about what he's doing."

Dole's legislative record appears singular, even contradictory. Following hardrock Republican stands, Dole voted against Medicare in the 1960s and much of President Johnson's War on Poverty programs. In the early 1970s he backed President Nixon's Vietnam War policies. In the last twenty years Dole has spoken out for a balanced-budget amendment, a line-item veto for the president, an amendment to ban burning the American flag, military and economic aid to the Nicaraguan contra rebels, President Reagan's Star Wars defense plan, Desert Shield, Desert Storm and Most Favored Nation trading status for China. He opposed many government mandates, health-care price controls, unpaid family and medical leave, taxpayer money for abortions and opening the military to gay Americans.

On the more moderate side, Dole's modest upbringing and disability have prompted him to lead battles for civil rights for women, minorities and the disabled; for expansion of nutrition programs for poor mothers and their children; for Eldercare programs for older Americans. And for protection of American farmers, including their taxpayer subsidies. He's spoken in favor of peace in the Middle East, Eastern Europe and Africa, though liberal critics at times disagreed with his proposals and views.

Dole's professional life has been consumed by years of public and private debate over hundreds of issues, amassing a record of wins, losses, and many ties. He was proud of his work on the 1983 Social Security bailout and on farm legislation since he arrived in Washington in the 1960s. President Bush cited Dole for persuading him to work for passage in 1990 of the Americans with Disabilities Act, a milestone in the advancement of workplace rights for disabled Americans, which Bush's predecessor Ronald Reagan had kept on the back burner.

Ralph Neas, who headed the National Leadership Conference on Civil Rights, a leading civil-rights advocacy organization in Washington, gave credit to Dole for his work during a dismal era. "Despite the hostility of the Reagan-Bush years on civil rights, legislatively Dole was the author of a compromise or catalyst for compromise on two dozen bills over the last decade," Neas said. He mentioned in particular the twenty-five-year extension of the Voting Rights Act approved in 1982, the Civil Rights Act of 1991, the disabilities act and a civil-rights restoration bill of 1984. "While there's no question the leadership conference and Senator Dole disagree on issues, and sometimes sharply, he has a commitment to improving civil rights."

Failure confronts all lawmakers. Dole labored through the 1980s against the federal deficit, winning passage in 1985 of a bold measure capping the growth of entitlement spending for Social Security, only to have President

Reagan back out. He fought to balance the federal budget without success. The deficit continued on its upward trajectory. Dozens of other amendments he sought were rejected, due perhaps in part at least to the Senate's Democratic majority. Sometimes one man cannot make a difference.

Dole's responsibilities as Senate Republican leader have summoned him to vouch for controversial Republicans in the 1980s and 1990s, among them Judge Robert Bork, former senator John Tower, Supreme Court Justice Clarence Thomas and Senator Bob Packwood. His defenses of these men alienated many Americans.

"What's a leader to do, if you can't stand the heat?" Dole said. Bork, he explained, was President Reagan's man. Dole worked with Tower, same college fraternity, too. "Packwood has been my friend on the Finance Committee," Dole said. "At least he deserves a fair hearing, which he hasn't had. If it's bad news, it's bad news. I think he's getting a little stronger. There's a poll in Oregon saying 50 percent of the people now think he should stay. He was way down in the 30s." Dole pushed Thomas' confirmation because of friendship with Thomas' mentor, Senator Jack Danforth of Missouri. "I like Clarence Thomas," Dole said. "I keep hoping he'll break out one of these days; we'll see some big decision that tells everybody who voted for him, 'You were right, you made the right choice.' "

Now that the shoe was on the other foot and Senate Majority Leader George Mitchell had to support President Clinton choices, Dole said with a wry glance, "I see Mitchell defending some of these nominees and I think, 'Geeminee, how can you do that, George? They're terrible people.' "

But that's politics, the war of ideas espoused by opposing parties. Dole expressed his general view of matters taken up by the Senate in one telling comment: "Anybody who can look somebody in the eye and say, 'There's no politics in this is crazy,' " Dole said. 'There's politics on both sides, there's always going to be politics. I don't say that's bad, it's probably healthy. There may be somebody over in that Senate who doesn't understand politics, but I doubt it. There are one hundred politicians over there." And all of them jousting for position where, despite the veneer of cordiality, fifty senators at any given moment believed they should be president.

Dole arrived in Congress at the dawn of the Cold War in 1960, a neophyte in the rules and customs of Washington, an unremarkable conservative. In the 1990s he has become the player's player, molding his style to political factors of the moment, part pragmatist, part moderate, part conservative, a politician of broad-ranging interests, from health care to campaign financing, food stamps to foreign policy. Senate colleagues have called Dole an authority on the process of the Senate. That means, said Robert Dove, a top aide to Dole, he's a "master of things more unwritten than written, understood than talked about, things done in small groups, through diplomacy and negotiating, where nobody gets to issue orders. The powers are very few, but the power of knowing who to talk to, what to do, how to close a deal are enormous."

And when Dole has been unsure of the technical rules of the "world's most deliberative body" he has turned to Dove, the Senate rulekeeper. Dove began working for the Senate in 1966, and served for years as its official parliamentary referee before joining Dole's staff in the late 1980s.

Dole's legislative style has been both a strength and a weakness. He is not one to frequently offer broad overhauls of national policy regarding the big issues of the day, but rather has introduced measures with dozens of incremental changes aimed to improve the existing situation. Critics in Congress and the media have complained he lacks a grand vision for America. Dole has tended to withhold his commitment or opinions on bills introduced by colleagues, both Democratic and Republican, until Senate approval seems possible, then has weighed in to broker a deal. "On most issues he's the one who steps forward and puts together the language and coalesces support," said Kansas Senator Nancy Kassebaum, Dole's Republican colleague. "If I said, 'What do we need to do on welfare reform?' I don't think Bob's somebody who sits down and spends a lot of time trying to figure out what to do. What he does very well is pull together, at the right moment, what becomes an approach that seizes the moment. Not to take away, but that is a great skill. The rest of us can be thrashing around for a couple of years or we get lost in the shuffle."

Over the years Dole has traveled a million miles, perhaps literally, experiencing a vast spectrum of campaigning in the twentieth century, humble to sophisticated. He began with the Bobolinks and Dole pineapple juice in the 1960s. By the 1990s, Dole was holding high-tech, high-dollar fundraising on the east and west coasts, scooping up donations from lobbyists and corporate moguls.

As his prominence has risen, Dole has capitalized on his name recognition to command two large money-raising organizations—Campaign America, and the Dole Foundation. Dole set up the foundation in 1984 as a non-profit charitable endeavor providing grants to help disabled Americans receive training and education. In addition to its meritorious work, critics have contended the foundation has been a means for big corporations to earn Dole's favor with large contributions, a charge that angers Dole.

Since 1978 Campaign America has handed out hundreds of thousands of dollars to Republican candidates for the Senate, the House, state governorships, state legislatures and local posts. On a February night in early 1994, Campaign America was holding a fund-raising event at the Willard, an imperial hotel just two blocks from the White House. Dole's well-heeled invitees strode in and anted up $1,000 donations for drinks and $5,000 donations for dinner to spend a couple of hours around Bob Dole, hear his pitch for "Seven more in '94"—the number of Senate Republicans needed to retake the majority—and a few jokes. The take that evening? A half-million dollars.

Dole has found a way to compartmentalize and live with the criticism and contradictions that raising money breeds. Among them, the tobacco industry has contributed substantial sums to Dole's campaigns, an irony because Dole has told family members he believed his brother Kenny died from smoking cigarettes.

To those who suggest Dole has become too influenced by special interest contributions, Dole says he operates by a personal code designed to keep him out of trouble. "I try to live like I think people at home would want me to live," Dole said. "I try to be open and candid, maybe candid to a fault sometimes. Try to be very careful with all these people coming in and out of your office. You're never certain. We've got a good, smart lawyer who looks at a lot of these requests, whether we should do it, how we should do it, so we're not in any compromising positions. Sometimes people don't understand why we can't do certain things. I don't make many phone calls to cabinet people or try to twist their arms, though some members do."

In the intrusive 1990s where no question for public officials is off-limits, Bob and Elizabeth Dole's relationship, like those of many public figures, has been the subject of occasional speculation. A rumor first appeared in the early 1990s that they had separated. A Dole source said that was untrue, but the rumor has again occasionally popped up.

With a vexed look, Dole said: "Nope. We're happily married. We try to spend time together, Sundays, and we go out to dinner pretty often. I don't know where that rumor got started, maybe Kansas City."

Although they looked around at houses in Virginia in the late 1980s, the Doles decided to stay in their Watergate apartment, crowded with a stair-stepper and treadmill exercise machines. Their marriage is unconventional, but both said it works for them.

"We have date nights," Elizabeth Dole said with a laugh. "Where it's no work, nothing, it's our night, stay up all night watching old movies or doing whatever we want to do. Sunday is the day we try to save. Now, the talk shows don't help much on that. We really do carve out the time we're going to save for us. We enjoy a lot of the same kinds of things, not getting out on the social circuit. We like to be home alone, shut that apartment door, putter around the kitchen, order in Chinese food. You just enjoy the simple things, really."

Heading the Red Cross since 1991, Elizabeth Dole has improved the safety of the half of the nation's blood supply collected by the Red Cross. She has raised more than $180 million for Red Cross disaster relief around the world and established standardized training for twelve thousand disaster relief workers. She defines the work as "a mission field," an endeavor complementing her abiding Christian faith.

"The fact that we both really love what we do, I think, enriches our marriage rather than takes away," Elizabeth Dole said.

When her own busy schedule allows, Robin Dole joins her parents for Sunday brunch. Dole enjoys the Hay Adams Hotel, one of Washington's most suave, for its biscuits and gravy, a down-home cholesterol bomb a health afficionado like Dole probably knows he should avoid. Robin, who has not married and works in governmental relations for a large real-estate company, has Bob and Elizabeth over to her house in Virginia for cook-outs. Despite opinions in the media that her father has changed since his first days in Washington, Robin Dole feels differently. "The way he is now is the way be has always been in my eyes," she said. "He's much more comfortable in his role now. It's all very natural for him now."

It is a captivating question to ponder: if Bob Dole had not been wounded a mere nineteen days before the shooting stopped in Europe and five months before World War II ended with the Japanese surrender, would he ever have entered politics? Would he have earned his law degree in Topeka, Kansas? Or would he instead today be making the rounds as a physician in a prominent hospital in Kansas City or healing neighbors in central Kansas? Like politics, medicine is a world unto itself. Rare is the physician who has served in Congress.

Bob Dole unequivocally has found his calling among the one hundred men and women of the United States Senate, on the anvil where the rules of Democracy are forged with fire and steel. The Senate has served as a testing ground to hone his ambition, competition, inquisitiveness and skills at brokering consensus.

That Senate also will inform Bob Dole's future. In the fall 1994 Congressional elections, more Democratic Senate seats will be up for election than Republican seats. As minority leader, Dole hopes to close the gap in the 56–44 Democrat-Republican ratio. Historically, the president's party tends to lose seats in Congress at the mid-term elections, which would favor Republicans. Should Republicans take seven seats in November, at this writing unlikely but possible, Dole might well be reelected majority leader again. Would he want to lead the Senate or run for the presidency? Could he try both?

"If Republicans did somehow manage to take back the majority in '94, decision time would be tough in Dole's office," said David Keene, the conservative consultant who has known Dole since 1978 and worked for him in Dole's unsuccessful 1988 presidential race. "Then he'd have to be giving up the best job he ever had for another job he knows he screwed up trying to get once before."

Republican Howard Baker, who was Senate majority leader from 1980 to 1984, agreed that Dole would face a dilemma. "It surprises me, frankly, but I think he's psychologically better as majority leader than as minority leader," Baker said. "Most people would have thought his role would tend more naturally as minority leader, as opposition leader." Baker also sees that job as innately limiting Dole's other consideration. "You've got a lot of publicity, a lot of name recognition, but also a lot of controversy, mostly because you have to take a stand on every peajeb issue that comes along," Baker said. "I'll tell you what: majority leader is the second best job in Washington. Right after president. But it is a terrible place from which to *run* for president."

In June of 1994 Dole took stands on two important issues that could help or hinder either of his political objectives for after the November elections. On June 11 Dole came out with his strongest to-date opposition to President Clinton's health care reform effort, setting up a possible show-down at the polls. Dole suggested that Republicans block any health care bill requiring employers to provide insurance for their employees, and should welcome a referendum on the issue in the November elections.

"Let the voters decide," Dole told those gathered at the Republican National Committee's Northeast regional meeting, according to the New York *Times*. "If they want the Clinton health care plan, then they'll vote for their candidates. If they want something else, they will vote for Republicans."

In a later interview, Dole said he thought polls showed many Americans opposed Clinton's health reform proposal, and that Republicans would not pay a price if no bill passed by November.

"Six months ago, I think they had a winner there," Dole said of Democrats using health care reform against Republicans. "I think now, with 58 or 59 percent saying put it off until next year, the bottom line is: Do it right. People don't like these deadlines."

At the end of June, 1994, Dole unveiled a health care plan with Bob Packwood of Oregon that immediately drew 38 other Republican cosponsors. It contained insurance reforms, subsidies for low-income Americans to buy insurance, aid in setting up voluntary insurance pools and partly eliminated the ability of insurance companies to deny new coverage to individuals and families because of preexisting health conditions, such as diseases, injuries or pregnancy. It did not contain universal coverage nor mandates that businesses provide their workers with insurance. The Clinton administration attacked it as inadequate for middle-class Americans and challenged Dole to support broader reforms.

"The big test is going to be health care reform," said Democratic National Committee Chairman David Wilhelm. "But for all his feints, his discussion of the goal of universal coverage, his one-time support of the (Republican Senator John) Chafee plan that would bring about universal coverage, as it gets closer to the time of the actual vote, he's pulling back and that could be, in part, because of his desire to run for president, and a judgment within the Republican party that a failure to play to the far right is just suicidal."

Dole also made a rare awkward step that might have consequences later in the year. On June 4, Virginia Republicans nominated former Marine Lieutenant Colonel Oliver North, a principal figure in the Iran-Contra scandal, as the Republican challenger for the Senate seat held by Democrat Senator Chuck Robb. North had been convicted of aiding and abetting the obstruction of Congress in its investigation of the scandal and was running a campaign ridiculing Congress as out of touch with Americans. The following day reporter Bob Schieffer asked Dole on CBS's "Face the Nation" television program if he would support North.

"I think it's going to take a while to sort that out," Dole said, speaking from Sarajevo in the former Yugoslavia, which he was touring at the time. "I hope to meet with the appropriate people sometime next week, but it's —it makes it very difficult for some in the Republican party."

Virginia's senior senator, John Warner, a Republican, had publicly spoken out against North. But Dole's comments, broadcast and published around the nation, triggered a backlash of conservative senators who proclaimed their support of North. Several days later Dole met with Marshall Coleman, a Republican running as an independent, and told him he could not support an independent candidate. He then met with North and endorsed North publicly. Dole would need every seat to win a Republican majority in the Senate. He avoided, however, a photo-op with North that would feed the two of them together to the nation's newspapers, magazines and television news shows. Instead he issued a brief statement.

"I told Ollie I will do everything possible to assist in his election to the U.S. Senate," Dole said. "Including, of course, campaigning for him in Virginia." Dole's Campaign America also donated $5,000 to North's campaign.

Within days, Coleman officially entered the race, as did former Virginia Governor Douglas Wilder, a Democrat running as an independent. Some conservatives grumbled privately about challenging Dole for his leadership post after the fall elections, acknowledged Senator Thad Cochran, a Mississippi Republican who said he thought complaints would die away. Newspaper columnists suggested that Dole had been persuaded to come around for North under pressure from conservatives and television evangelist Pat Robertson, a leader of the Christian right, constituencies he would want for 1996.

"Aw, it's been interpreted about fifty different ways," Dole said in an interview. He explained that he had promised Coleman he would meet with him before offering an endorsement, and, once done, he decided to endorse the Virginia Republican party's choice, which was North. One California state lawmaker had said that he should endorse North, but he had not spoken with others or Robertson.

Clearly such maneuverings demonstrate that on the cusp of his seventy-first birthday, the lure of the presidency still seems to sway Bob Dole and that he is gearing up for a possible third quest. He stopped merely enjoying the speculation soon after Christmas of 1993. Over a dinner one evening at the Watergate Dole first talked seriously about running in 1996 with Elizabeth, Robin, Chief of Staff Sheila Burke, Jo-Anne Coe who runs Campaign America, and three top aides from his 1988 team, Tom Synhorst, Bill Lacy and Mari Maseng Will. The consensus was: test the waters.

Barring unforeseen complications, Dole seems to be laying the necessary groundwork, raising money, traveling the nation, setting up regional political directors through Campaign America that could roll over into a presidential campaign staff.

If he launched a presidential bid, there would be daunting complications for him: his own record of having failed twice before and the fact that other Republicans considering 1996—Bill Bennett, Jack Kemp, James

Baker, Lamar Alexander, Dan Quayle—are not in the Senate and can distance themselves from the failures and controversy of government.

Another significant factor might weigh against him: age. Bob Dole would be roughly five months younger than Ronald Reagan was when Reagan was elected to his *second* term in 1984. "Ronald Reagan had a whole youthful upbeat way of looking at things," said Kevin Phillips, a political theorist and author. "It wasn't what somebody would think of as a crabby senior-citizens viewpoint. You could make the case Reagan was out to lunch half the time, because that's the way he looked at things. But Dole has this dour demeanor, and as he gets older it'll make the caricature easier. Now, it may be after four years of Clinton and the Romper Room, there's going to more of a premium on age. While that may be true, I don't think it'll be wanting a president in his early seventies whose principal training has been legislative gut-fighting. People are more likely to want some upbeat outsider type.

"For Dole to want to do it it's got to look like it's very winnable and that the party would come together behind him," Phillips continued. "They'd do that because they'd figure he could talk Ross Perot out of the race, do some deal with the Perotistas. It could be the one time in his life when all the stars came in a row for him."

To some, the perception of Dole as Republican leader playing politics against the Clinton administration on health care, the budget and foreign policy could be too off-putting for 1996. But despite all the negative factors, Dole still seems the man to beat for the Republican nomination.

"People say in this business there's nothing that makes a politician madder than to find out the other guy has been playing politics," Russell Long, the Louisiana Democrat who worked with Dole on the Senate Finance Committee through the mid-1980s, said in his southern timbre. "Bob's been playing some politics, but why not? If he hopes to be president of the United States he'd better play some politics. Statesmanship will only get you so far. At some point you've got to be practical and tell people what they want to hear. It's been a real enjoyable experience working with Bob and his lovely wife. I think Bob would make the country a good president. It seems to me he's worked at it long enough, why, he's entitled to that Republican nomination."

Ed Feulner, president of the Heritage Foundation, a conservative think tank in Washington, said: "At this stage, because of his commanding presence and his universal acceptability, he's kind of the eight-hundred-pound gorilla in the arena. I've got Jack Kemp and Bill Bennett under my wing, love them both, but whenever anybody talks about this sort of thing,

Dole's is the first name that comes up. Dole, I think, has gotten over the meanness that people used to attribute to him. He's tough but he listens."

And former President Gerald Ford had a similar assessment. "I think Bob Dole would be a good president or I wouldn't have selected him as my running mate in '76," said Ford. "That's the best evidence of why I believe he would make a good president, because if we'd been elected and I'd died, I would have had full faith in him to be a good chief executive. I still believe that. Bob's performing today a first-class role as the leader in the opposition. There's nobody else doing that effectively. And I don't know where he gets all the energy. He's a strong, tough guy."

As he talked about why he might seek the Republican nomination in 1996, Bob Dole's words conveyed a greater likelihood of running than not. "I still think leadership is the key, I think it's all about leadership," Dole said, wheels seemingly already turning inside his head on the theme that could capitalize on his attributes. "I think the American people may be looking for strong leadership by '96. Somebody who's been tested everywhere, didn't always succeed but has been tested. Somebody who has a name before they get there, a reputation, integrity, honesty, candor, whatever, failure. But I haven't made that decision and if I don't make it I still think I've had a good political career and made a difference in a lotta things. If I did decide I think it'd be easier. I think I could get just about anybody I wanted in my campaign. Probably raise the money. I think we've got a strong base of support in the key early states, as opposed to '88, where George Bush, properly so, was selected by Ronald Reagan.

"If we look at it after the election in early '95, my guess is we'd have to do it around Lincoln's birthday, somewhere in there. When you did, you'd have to be set, you'd have to have twenty-five gurus out there with money in the bank, you'd have to have your team. And you'd have be, as Bush used to say, 'Ready from day one.' "

Would his wife support a fourth wild ride on a national campaign? "It's such a personal decision that he has to be the one to ultimately decide that," Elizabeth Dole said. "I'm very supportive, I think he'd be a great president. If he decided he wanted to do it, sure. But I really don't know. Everybody's always trying to say, 'Aw, he's going to do it, isn't he?' But he doesn't know."

Perhaps Marlin Fitzwater, who hovered over Ronald Reagan's and George Bush's shoulders for ten years and observed their drive from inches away, offers the most insightful assessment: "I'm sure he's going to run. He's got the fire and the hunger, and once you've got it you don't get rid of it."

To some Republicans, a dream ticket for 1996 would match Bob Dole's experience with the attractiveness of Colin Powell, the former chairman of the Joint Chiefs of Staff who became an American hero in handling political and military demands that resulted in the success of Operation Desert Storm in 1991. Dole said: "I'd like to talk to him about '96. Straight out."

Powell's positive demeanor could mute Bob Dole's rough edges, while Dole's stature as a congressional leader could provide Powell a good training ground, if he needs one politically, for a run for the presidency himself. As a black American, Powell might draw African-Americans to the sorely lacking Republican party, something Dole has strived for over the last two decades. Yet Powell may be considering running for the presidency himself, or as a vice-presidential mate with another Republican, or even a Democrat.

Have Powell and Dole chatted about 1996? "No," said Colin Powell. "We exchange notes. He wrote me a nice note concerning my Howard [University] commencement speech, and I wrote him back. We see each other because his wife works as head of the Red Cross. We see them both through professional political connections as well as through Red Cross activities, because I was on the board of directors of the Red Cross."

While that's a pretty tenuous link, these sorts of casual and professional connections are what make Washington go around.

Powell might consider joining Dole, if Dole enters the race, because, for all his quirks, Bob Dole is a powerful force on the American political scene. By dint of his heat-lightning personality, Dole has become one of a select few American politicians as familiar to the citizenry as movie actors and sports heroes. And he is the last World War II hero still dominating American politics. A Dole-Powell ticket could offer the nation two war heroes from victorious conquests.

"For all Bob Dole's wonderful qualities, his warts, whatever they are, he's a marvelous story of what this country's all about," asserted his friend Democrat Robert Strauss. "A fellow that came from where he came from, managed to get himself an education, terribly wounded fighting for his country, for freedom all over the world, surviving with help of a fund made up of pennies to dollars contributed by neighbors to give him a chance. That's a helluva story. He's very, very partisan, sometimes too partisan, and I've told him so. He doesn't get offended when I say that to him. As far as the [Republican presidential nomination] goes, if he got it he'd be very formidable. If he got it, I'd be on the other side from him. And he and I would be as good friends the day after the election as we are today."

In the final measure, Bob Dole clearly is a truly American politician, as questing as its pioneers, a flawed but fascinating titan. Yet the achievement of his life, regardless of what different people think of his political positions and views, is not that he simply endured the vicissitudes of politics for more than thirty years. It is that even though nothing has ever come easy for Bob Dole, he has never surrendered. He has always been primed for the next fight, playing the game with fierce devotion, seeking to make a difference. *He* has never given up, never given in.

After Richard Nixon's funeral in April of 1994, Republican senators and old Nixon hands boarded their jet. They settled in for the five-hour flight east. At one in the morning Bob Dole looked back from his seat and noticed the captive audience. He walked back to shake the shoulders of senators. "Let's talk about health care!" he said. Some joined him and his chief of staff as through the dark night the plane flew toward Washington, lights on in the forward cabin, high above sleeping towns like Russell, Kansas.

PERMISSIONS

INDEX

241